Ethical Dilemmas in the New Millennium (I)

Associate Editor
Gaile M. Pohlhaus

Editorial Assistant
Patricia M. Fry

Ethical

Dilemmas

in the

New

Millennium (I)

Francis A. Eigo, O.S.A.
Editor

The Villanova University Press

G

BJ
1249
E79
2000
v. 1
c. 2

Library of Congress Cataloging-in-Publication Data
Ethical dilemmas in the new millennium (I) /
    Francis A. Eigo, editor.

        p.   cm. — (Proceedings of the Theology Institute of
    Villanova University ; v. 32)
        ISBN 0-87723-069-2
        1. Religious ethics. 2. Ethics, Modern—20th century.   I. Eigo,
    Francis A.   II. Series.
    BJ1188.R45 2000   00 033377
    291.1'75—dc21   CIP

b13710722

Dédié

à

Will,

né à la fête

de

Saint Joseph

Contents

Contributors

CHRISTINE E. GUDORF, a member of the Religious Studies faculty of Florida International University, is the recipient of a number of honors and awards, has conducted seminars, lectured widely, served as a consultant for numerous groups, has enjoyed a variety of administrative positions and membership in prestigious professional societies. In addition to contributing to a number of scholarly journals and books, she has coedited *Women's Consciousness, Women's Conscience* and *Christian Ethics*, coauthored *Religious Ethics*, and authored *Victimization: Examining Christian Complicity* and *Body, Sex, and Pleasure: Reconstructing Christian Sexual Ethics*.

M. CATHLEEN KAVENY, on the faculty of the University of Notre Dame Law School, has received a number of honors and awards, is a member of various editorial boards, has published in many scholarly journals and books, has delivered papers before learned societies, and has contributed book reviews to such publications as *Theological Studies*.

JAMES F. KEENAN, S.J., teacher (Weston School of Theology), lecturer, consultant, member of professional organizations, recipient of various awards and honors, contributor to any number of journals and books, coeditor of several books, is the author of such works as *Goodness and Rightness in Thomas Aquinas' Summa Theologiae* and *Virtues for Ordinary Christians*.

JUDITH A. MERKLE, S.N.D.deN., presently on the faculty of Niagara University, has served in many professional capacities in this country and abroad: writing book reviews in such journals as *Theological Studies*, presenting papers before learned societies, taping instructional videos, engaging in various consultative activities, working in parishes, addressing Church groups and religious congregations, joining professional organizations, and, not least of all, authoring such books as *A Different Touch* and *Committed by Choice*.

ANNE E. PATRICK, S.N.J.M., professor of religion at Carleton College in Northfield, Minnesota, has made many contributions to professional activities: past president of the CTSA, director of the Society of Christian Ethics, editor of the Religious Book Club, founding president of the Washington, D.C., Council of Religious Women, chairperson of the Committee on Women in Church and Society of the NAWR, pioneer in the Women's Ordination Conference, delegate of Sisters Uniting to the International Women's Year Tribute in Mexico City (1975), assistant in establishing the International Network of Societies for Catholic Theology to whose steering committee she was elected, author of writings on religious, ethical, and literary themes that have appeared in many books and periodicals. Continuum Publishing Company has recently released a paperback edition of her 1996 book, *Liberating Conscience: Feminist Explorations in Catholic Moral Theology.*

KEVIN WM. WILDES, S.J., Associate Director of the Kennedy Institute of Ethics and Assistant Professor in the Department of Philosophy of Georgetown University, with a secondary appointment as Assistant Professor in the Department of Medicine at the University School of Medicine, and a Senior Scholar of the Kennedy Institute of Ethics and the Center of Clinical Bioethics, serves as Associate Editor of *The Journal of Medicine and Philosophy* as well as Associate Editor of *The Philosophy and Medicine* book series and as Coeditor of the *Clinical Medical Ethics* book series and *The Journal of Christian Bioethics* and the book series, *Philosophical Studies in Contemporary Culture.* He is editor of such books as *Birth, Suffering, and Death; Critical Choices and Critical Care; Choosing Life,* and *Infertility,* as well as author of the forthcoming book, *Moral Acquaintanceship: Methodology in Bioethics.*

Introduction

This thirty-second volume of the *Proceedings of the Villanova University Theology Institute* focuses on several ethical dilemmas in the new millennium. After the introductory essay by James Keenan, Christine Gudorf treats the topic of sexual morality; Kevin Wildes, bioethics; Judith Merkle, social ethics; Anne Patrick, feminist ethics; M. Cathleen Kaveny, ethics and civil law.

For their assistance to me in any number of ways I am grateful to the following: Judith Dwyer; the Theology Institute Committee; the presiders (Pat Laferty, Jim McCartney, Bill Werpehowski); Gaile M. Pohlhaus (coordinator/associate editor); Patricia M. Fry (assistant coordinator/ editorial assistant); the essayists; and the Administrators of Villanova University for their enthusiastic assistance.

Francis A. Eigo, O.S.A.
Editor

Fundamental Moral Theology in the New Millennium

James F. Keenan, S.J.

I. My Premise

Calling our attention to the need to correct an enormous oversight, Charles Curran opens his new book with these words: "Catholic moral theology in the past has paid little or no explicit attention to the Church and its influence on the discipline."[1] In this essay, I agree with Curran and argue that, now more than ever, Catholic moral theologians need to address the life of the Church.

Here, I think of two particular persons who have set a standard for this. First, Charles Curran established the concept of academic freedom in *de facto* (though not *de jure*) Catholic universities. By his own actions and writings, he established freedom of discourse and critical reflection as a value that should be recognized in ecclesiastical contexts as well as in theological and civil ones.[2]

Another is Christine Gudorf who consistently asks whether Church teachings and practices are ethical. Gudorf addresses not only her readers and colleagues, but her Church as well. She has critiqued the ecclesiastical application of the seamless garment issue, ecclesiastical conduct in the case of Charles Curran, and ecclesiastical behavior in the face of women who are victims of violence. As a feminist theologian, she examines the practical life of the Church and, in particular, has insisted on justice as the standard of all teaching on sexual ethics.[3]

These two persons, one a diocesan priest, the other a laywoman, show us that moral theology no longer operates in a clerical domain. Since most moral theologians are lay persons, we must more self consciously acknowledge the ecclesiastical responsibilities that

1

fall to us as a result of our training, competency, and profession. Indeed, much of the extraordinary growth in the writing of moral theologians today results from the declericalization of morals and from the variety of points of view that were never really entertained by cleric theologians before. These contributions that directly affect ethicists and their students must be directed to Church members and leaders as well.[4]

For instance, I just participated in a book length project with the Mennonite theologian, Joseph Kotva. In *Practice What You Preach: Virtues, Ethics and Power in the Lives of Pastoral Ministers and Their Congregations*, twenty-three Christian ethicists engage the ethics of their respective Churches. Contributors discuss the screening of seminary candidates and subsequent promotion processes, pay scales and the treatment of women religious, the ethics of intercommunion and inclusive language. These contributors look at a variety of Church practices and ask the question, "but is it ethical?"[5]

I also edited a book this year, called *Catholic Ethicists on HIV/AIDS Prevention*. In that book, thirty-six moralists, six from each continent, talk about their local problems with HIV prevention and the moral theological resources that could be used to help Catholic communities understand that the moral tradition exists to prevent the spread of HIV.[6]

We moralists need to remind one another that our competency in moral theology is not only for the academy (would that we accomplished something there!), but also for the Church. We must realize how political (in the full Aristotelian sense of the word) we should be. Unfortunately, however, we moralists present ourselves as thinkers instead of as practical theologians aware of Church polity.

In saying this, I do not at all deny the Magisterial authority of our episcopal leadership, but I want to insist on the authority that moral theologians have as well. We must exercise that authority by addressing what our Church teaches as moral theology and the way it practices its mission.

Here, I think of the recent investigations of theologians like Tissa Balasuriya, Anthony DeMello, and, more recently, Jacques Dupuis. While many debate over the proper theological and canonical standards of these cases, ethicists must pose the question whether ethical imperatives are equally observed. Similarly, in questions about women and leadership in the Church, we must ask, not only what our ecclesiology permits, but also what ethics demands.

One of the great interests among ethicists today is how can we respect local culture while observing universal standards. That very important question, which will be raised throughout the new century, must be applied to the Church: though it has its own local culture which is shaped by its practices and canons, still, fundamental universal standards must serve as critical tools for analyzing Church conduct. Not only are universal ethical standards available, however; within the Church's own ethical tradition is a rich legacy that needs to be critically applied to the exercise of power and authority in the Church today. This essay, then, is written in the hope of creatively engaging the ecclesial context in which we live and in which we propose our understanding of ethics.

II. A Good Quote from a Hundred Years Ago about the Fundamental Dualism in Practical Theology

In the beginning of the twentieth century, fundamental moral theology began with a major innovation: for the first time a manual of moral theology appeared in English. In *A Manual of Moral Theology* (1906), the English Jesuit moralist Thomas Slater (1855-1928) acknowledged that his was the first book "to present the common teaching of the Catholic moral theologians in an English dress." After commenting that other vernacular versions in German, Italian, Spanish, and French were successful, he then acknowledged that among Protestants "the moral theology of the Catholic Church is little understood and constantly misrepresented and maligned. Of course it does not merit the bad reputation which has been fastened on it by Protestant and Jansenist slander." The purpose of his Preface was, however, to justify moral theology's singular and exclusive concern about sin. He wrote:

> It is the product of centuries of labor bestowed by able and holy men on the practical problems of Christian ethics. Here, however, we must ask the reader to bear in mind that the manuals of moral theology are technical works intended to help the confessor and the parish priest in the discharge of their duties. They are as technical as the text-books of the lawyer and the doctor. They are not intended for edification, nor do they hold up a high ideal of Christian perfection for the imitation of the faithful. They deal with what is of obligation under pain of sin; they are books of moral pathology. They are necessary for the Catholic priest to enable him to administer the sacrament of Penance and to fulfill other duties.

By focusing on sin, Slater affirmed, too, that there was no need for moral theology to engage spiritual or ascetical theology, that is, a theology that promoted the spiritual betterment of oneself. He noted the "very abundant" literature of ascetical theology, but added that "moral theology proposes to itself the much humbler but still necessary task of defining what is right and what wrong in all the practical relations of the Christian life... The first step on the right road of conduct is to avoid evil."[7]

Slater's opinions were shared by all his contemporary moral theologians. Thirty years later, another English Jesuit moralist, Henry Davis, wrote: "It is precisely about the law that Moral Theology is concerned. It is not a mirror of perfection, showing man the way of perfection."[8] Spiritual or ascetical theology helped devout persons pursue Christian perfection; moral theology assisted priests in their role as confessors.[9]

III. A Fundamental Dualism in Practical Theology

This fundamental dualism in practical theology has done enormous harm to the life of the Church.[10] In this essay, I argue that the fundamental revisionism of the past century was an explicit attempt both to overcome this dualism and to have an integrated vision of moral theology. As we stand facing the millennium, no task is more urgent for fundamental morals than the continuation of this project: the future of moral theology is found by situating it in spirituality. In the words of the French novelist, André Malraux, "le XXIème siècle sera spirituel ou ne sera pas"[11] ("The twenty-first century will be either spiritual or it will not be at all.").

To make my case, I first demonstrate the seriousness of the dualism, then explore the contribution of ascetical theology, highlight three contemporary trends that advance the contemporary project to overcome dualism, and conclude with a case.

I begin by mentioning three effects of the dualism. First, Church leadership phrases moral theology in the language of moral pathology. *Veritatis Splendor*, for example, went to great pains to argue the necessity of intrinsic evil in order to preserve the objectivity of moral truth.[12] The Dominican, Herbert McCabe, noted that that claim showed that the encyclical was firmly in the tradition of the moral manuals and not in the spirit of Vatican II. Moreover, he added, as others also have claimed, that the concept of intrinsic evil is a fundamentally antiThomistic one.[13] Like the writers of *Veritatis Splendor*, some bishops and other Church leaders today effectively define good Catholic identity by listing those actions which the Church deems immoral: capital punishment, abortion, birth control, homosexual activity, divorce and remarriage. The contemporary public stance of Church leaders defining Catholicism by what it avoids as opposed to what it loves and pursues reflects Catholic moral theology's fifteen hundred year history of reflecting only on sin. But, it also reflects the contemporary abandonment both of any real ascetical theology and of the centrality of the sacramental life in ecclesiastical consciousness.

Second, even though the first ethical principle for all persons is to do good and avoid evil, as a matter of fact, the fundamental dualism left moral theology to consider solely the evil to be avoided. In this economy, ordinary Christians were not charged with becoming better disciples; rather, they were warned against becoming worse: avoid sin, and, if you cannot, confess.

For this reason, many Catholics look at critically complex issues one sidedly: a direct abortion of an already doomed fetus to save a woman's life is considered wrong because we look only at the evil (killing the fetus) instead of promoting the good (rescuing a woman's life). Likewise, many fear giving adequate pain relief (a good) lest it cause death (an evil). Similarly, we hesitate to promote HIV prevention because avoiding evil (compromising our teaching on birth control) is always more important than doing the good (halting the spread of a pandemic).

This dualism had a third effect: it promoted a distorted understanding of sin. When moral theology is integrated with spiritual theology, sin is simply defined as not bothering to love. For instance, in the parable of the Good Samaritan (Lk 10: 25-37), sin appeared in the priest and the Levite who passed by the wounded man. In that parable, those who actually did harm were not even mentioned, because the issue of goodness and sin was not whether one harmed or not, but whether one loved or not. Likewise, in the story of the rich man and Lazarus (Lk 16: 19-31), the rich man was damned to hell for not taking care of his fellow human being who hungered at the rich man's door steps. This same insight about sin reappeared in Matthew 25 (31-46); in the Last Judgment, those cast into hell fire were those who did not feed the hungry, clothe the naked, or visit the imprisoned.

In the first centuries of Christianity, sin was not bothering to love. The early Church recognized that the first movement of salvation was from God who through Christ invited Christians to walk with him along his way by his grace. Moral goodness, then, was the human response to God's first movement. Contrariwise, sin or moral badness was not bothering to respond.

The Patristic tradition, using journey imagery, appreciated the importance of this responsive movement. Failing to move ahead on the way of the Lord or simply standing on that way was considered sin or badness. Gregory the Great wrote: "Certainly, in this world, the human spirit is like a boat foolishly fighting against the river's rush: one is never allowed to stand still, because unless one forges ahead, one will slide back downstream."[14]

Later, from the ascetical tradition of the twelfth century, Bernard wrote: "Not to progress on the way of Life is to regress."[15] As we shall see later in this essay, Thomas Aquinas was evidently influenced by this ascetical theology and in his *Summa* rejected the idea of separating moral theology from ascetical theology. Thus, he took the insights of Gregory, Bernard, and others and offered his own motto regarding sin: "To stand still on the way of God is to go backwards."[16] Sin or badness was not bothering to respond to the Lord who calls us to move forward.

Sin was not fundamentally choosing the wrong or even the failure to choose the right; it was antecedent to choice. Sin was not bothering to love.[17] This notion of sin, absent in most moral theology from the fifth to the twentieth centuries, remained alive wherever ascetical theology was in place. For instance, *The Spiritual Exercises of Ignatius* proposed the famous colloquy with Jesus on the cross. Exercitants were invited to entertain three questions: "What have I done for Christ?," "What am I doing for Christ?," "What ought I do for Christ?" The questions were not between what right things ought they do versus what wrong actions they ought to avoid. Rather, the questions concerned whether they were bothering to do anything at all for Christ.

As we turn now to examine ascetical theology, I offer two preliminary comments. First, I am more interested in the ascetical texts from the twelfth through the sixteenth centuries. I find the later ascetical manuals, from the seventeenth to the twentieth centuries, unimaginative at best. They were, after all, authored by the same people who gave us the moral manuals! Second, I will use the terms spiritual and ascetical theology interchangeably, since the distinction between them was not made until the eighteenth century.[18]

IV. A Look Back into History

When we think of the history of ascetical theology,[19] we should start with the twelfth century. "The twelfth century has long been seen as a turning point in the history of Latin spirituality," claims Bernard McGinn. "[T]here can be no argument that the twelfth century was fascinated with the mystery of the human person as *imago Dei* and brought to the study of this mystery a systematic ordering mentality not seen before." Through Aelred of Rievaulx's spiritual friendship, Abelard's insistence on the conscience, Bernard of Clairvaux's location of the image of God in human freedom, Hildegard of Bingen's knowledge of the way of the Lord and her appreciation of the goodness of the human body and the delight of the passions, and Richard of St. Victor's understanding of the interpersonal human subject as an image of the three-personed God, the theologians of the twelfth century developed a powerful relational anthropology as a basis for their spirituality.[20]

Caroline Walker Bynum agrees with McGinn: "No period was ever busier creating structures for its piety than the twelfth century."[21] Like McGinn, she, too, examines Bernard of Clairvaux, who with "other 'new monks' stressed discovery of self — and of self-love — as the first step in a long process of returning to the love and likeness of God, a love and likeness in which the individual is not dissolved into God but rather becomes God's partner and friend."[22] Bernard's spirituality, as well as that of his contemporaries, drew deeply from the Scriptures and cultivated in a particular way a devotion to the humanity of Jesus, which moved readers into greater intimacy with Jesus and with those who shared the devotion.[23] In developing a highly relational anthropology, then, the twelfth century never compromised the person and, in fact, discovered "the self, the inner mystery, the inner man, the inner landscape." Nonetheless, the discovery of the self did not mean the endorsement of individualism; as Bynum argues, the twelfth century "also discovered the group in two very precise senses: it discovered that many separate 'callings' or 'lives' were possible in the Church, and it elaborated a language for talking about how individuals became a part of them (the language of 'conforming to a model')."[24]

After the twelfth century, we can turn to the writings of Jean Gerson (1363-1429) or *Showings* of Julian of Norwich (1382-1416). Later, the sixteenth century marked the birth of modern spiritual theology. Here, we can think of Desiderius Erasmus' *Enchiridion militis christiani* (1503) and *De praeparatione ad mortem* (1534), Ignatius of Loyola's *Exercitia Spiritualia* (1548), Johannes Justus Lanspergius' *Epistola Salvatoris ad quandam animam fidelem* (1554), Luis de Granada's *Libro de la oración y meditación* (1544) and *Doctrina espiritual* (1587), *Camino de perfección* of Teresa of Avila (1515-1582), Robert Persons' (or Parsons') *Christian Directory* (1583), Lorenzo di Scupoli's *Il combattimento spirituale* (1588), *The Practice of Perfection and Christian Virtues* of Alfonso Rodriguez (1538-1616), and Francis de Sales' *Introduction à la Vie dévote* (1609). I believe that most contemporary moral theologians would find more congruency between their contemporary thoughts and these works than they would with any moral manuals written over the past four hundred years.

V. The Contribution of Ascetical Theology to the Reform of Moral Theology

In light of those works, I propose ten instances of what ascetical theology offers to moral theology.[25] First, the ascetical texts were decidedly *based on Scripture*, and the moral manuals were not. When Vatican II admonished moral theologians to draw more fully on the Scriptures, they had nothing in their own tradition of four hundred years to turn to as a reference point. In practical theology, only ascetical theology grew out of a Scriptural foundation.

Second, the ascetical texts *animated* readers' devotional and moral practices. Without these texts, moral practices were animated by fear of damnation; with them, they were animated by the pursuit of Christ. Moreover, by their Christological focus, they provided a relational context for the motivation of moral practices. In turn, the moral life became considered by the devout as a response to the initiative from God in their spiritual relationship with Christ. Here, then, the theological framework of "call and response," so important in postVatican II writings, found its practical application: Being moral meant being a grateful disciple.

This animation was commonly called "a conversion." Conversion for ascetical writers was not turning away from an earlier held belief and a subsequent turning toward Christianity. Rather, the one undergoing conversion was already baptized; conversion was a process of both deeply interiorizing what one had already confessed and making those confessional claims the integrating force of one's life. Robert Persons' (or Parsons') famous *Christian Directory* was a clear example of ascetical literature leading readers to conversion.[26]

Third, the moral life was, therefore, no longer understood by the devout Christian as the simple avoidance of sin. Whenever ascetical theology amplified moral theology, the latter defined itself as primarily interested in *the increase of charity.* Just as the ascetical texts fostered *union with Jesus Christ,* devout Christians could also interpret their moral lives as disciples who seek union with the Lord. The intimacy that the ascetical theology proposed was consistently evident in their texts, whether Julian of Norwich's *Showings,* Johannes Lanspergius' *Epistle from Jesus to a Soul,* or Ignatius of Loyola's *Spiritual Exercises.* The end of ascetical theology eventually became also *the end of moral theology,* as Gérard Gilleman and René Carpentier had argued.[27]

Fourth, ascetical theology introduced *moral effort or striving* as a key concept for capturing the moral goodness of the agent. This notion of striving was rooted in ascetical theology's overriding interest in charity[28] and later occasioned recognition of the distinction between goodness and rightness.[29] Striving particularly manifested itself in the ascetical theology that accentuated the metaphor of the struggling soldier as found in Erasmus' *Enchiridion* or Lorenzo Scupoli's *Spiritual Combat.*[30] When moral theology also appropriated the concept of striving, it located the cause of striving, charity, in the heart of the disciple. This turn to the heart conveyed the goodness of deep human desire, captured human aspiration and longing, and finally prompted moral theology once again to talk about love.[31]

Fifth, likewise ascetical theology presented the *passions positively*, not as sources of sinful inclinations, but as forces that, when properly trained, would assist the devout Christian in the way of the Lord. Hildegard of Bingen celebrated the wisdom of the passions, and Ignatius taught Christians to discern God's will through their affections. This appreciation of the passions occurred in ascetical theology when a positive anthropology (*imago Dei*), a positive goal (union with Christ), and a positive way (*imitatio Dei*) coupled with a respect for the importance of a person's experience of God. This appreciation of the passions was emblematic of the appreciation that ascetical writers had of the entirety of the readers' experiences. Unlike moral manuals, ascetical manuals asked their readers to reflect on their own experiences to see whether they validated the truth claims that ascetical writers made.

Sixth, the ascetical works also prompted *an attentiveness to the ordinariness of life*. Though ascetical works began as little more than prayer manuals, in time they became meditations that pursued union with Christ in one's ordinary existence.[32] The engagement of ordinariness demonstrated the comprehensiveness of the scope of ascetical theology; in ordinariness, ascetical theology encountered humanity completely, as Julian shows us. For that reason, the *imitatio Christi* aimed to depict the ordinariness of Jesus' human life. That ordinariness is elsewhere well captured in the very successful *The Christian Man's Guide* (1630) by Alfonso Rodriguez which went through fifty editions and was translated into twenty-three languages: each of the two treatises is entitled "The Perfection of Our Ordinary Actions." Aquinas, too, captured the inclusiveness of the ordinary and applied it to the moral life when he insisted that every human action is a moral action.[33] The ordinary rescues moral theology from its restricting tendency to study only sinful or controversial actions.

Seventh, as they developed, the ascetical manuals specifically *addressed the occupations and vocations* of their readers. This specificity is well conveyed, for instance, in a recent essay that investigates the prayers for midwives at the time of childbirth.[34] Nowhere was the particular vocation of readers more specifically treated, however, than it was in the lives of the saints. In ascetical literature, the saint became an exemplar for readers trying to live out their vocations.[35] One pair of saints who became incredibly comprehensive were Martha and Mary who, until recently, were often depicted together so as to uphold the necessity of both active and contemplative vocations.[36]

Eighth, ascetical theology's powerful interest in anthropology, therefore, finally prompted moral theology in this century to be concerned, not simply with negative external actions that were to be avoided, but, more importantly, with *an interior character to be positively developed*. Thus, Thomas Aquinas' interest in the virtues in the thirteenth century was not simply due to the retrieval of Aristotle. Rather, the virtues emerged earlier in the ascetical theology of the twelfth century that conceived and nourished the religious movements that developed at the end of that century. That theology guided the new religious orders into their relationships with Christ. Thomas, like others in the newly established Franciscan and Dominican orders, grew up in a culture that promoted the virtues as the proper vehicles for growth as a devout disciple, and he, like others, introduced them into his moral theology. Not surprisingly, then, he concluded his treatment of the virtues in the *Pars Secunda* with questions concerning the devout life.[37]

Ninth, the ascetical texts also introduced *exercises*, not only for devotional practices, but also for acquiring those virtues. While the moral manuals directed persons away from (sinful) actions, the ascetical texts directed readers to the practice of actual consistent, concrete positive actions. As de Guibert notes, asceticism meant "to make someone adept by exercises."[38] Exercise became key, then, for understanding the development of the ascetical and virtuous personality. In fact, Aquinas used the word "exercise" basically to convey growth in two areas of life: in the ascetical schools of perfection and in the acquisition of the cardinal virtues.[39] Clearly, the insights of the latter derived from the former.

Implicit in this notion of exercise was a profound regard for the person as embodied. Persons did not become virtuous by intentionality alone or by simple wishful thinking, but only by the habitual practice of particular kinds of action that could eventually become for the practitioner a second nature. In fact, the virtues were basically strengths resulting from the right exercise of the passions. In ascetical literature, at least from the twelfth through sixteenth centuries, the passions and the body were not suppressed, but engaged.

Tenth, the ascetical manuals strongly advocated the primacy of the conscience. While the moral manuals' writings on conscience developed a sin taxonomy where confessors scrutinized a penitent's conscience as some *thing* subject to examination, in the ascetical texts, the conscience was that by which the Christian grew in union with Christ. Written in the vernacular for lay persons, the ascetical texts addressed readers who were striving to take care of their souls and of their neighbor. They were self directed, a virtue that Lottin recognized and developed in this century.[40]

It is not coincidental, then, that, while Peter Lombard preferred Church teaching to the human conscience, Thomas Aquinas was able to insist, on three occasions, that on this point the Master of the Sentences had erred: it was better to die excommunicated than to violate one's conscience.[41] Thomas had what Peter did not: the experience of the twelfth and thirteenth centuries' extraordinary evangelical and spiritual activity that found in the conscience what *Gaudium et Spes* 16 accurately described, seven hundred years later, as the voice of God.

In each of these ways, then, ascetical theology amplified the scope, competency, and subject of moral theology. By emphasizing a Scripture based, holistic, self directed, embodied, and relational practical theology, ascetical theology offered moral theology a way of exploring broadened and positive agenda for examining the ethical life.

VI. Setting Agenda for the Next Century While Acknowledging the Dark Side of Ascetical Theology

The darker side of ascetical theology is more appropriately from the same period as that of the moral manuals, that is, from the seventeenth century to Vatican II. When contrasted to the moral manuals, this ascetical theology still provided a richer, deeper, affectively strong practical theology. However, certain real problems emerged from this theology.

While the twelfth century marked the discovery of the self and the thirteenth celebrated evangelization and, with it, the birth of the Renaissance leading up to the age of discovery in the sixteenth century, the subsequent centuries were an institutionalization of the foregoing. Rather than the new, the creative, and the exceptional, the neoScholastic texts from the seventeenth to the twentieth centuries highlighted a distinct preference for the universal, the eternal, and the immutable. If the language of virtue characterized the twelfth through sixteenth centuries, the language of law dominated the later centuries. In this context, the conscience, which was so powerfully promoted and defended by Thomas, Erasmus, and Ignatius, is inhibited into subservience in most later texts.

Virtue still appeared in the context of law, but it functioned, not as a guide to human flourishment, but rather as a restraint. For instance, the virtue of prudence functioned from the twelfth to the sixteenth centuries as the practical, self directing wisdom for consistently moving forward; from the seventeenth century on, it was the virtue of caution, reluctance, and self restraint.[42]

The Christological images that these ascetical writings promoted also contributed to this inhibiting anthropological vision. The imitation of Christ never really extroverted in later devotional literature. From the humble one born in a manger, to the pietistic one who sought prayerful places, to the obedient one in the Garden, or the patient one on the cross, Catholic devotional literature for the last three centuries found plenty of virtuous images of the humble, obedient, pietistic, patient Christ for the pious reader. But, those images did not include the Christ who fed, taught, healed (on the Sabbath!), served, welcomed the stranger, et cetera.

Thus, virtues dealing with human flourishment, imagination, justice and fairness, friendship, and personal growth appeared almost exclusively in the earlier ascetical texts, where there was a richer and more active Christological vision. But, later the obedient Jesus who became the reigning Christ the King wanted virtues that were ancillary ones like obedience, patience, chastity, meekness, steadfastness, and temperance, that served to help us carry out his laws. They controlled the human spirit, harnessed the human passions, and sublimated any sense of personal uniqueness.

Though we are familiar with the triumphalistic ecclesiology of this period, we should recognize that, not only did the decisions of the hierarchy foster the ethos that predominated during this time, but the moral and ascetical texts did also. In particular, the anthropological identity that the ascetical texts offered harnessed women with a piety that served well the patriarchal world that the hierarchical Church actively promoted.

Women were, and are, routinely and systematically ignored for their leadership and sanctity. For instance, between 1000-1900, eighty-seven percent of those who were canonized saints were men.[43] Women were not only overlooked, but the model of virtue that was proposed to them was designed to "keep them in their place." Exploring the "social dynamics of virtue," Anne E. Patrick remarks on the process of canonizing Maria Goretti and notes the underlying anthropological vision that was proposed: maintaining a woman's own sexual purity was more important than was any other task she could perform; if necessary, she should die for the cause. Against that iconography, Patrick invites us to explore an entirely different notion of virtue, embodied, for instance, in the intelligence, vision, and care for the marginalized as witnessed in the life of Dorothy Day.[44]

The ascetical theology for the last three centuries provided, too, a virtual stranglehold on the passions as well. While Hildegard, Julian, Ignatius, and Lanspergius looked to the passions to discover the way intimacy with Christ could be achieved, the more recent texts singularly aimed to control them. Patricia Beattie Jung has convincingly argued that moral theology needs to attend to the deep, rich, energetic roots that the passions provide and that contemporary writers like Paul Ricoeur so eloquently advance. The passions offer to us their own rich way of absorbing and grasping the highly charged, relational world in which we live.[45]

Finally, since the ascetical manuals of the past three centuries were as inhibiting as the moral manuals, they were also hardly relational. While Jean Gerson, Desiderius Erasmus, and Martin Luther, for instance, stressed the virtue of neighbor love, later ascetical texts were much more concerned with protecting oneself prudentially than they were with aiding one's neighbor. In fact, many texts warned readers to beware of the company they kept.

One could illustrate the difference between the earlier and later ascetical theology with the fact that the former recommended hospitality, while the latter hardly mentioned it. Those earlier writings reflected the hospitality that we find in the Scriptures and in the early Church practices. Similarly, contemporary attempts to reflect on the virtue and practice of hospitality in the Christian tradition almost always return to Scriptural narratives and injunctions and early Church practices.[46] Earlier ascetical theology, then, was relational, positive, embodied, and self directing; later ascetical theology was not.

As we look forward toward a more integrated vision of moral/ascetical theology, I suggest three important contemporary trends for the future of moral theology: autonomous ethics from Europe, virtue ethics from the United States, and liberation ethics from Latin America. I note, here, as we proceed, that most of my argument is written from a feminist perspective: by promoting an integrated, embodied ethics that is suspicious of historical retrieval which does not discern the difference between patriarchal and egalitarian-feminist paradigms of ethics[47] and which insists on the primacy of an individual's experience while claiming a constitutively relational anthropology and endorsing the option for the poor, I argue that the future of fundamental moral theology is constitutively feminist.[48]

VII. The Autonomous Christian

Undoubtedly, the most important contribution out of Europe these last twenty years is an autonomous ethics in the context of faith.[49] This ethics, articulated by Alfons Auer, who used, among others, the insights of Lottin, Tillman, and Fuchs, rests on an ethical and a theological claim.[50] First, all moral reasoning must be arguable and communicable, that is, ethics is not a matter of fiat or obedience, but of understanding, truth, and judgment. As an *ethical* claim, the autonomy of moral reasoning refers, then, to the rational character of moral statements. Second, because we are created in the image of God and redeemed by Christ, we can take our call to discipleship seriously only if we acknowledge the primacy of the conscience and the individual Christian responsibility to form it. As a *theological* claim, then, the autonomy of moral reasoning holds that the specificity of Christian ethics cannot be primarily found in specific moral teachings, but rather in its promotion of the personal conscience where God animates the person to follow Christ. As a thesis about *Church teaching*, then, the autonomy of moral reasoning helps protect the conscience from being overthrown by any outside authority, in general, or the Magisterium, in particular. The Church's teaching must be made plausible by dialogue and rational argument to all people of good will.

In this context, then, faith provides a new horizon of meaning for moral living. A unified understanding of faith and reason allows us to see that moral norms are not naïvely derived from faith because faith does not replace the responsibility of human reason, but exerts an integrating, criticizing, and stimulating effect on the reasoning process. This reasoning builds, then, on Augustine's insight that God is closer to us than we are to ourselves.[51] This way of thinking takes seriously the immediacy of God's presence and aims to draw out and communicate all the ethical implications of faith. To be sure, moral truths cannot be deduced from truths of faith, but, as Klaus Demmer says, "genuine theology leads to a fundamental change in our way of thinking."[52] Faith provides, then, an orientation to all of reality and a theological anthropology that serves as the hermeneutical key with which to unlock the meaning of normative human nature.

In pursuing the agenda of autonomy, a responsible ethics locates the conscience as the privileged point of departure for determining right conduct, but it does so appreciating the dangers of subjectivity. In his new book, Sabatino Majorano places the conscience between the extremes of subjectivism and objectivism. On the one side, a conscience that denies truth contradicts its very self; a conscience that does not recognize truth, but sees it as an imposition, is not truly human. On the other hand, conscience cannot deny its hermeneutic task: when conscience is reduced to simply serving norms or an ideology, conscience is dead.[53]

Brian Johnstone locates the responsible conscience between two extremes: a conscience that makes up its own moral values solipsistically and a submissive conscience that simply heeds the "objective" law.[54] Johnstone names this midpoint between the Scylla and Charybdis of subjectivism and objectivism "critical conscience within a living tradition."[55] He introduces "solidarity" to consider the social formation of the conscience and argues that a proper notion of conscience requires one to "think with the other," especially the oppressed, in order to challenge critically the established forms of domination and to become self purifying through self criticism.

Evidently, autonomous ethics has undergone a significant shift in recent years.[56] While arguing that the moral task for each person is to realize the anthropological gifts that all of us have been given, it adds now that we are constitutively relational and that that relationality is with nature, God, and humanity.

In describing our relationality with nature, theologians offer a reintegration of humanity and nature that does not diminish our ability to reflect on our place in nature and the possibilities we have of consciously intervening and directing it.[57] Our interaction with nature will reflect both our responsibility for nature of which we are always a part and our ability to mold nature in light of human purposes.[58] Our interventions into nature, in other words, will reflect our commitment to respect and enhance the conditions of future human action in the world. This insight of the Europeans has enormous repercussions for the growing field of environmental ethics.

Our relationality with God begins with the recognition that we are in God's image. In particular, being in the image of a triune God means that our nature is, like God's, constitutively relational. The ramifications of this were noted in the twelfth century by Richard of St. Victor and in the twentieth century by Catherine LaCugna[59] and Margaret Farley.[60] Recently, Edward Vacek has argued that relationship with God is not primarily elective, but originally natural. Each person as creature must rediscover her/his connectedness to God.[61]

To discuss our relationship with fellow human beings, I will turn to the virtues, but, in concluding this section, I want to note that moralists must, for the next century, advance the claims of the Christian conscience, not only by defending its primacy and insisting on its social dimension, but also by providing clear accessible tools that help people from a variety of backgrounds form their own consciences. Moralists must develop a variety of pedagogical skills in order to help others understand better the call to form and heed their consciences.

Moreover, moralists must remind hierarchical leaders of their responsibility to awaken in the community of faith an understanding of the demands of conscience. This means, not that they provide Church members with a list of rules to obey, but, rather, that they preach and teach, as Paul and Aquinas did, the primacy of conscience as an identifiable trait of being Christian.[62]

VIII. Development of Virtues

Though often unacknowledged, the recent retrieval of virtue ethics is certainly indebted to the work of ascetical theology.[63] As Slater and other ethicists noted, ascetical theology alone promoted the virtues as positive dispositions for Christian growth. Not surprisingly, then, any return to the virtues would prompt eventually an historical turn to the ascetical theology that sustained them during these last four centuries. The writings of William Spohn provide a perfect example of this insight. In three successive essays, he noted, first, a renewed interest in the passions, then, the virtues and, finally, spirituality.[64] Any retrieval of the virtues leads us back to their context, spiritual theology.[65]

Not only are the virtues a natural expression of the moral life that could evolve from an ascetical theology, but they also provide Christians with a healthy program for conscience formation and development. Yet, these virtues must take into account the relationality of human nature.

Not only have twelfth century ascetical writers and, more recently, European Christian ethicists insisted on the relational as normative anthropology. Paul Lauritzen, for instance, has done an important synthesis of recent works on morality and the self in narrative ethics and argues that "the narrative self is necessarily a social and relational self." A relational view of the self requires a reexamination of our understanding, not only of the self, but of morality.[66]

To accommodate this relational anthropology, I have proposed elsewhere a new model for the cardinal virtues.[67] Aquinas' cardinal virtues perfect an individual person's powers (the will, the practical reason, the irascible and the concupiscible). I propose, instead, that virtues perfect, not parts of an individual, but, rather, ways that we are constitutively related.

As persons, we are relational in three ways: generally, specifically, and uniquely, and each of these relational ways of being demands a cardinal virtue: as a relational being in general, we are called to justice; as a relational being specifically, we are called to fidelity; as a relational being uniquely, we are called to self care. These three virtues are cardinal. Unlike Thomas' structure, none is ethically prior to the other; they have equally urgent claims, and they should be pursued as ends in themselves. Thus, we are not called to be faithful and self caring in order to be just, nor are we called to be self caring and just in order to be faithful. None is auxiliary to the others. They are distinctive virtues with none being a subset or subcategory of the other. They are cardinal. The fourth cardinal virtue is prudence which determines what constitutes the just, faithful, and self caring way of life for an individual.

Let me consider each way that we are relational. First, our relationality generally is always directed by an ordered appreciation for
the common good in which we treat all people as equal. We belong
to humanity and are expected to respond to all its members in general equally and impartially. Paul Ricoeur notes that from Aristotle
to Rawls justice is always associated with equality,[68] and, as Bernard
Williams notes, justice is about ordering all our interior dispositions so that in our relationship with anyone the claim of equality
originates from within.[69]

If justice urges us to treat all people equally, then fidelity makes
distinctively different claims on us. Fidelity is the virtue that nur-
tures and sustains the bonds of those special relationships that we
enjoy whether by blood, marriage, love, or sacrament. Fidelity
means that we should treat with special care those who are closer
to us. Thus, if justice rests on impartiality and universality, fidelity
rests on partiality and particularity.[70]

Fidelity here is like Reinhold Niebuhr's love in his "just-love"
dialectic.[71] It is also like the claim that Carol Gilligan made in her
important work, *In a Different Voice*.[72] Gilligan criticized Kohlberg
for arguing that full moral development was found in the person
who could reason well about justice as impartial and universal. She
countered that the human must aim both for the impartiality of
justice as well as for the development of particular bonds.

Fidelity also captures the concern of contemporary moral theologians and ethicists. It expresses, for instance, the covenant
ethics of the late Paul Ramsey,[73] the friendship ethics of Gilbert
Meilaender[74] and Paul Wadell,[75] the loyalty ethics of George
Fletcher,[76] the commitment ethics of Margaret Farley,[77] and the
love-justice model of William Werpehowski.[78]

Paul Ricoeur, also, studies these two virtues as dialectical. Rather
than reducing one to the other, eliding the two together, or
placing the two in a pure and simple dichotomy, Ricoeur places
them in a "tension between two distinct and sometimes opposed
claims."[79] Ricoeur's insight that the virtues are distinct and at times
opposing stands in contrast to Thomas' strategy of the cardinal
virtues where justice is supported by fortitude and temperance and
none contradicts, opposes, or challenges the claims of the other.
But, today, many argue that only when one cardinal virtue stands
on equal footing with another cardinal virtue can there be a
dialectical tension wherein the virtues challenge and define one
another, and, as Ricoeur suggests, "may even be the occasion for
the invention of responsible forms of behavior."[80]

Neither of these virtues, however, addresses the unique relationship that each person has as a moral agent with oneself.[81] Care
for self enjoys a considered role in our tradition, as, for instance,

the command to love God and one's neighbor as oneself. Thomas, too, through his order of charity,[82] developed the love of self that Stephen Pope[83] and Edward Vacek[84] each addresses in his works.

Finally, prudence has the task of integrating the three virtues into our lives, just as it did when it was among the classical list of the cardinal virtues.[85] Thus, prudence is always vigilant, looking to the future, trying not only to realize the claims of justice, fidelity, and self care in the here and now, but also calling us to anticipate occasions when each of these virtues can be more fully acquired. In this way, prudence is clearly a virtue that pursues ends and effectively establishes the moral agenda for the person growing in these virtues.[86] But, these ends are not in opposition to, nor in isolation of, one another. Rather, prudence helps each virtue to shape its end as more inclusive of the other two.

Inasmuch as all persons in every culture are constituted by these three ways of being related, by naming these virtues as cardinal, we have a device for talking cross culturally. Still, this device is based on modest claims. The cardinal virtues do not purport to offer a picture of the ideal person or to exhaust the entire domain of virtue. Rather than being the last word on virtue, they are among the first, providing the bare essentials for right human living and specific action. Thus, inasmuch as the word cardinal derives from the word hinge, the cardinal virtues provide a skeleton of both what human persons should basically be and at what human action should basically aim. All other issues of virtue hang on the skeletal structures of both rightly integrated dispositions and right moral action.

IX. Liberation Ethics

One major reason for discussing cross culturally is to consider the option for the poor and marginalized. Though there is much else that we can take from Latin America's enormous contribution of liberation ethics,[87] the option for the poor[88] has become an essential universal expression of the Christian identity. The extraordinary success of the option for the poor entering into the canon of identifiable Catholic values is attributed, in part, to spirituality: the self understanding of communities of faith, in the light of the Gospel, saw and appropriated the option as a constitutive expression of being in union with God.

The option for the poor means that the poor and marginalized have a privileged perspective and relationship with God who dwells with them. Anyone who wants to draw near to God, therefore, must draw near to those who enjoy this privilege.

It is on this insight that I wish to close, illustrating my point by turning to an urgent matter. I have argued that we need an integrated moral theology that upholds individual conscience and yet is profoundly ecclesial and profoundly relational, that respects cultures and yet can promote cross cultural dialogue. I have also argued that moralists must address the ordinary, be practical in their teaching, and become more aware of the service they can provide to the Churches. We must propose to the Church ways to improve the character of our membership as ethically embodying the Gospel.

For the millennium, I propose to our Churches that we work to end violence against women. This challenge is long overdue: when we examine the literature on violence against women and, in particular, domestic abuse, this enormous topic and its all too common practice remain on the margins of Church reflection and professional ethical writings.[89]

First, we need to recognize that the Churches lack a will to respond to it. Despite the amount of violence done against women, we do not hear about it in our sermons, parish meetings, or the prayers of the faithful. The practice of domestic abuse has not been critiqued by bishops, preachers, or ethicists. The movements that we see against violence in the form of capital punishment, abortion, and euthanasia vastly overwhelm any conscious, organized, and reflective attempts to address the much more familial instance of domestic abuse.

Second, we need to be converted to a will to eradicate domestic abuse and the systemic supports that make it happen. We need to become resolved in our deepest convictions that our inability is due to a willfulness that has accommodated domestic violence into ordinary life.

Third, we need to repent, individually and communally, for not bothering to examine the causes and occasions of violence against women. We need to recognize that our ignorance was culpable.

Fourth, we need to recognize that men are the causes of most domestic violence and that we continually see instances of male rage played out, whether in a Columbine High School or on a crowded highway. We need to ask why, if we are so interested in violence in the form of abortion, euthanasia, and capital punishment, we are not more vocal about forms of violence that are more ecclesial and domestic. We need to see that male violence — whether in the shotgun view of a high schooler or the bullying stance of a prelate — is a violence at home with a variety of social, cultural, legal, and ecclesial structures.

Fifth, we need to learn more about domestic abuse by listening to those victims who have developed voices that can instruct and inform us. We need to encourage the work of narrative to capture these experiences, so that we can learn to recognize the way systematically domestic violence is protected by our laws, culture, and religion. Those narratives will hopefully lead us to examine the civil and ecclesial structures that directly and indirectly prolong this extraordinary barbaric conduct.

Sixth, in light of that recognition, conversion, repentance, and learning, we need to become vigilant as to the causes that prompt it, the structures that support it, and the methods that hide it. In our vigilance, we need to be ready to act. We need to recognize that no option for the poor can be better realized than that of standing with women whose well being is threatened.[90]

Seventh, since domestic abuse is transculturally ordinary,[91] we need to propose virtues to build up a social anthropology that promotes through justice the actual and full equality of all men and women, through fidelity a marital love that rejects the use of force in family life, and through self care the recognition that no one, created in the image of God, should allow herself/himself to remain in a situation of being victimized by brute force.

Only when the depth of one's ascetical commitments is called in faith to be expressed in the moral life will we have an effective, life giving moral theology that can lead the entire Church toward its mission. We need urgently to develop it now.

NOTES

[1]Charles E. Curran, *The Catholic Moral Tradition Today: A Synthesis* (Washington, D.C.: Georgetown University Press, 1999), 1. For an example of the way differing ecclesiologies influenced moral theologians at the beginning of the twentieth century, see his *The Origins of Moral Theology in the United States: Three Different Approaches* (Washington, D.C.: Georgetown University Press, 1997).

[2]Of his many works, two that he edited that dealt with freedom of discourse are *Absolutes in Moral Theology?* (Washington: Corpus Books, 1968); with Richard A. McCormick, *Dissent in the Church* (New York: Paulist Press, 1988). On a narrative of his own practical efforts, see *Faithful Dissent* (Kansas City, MO: Sheed & Ward, 1986).

[3]Christine Gudorf, "The Case of Charles Curran: Sexuality, Reality and the Law," *Christianity and Crisis* 46 (1986), 151-54; "To Make a Seamless Garment, Use a Single Piece of Cloth," in Patricia Beattie Jung and Thomas Shannon, eds., *Abortion and Catholicism* (New York: Crossroad, 1988), 279-96; "Encountering the Other: The Modern Papacy on Women," *Social Compass* 36 (1989): 295-310; *Victimization: Examining Christian Complicity* (Philadelphia: Trinity Press International, 1992); "The Worst Sexual Sin: Sexual Violence and the Church," *Christian Century* 110 (1993), 19-21; *Body, Sex, and Pleasure: Reconstructing Christian Sexual Ethics* (Cleveland: Pilgrim Press, 1994).

[4]On the change from clergy to lay theologians, see Richard McCormick, "Moral Theology 1940-1989: An Overview," *Theological Studies* 50 (1989): 3-24.

⁵James F. Keenan and Joseph Kotva, *Practice What You Preach: Virtues, Ethics, and Power in the Lives of Church Ministers and Their Congregations* (Franklin, WI: Sheed and Ward, 1999).

⁶James F. Keenan with Lisa Sowle Cahill, Jon Fuller, and Kevin Kelly, *Catholic Ethicists on HIV/AIDS Prevention* (New York: Continuum, 2000).

⁷Thomas Slater, *A Manual of Moral Theology*, 2nd ed., 2 vols. (New York: Benziger Brothers, 1908), I: 5-6.

⁸Henry Davis, *Moral and Pastoral Theology* (London: Sheed and Ward, 1941), I, 4.

⁹Héribert Joné made the same point in his *Moral Theology*, distinguishing his work from what "is concerned with the attainment of Christian perfection." Cf. H. Joné, *Moral Theology* (Westminster, MD: Newman Press, 1959), 1. In another work, as quoted in Henry McAdoo, *The Structure of Caroline Moral Theology* (London: Longmans, 1949), 10-11, Slater wrote that the object of moral theology "is not to place high ideals of virtue before the people and train them in Christian perfection...its primary object is to teach the priest how to distinguish what is sinful from what is lawful...it is not intended for edification nor for the building up of character." For a discussion on the differences between English Protestant writings and Roman Catholics on this point, besides McAdoo, see Thomas Wood, *English Casuistical Divinity during the Seventeenth Century* (London: SPCK, 1952). On the overall impact of these manuals on moral theology, see John Mahoney, *The Making of Moral Theology* (Oxford: Oxford UP, 1989), 1-36; John Gallagher, *Time Past, Time Future: An Historical Study of Catholic Moral Theology* (New York: Paulist Press, 1990). More specifically, see the manualists as they worked in the United States in Charles Curran, *The Origins of Moral Theology in the United States: Three Different Approaches.* On the penitentials, see *Medieval Handbooks of Penance*, ed. John T. McNeill and Helen M. Gamer (New York: Columbia UP, 1990); James Dallen, *The Reconciling Community* (New York: Pueblo Pub. Co., 1986); Bernard Poschman, *Penance and Anointing of the Sick* (New York: Herder and Herder, 1964). On the confessional manuals, see Kilian McDonnell, "The *Summae Confessorum* on the Integrity of Confession as Prolegomena for Luther and Trent," *Theological Studies* 54 (1993): 405-26. On casuistry, see Albert Jonsen and Stephen Toulmin, *The Abuse of Casuistry: A History of Moral Reasoning* (Berkeley: University of California Press, 1988); *Conscience and Casuistry in Early Modern Europe*, ed. Edmund Leites (New York: Cambridge UP, 1988); and, *The Context of Casuistry*, ed. J. Keenan and T. Shannon (Washington, D.C.: Georgetown UP, 1995).

¹⁰See the argument in John Mahoney, *op. cit.* See also Richard McCormick, "Self-Assessment and Self-Indictment," *Religious Studies Review* 13 (1987): 37-44.

¹¹Quoted in Johann Verstraeten, "Perspectives for a Spirituality of the Laity in the Twenty-First Century and the Rediscovery of the Meaning of Professional Life" (unpublished paper), at 13.

¹²Pope John Paul II, *Veritatis Splendor* (Washington: United States Catholic Conference, 1993).

¹³Herbert McCabe, "Manuals and rule books," in John Wilkins, ed., *Considering Veritatis Splendor* (Cleveland: Pilgrim Press, 1994), 61-68. On the historical development of the concept, "intrinsically evil," see John

Dedek, "Intrinsically Evil Acts: The Emergence of a Doctrine," *Recherches de théologie ancienne et médiévale* 50 (1983): 191-226; "Intrinsically Evil Acts: An Historical Study of the Mind of St. Thomas," *The Thomist* 43 (1979): 385-413; "Moral Absolutes in the Predecessors of St. Thomas," *Theological Studies* 38 (1977): 654-80. Dedek argues that the fourteenth century opponent of Thomas Aquinas' writings, Durandus of St. Pourcain, fathered the concept. In many ways, *Evangelium Vitae* was a striking improvement over *Veritatis Splendor*'s insistence on pathological language. See Kevin Wildes, ed., *Choosing Life: A Dialogue on Evangelium vitae* (Washington, D. C.: Georgetown UP, 1997); Reinhard Hutter and Theodor Dieter, eds., *Ecumenical Ventures in Ethics: Protestants Engage Pope John Paul II's Moral Encyclicals* (Grand Rapids, MI: Eerdmans, 1997).

[14]"In hoc quippe mundo humana anima quasi more navis est contra ictum fluminis conscendentis: uno in loco nequaquam stare permittitur, quia ad ima relabitur, nisi ad summa conetur" (Gregory, *Reg. Past.*, p. III, c. 34: *ML* 77, 118c).

[15]"In via vitae non progredi regredi est" (Bernard, *Serm II in festo Purif.*, n. 3: *ML* 183, 369 C).

[16]"In via Dei stare retrocedere est." Thomas attributes the quote to Bernard in *In III Sen* d29,a8,qla2,1a, and to Gregory in *ST* II-II,24,6 ob3.

[17]Stanley Hauerwas and David Burrell, "Self-Deception and Autobiography: Reflections on Speer's *Inside the Third Reich*," in *Truthfulness and Tragedy* (Notre Dame: University of Notre Dame Press, 1977), 82-98, argue that, unlike the other Nazi leaders, Speer's wickedness was most ordinary. While leading a fine family life, he made certain he was not bothered with knowledge of the concentration camps.

[18]The distinction seems to have appeared first in the writings of G. B. Scaramelli (1687-1752); thus, after the period I am interested in. See T. A. Porter, "Spiritual Theology," in *New Catholic Encyclopedia* (San Francisco: McGraw Hill, 1967), XIII, 588-90.

[19]Joseph de Guibert, *The Theology of the Spiritual Life* (New York: Sheed and Ward, 1953); Jean Leclercq, François Vandenbroucke, and Louis Bouyer, *History of Christian Spirituality* (London: Burns and Oates, 1968); *Christian Spirituality*, ed. Bernard McGinn and John Meyendorff (New York: Crossroad, 1985); Caroline Walker Bynum, *Jesus as Mother: Studies in the Spirituality of the High Middle Ages* (Berkeley: University of California Press, 1982).

[20]Bernard McGinn, "The Human Person as Image of God," *Christian Spirituality*, 312-30, at 323. While the twelfth century marks the enormous systematic development of ascetical texts, a few appear earlier, e.g., Dhuoda's *Manual for My Son* (843) and Jonas of Orléans' treatise, *Instruction of the Laity* (c. 828). See Jacques Fontaine, "The Practice of Christian Life: The Birth of the Laity," *Christian Spirituality*, 453-91.

[21]Bynum, "Did the Twelfth Century Discover the Individual?," *Jesus as Mother*, 82-109, at 109.

[22]Ibid., 86.

[23]François Vandenbroucke, "Lay Spirituality in the Twelfth Century," *History of Christian Spirituality*, 243-82.

[24]Bynum, 106.

[25]I develop this elsewhere: "Spirituality and Morality: What's the Difference?," in *Method and Catholic Moral Theology: The Ongoing Reconstruction*, ed. Todd Salzman (Omaha: Creighton University Press, 1999), 87-102.

[26]See my "How Casuistic Is Early British Puritan Casuistry? Or, What Are the Roots of Early British Puritan Practical Divinity?," in *The Jesuits: Cultures, Sciences, and the Arts*, ed. John O'Malley et al. (Toronto: Toronto University Press, July, 1999).

[27]Gérard Gilleman, *Le primat de la charité en théologie morale: essai méthodologique* (Louvain: E. Nauwelaerts, 1952); *The Primacy of Charity* (Westminster, MD: Newman Press, 1959).

[28]I have done some work on this in *Goodness and Rightness in Thomas Aquinas' Summa Theologiae* (Washington, D.C.: Georgetown University Press, 1992); "Distinguishing Charity As Goodness and Prudence As Rightness: A Key to Thomas' *Pars Secunda*," *The Thomist* 56 (1992): 407-26; "A New Distinction in Moral Theology: Being Good and Living Rightly," *Church* 5 (1989), 22-28; see Conrad van Ouwerkerk, *Caritas et Ratio: Etude sur le double principe de la vie morale chrétienne d'après S. Thomas d'Aquin* (Nijmegen: Drukkerij Gebr. Janssen, 1956).

[29]The distinction has been extensively used by Europeans, especially by Bruno Schueller, *Die Begruendung sittlicher Urteile* (Duesseldorf: Patmos, 1980); "Neuere Beitraege zum Thema 'Begruendung sittlicher Normen'," in *Theologische Berichte* 4, ed. Franz Furger (Zurich: Benziger Verlag, 1974), 109-81. See also Charles Curran and Richard McCormick, eds., *Readings in Moral Theology No. 1* (Mahwah: Paulist Press, 1979), 184-98; *Readings in Moral Theology No. 2* (New York: Paulist Press, 1980), 207-33. See also Josef Fuchs, *Christian Morality: The Word Becomes Flesh*, trans. Brian McNeil (Washington, D.C.: Georgetown UP, 1987); Klaus Demmer, *Deuten und Handeln* (Freiburg, Switzerland: Universitaetsverlag, 1985); Louis Janssens, "Ontic Good and Evil: Premoral Values and Disvalues," *Louvain Studies* 12 (1987): 62-82; Bernard Hoose, *Proportionalism* (Washington, D.C.: Georgetown University Press, 1987). In the United States, see Richard McCormick, "Bishops as Teachers, Scholars as Listeners," in *The Critical Calling* (Washington, D.C.: Georgetown University Press, 1989), 95-110; *Notes in Moral Theology* 1981-1984 (Lanham, MD: University Press of America, 1984).

[30]See Philip Sheldrake, *Images of Holiness: Explorations in Contemporary Spirituality* (London: Darton, Longman and Todd, 1987), who discusses the "spirituality of struggle." Also see Jean Leclerq's discussion of the "Christian Hero," in *History of Christian Spirituality*, 60-2.

[31]Stephen Pope, *The Evolution of Altruism and the Ordering of Love* (Washington, D.C.: Georgetown University Press, 1994); Edward Collins Vacek, *Love, Human and Divine: the Heart of Christian Ethics* (Washington, D.C.: Georgetown University Press, 1994). See also James Keating, "Listening to Christ's Heart: Moral Theology and Spirituality in Dialogue," *Milltown Studies* 39 (1997): 48-65; "The Good Life," *Church* 11.2 (1995), 15-20; Mark O'Keefe, *Becoming Good, Becoming Holy: On the Relationship of Christian Ethics and Spirituality* (Mahwah: Paulist Press, 1995).

[32]In particular, the ordinary was caught in domestic life; see Martin Thornton, *English Spirituality* (Cambridge, MA: Cowley, 1986), 215-17.

[33]Thomas Aquinas, *Summa Theologiae* I. II. 1. 3c; see my discussion of this claim in "Ten Reasons Why Thomas Aquinas Is Important for Ethics Today," *New Blackfriars* 75 (1994): 354-63.

[34]Colin Atkinson and William Stoneman, "'These griping greefes and pinching pangs': Attitudes of Childbirth in Thomas Bentley's *The Monument of Matrones* (1582)," *Sixteenth Century Journal* 21 (1990): 193-203.

[35]See Vandenbroucke, "Lay Spirituality in the Twelfth Century," 254-57.

[36]See Giles Constable, "The Interpretation of Martha and Mary," in *Three Studies in Medieval Religious and Social Thought* (New York: Cambridge University Press, 1995), 1-142.

[37]See the interest Aquinas had in the formation of young Dominicans in Leonard Boyle, *The Setting of the Summa Theologiae of Saint Thomas* (Toronto: University of Toronto Press, 1982); see also Simon Tugwell's lengthy introduction to Aquinas in *Albert and Thomas: Selected Writings* (New York: Paulist Press, 1988), 201-352. There, too, we see Thomas' "spiritual writings." See also Simon Tugwell, ed., *Early Dominicans: Selected Writings* (New York: Paulist Press, 1982).

[38]de Guibert, 5.

[39]See my discussion on the word "exercise" in Thomas' writings in *Goodness and Rightness in Thomas Aquinas' Summa Theologiae*, 50-52.

[40]Odon Lottin, *Psychologie et morale aux XIIième et XIIIième siècles*, 6 Tomes (Louvain:Abbaye du Mont César, 1942-57); *Morale Fondamentale* (Tournai: Desclée, 1954). See Mary Jo Iozzio, *Self-Determination and the Moral Act: A Study of the Contributions of Odon Lottin, O.S.B.* (Leuven: Peeters, 1995).

[41]Thomas Aquinas, *Scriptum super libros Sententiarum*, IV, 38. 2. 4 q.a 3; see also IV, 27. 1. 2. q.a. 4 ad3; IV, 27. 3. 3 expositio.

[42]John Treloar, "Moral Virtue and the Demise of Prudence in the Thought of Francis Suarez," *American Catholic Philosophical Quarterly* 65 (1991): 387-405.

[43]Philip Sheldrake, "Spirituality in History: A Social Perspective," *The Way Supplement: Spirituality and Social Issues* 63 (1988): 38-50, at 45.

[44]Anne E. Patrick, "Narrative and the social dynamics of virtue," in Dietmar Mieth and Jacques Pohier, eds., *Changing values and virtues* (Edinburgh: T & T Clark, 1987), 69-80.

[45]Patricia Beattie Jung, "Sanctification: An Interpretation in Light of Embodiment," *Journal of Religious Ethics* 11 (1983): 75-94; see also Paul Lauritzen, "Emotions and Religious Ethics," *Journal of Religious Ethics* 16 (1988): 307-24.

[46]For the most part, the best work on the topic of hospitality looks to the early Church where the spiritual theology animated the moral imperative to welcome the stranger. See John Elliott, *A Home for the Homeless: A Sociological Exegesis of I Peter, Its Situation and Strategy* (Philadelphia: Fortress, 1981); David Gowler, "Hospitality and Characterization in Luke 11:37-54," *Semeia* 64 (1994): 213-51; L. Gregory Jones, "The virtues of hospitality (2 Kgs 4:8-17; Lk 10:38-42)," *Christian Century* 109, (1992), 17-24; E. A. Judge, "The Quest for Mercy in Late Antiquity," in *God Who Is Rich in Mercy*, ed. P. T. O'Brien (Sydney: Macquarie University Press, 1986), 107-21; James Keenan, "Hospitality," in *Virtues for Ordinary Christians* (Kansas City: Sheed and Ward, 1996), 106-11; "Jesuit Hospitality?," in Martin Tripole, ed., *Promise Renewed: Jesuit Higher Education for a New Millennium* (Scranton:

Scranton UP, 1999); John Koenig, *New Testament Hospitality: Partnership with Strangers as Promise and Mission* (Philadelphia: Fortress, 1985); "New Testament Hospitality," *America* 155 (1986), 6; Julia Kristeva, *Strangers to Ourselves* (New York: Columbia University Press, 1991); Victor Matthews, "Hospitality and Hostility in Genesis 19 and Judges 19," *Biblical Theology Bulletin* 22 (1992): 3-11; "Hospitality and Hostility in Judges 4," *Biblical Theology Bulletin* 21 (1991): 13-21; Wayne Meeks, *The First Urban Christians* (New Haven: Yale University Press, 1983); Thomas Ogletree, *Hospitality to the Stranger: Dimensions of Moral Understanding* (Philadelphia: Fortress Press, 1985); Parker Palmer, *A Company of Strangers* (New York: Crossroad, 1986); Robin Scroggs, "The Social Interpretation of the New Testament," *New Testament Studies* 26 (1980): 164-79; Marta Sordi, *The Christians and the Roman Empire* (Norman: University of Oklahoma Press, 1986). For me, the finest account was in Rodney Stark, *The Rise of Christianity: A Sociologist Reconsiders History* (Princeton: Princeton UP, 1996). For the most insightful argument for a new direction in the practice of hospitality, see Christine Pohl, "Hospitality from the Edge: The Significance of Marginality in the Practice of Welcome," *Annual of the Society of Christian Ethics* (1995): 121-36.

[47]Anne E. Patrick, *Liberating Conscience: Feminist Explorations in Catholic Moral Theology* (New York: Continuum, 1996). See also her "Power and responsibility: changing paradigms of virtue [patriarchal and egalitarian-feminist paradigms]," in William O'Brien, ed., *Jesuit education and the cultivation of virtue* (Washington, D.C.: Georgetown UP, 1990), 31-49.

[48]A helpful reader on this enormous topic is Charles E. Curran, Margaret A. Farley, and Richard A. McCormick, eds., *Feminist Ethics and the Catholic Moral Tradition* (New York: Paulist Press, 1996). For an integrated theory, see Christina Traina, *Feminist Ethics and Natural Law: The End of the Anathemas* (Washington, D.C.: Georgetown UP, 1999); Denise Lardner Carmody, *Virtuous Woman: Reflections on Christian Feminist Ethics* (Maryknoll, N.Y.: Orbis Books, 1992).

[49]See our extended discussion of this: James Keenan and Thomas Kopfensteiner, "Moral Theology out of Western Europe," *Theological Studies* 59 (1998): 107-35.

[50]See the recent collection of Auer's work; in particular, "Die Bedeutung des Christlichen bei der Normfindung," in *Zur Theologie der Ethik* (Freiburg: Herder, 1995), 208. His interest in the thesis from an ecclesiological perspective stems from an early article: "Nach dem Erscheinen der Enzyklika *Humanae vitae* — Zehn Thesen über die findung sittlicher Weisungen," *Theologische Quartalschrift* 149 (1969): 78-85; the classical work remains his *Autonome Moral und Christlicher Glaube* (Düsseldorf: Patmos, 1984).

[51]Augustine, *Confessions*, III 6, 11; *PL* 32, 683.

[52]Klaus Demmer, "Die autonome Moral — einige Anfrage an die Denkform," in Adrian Holderegger, ed., *Fundamente der theologischen Ethik. Bilanz und Neuansätze* (Freiburg: Herder, 1996), 261-76, at 262.

[53]Sabatino Majorano, *La coscienza. Per una lettura cristiana* (Milan: Edizioni San Paolo, 1994). See also Marian Nalepa and Terence Kennedy, eds., *La Coscienza Morale Oggi* (Rome: Editiones Academiae Alphonsianae, 1987).

[54]Marciano Vidal, "Conciencia," *Diccionario de ética teológica* (Navarra: Estella, 1991), 107. See Patricia Lamoureux's thoughtful critique, "The Criterion of Option for the Poor and Moral Discernment: The Vision of Marciano Vidal," *Louvain Studies* 21 (1996): 261-87.

[55]Brian Johnstone, "Solidarity and Moral Conscience: Challenges for our Theological and Pastoral Work," *Studia Moralia* 31 (1993): 65-85, at 85.

[56]See the important survey by Franz Furger, "Christlich-theologische Ethik-angefragt und in Frage gestellt," *Theologie der Gegenwart* 39 (1996): 209-34.

[57]Enrico Chiavacci, "Für eine Neuinterpretation des Naturbegriffs," in Dietmar Mieth, ed., *Moraltheologie im Abseits? Antwort auf die Enzyklika Veritatis Splendor* (Freiburg: Herder, 1994), 110-28; Philipp Schmitz, "Natur im ökosystematischen Denken," in Bernhard Fraling, ed., *Natur im ethischen Argument* (Freiburg: Herder, 1990), 110-12.

[58]Klaus Demmer, "Natur und Person: Brennpunkte gegenwärtiger moraltheologischer Auseinandersetzung," *Natur im ethischen Argument*, 64-70.

[59]Catherine Mowry LaCugna, *God for Us: The Trinity and Christian life* (San Francisco: Harper, 1991).

[60]Margaret Farley, "New Patterns of Relationship: Beginnings of a Moral Revolution," *Theological Studies* 36 (1975): 627-46. She also develops this in "Fragments for an ethic of commitment in Thomas Aquinas," in David Tracy, ed., *Celebrating the Medieval heritage: a colloquy on the thought of Aquinas and Bonaventure* (Chicago: University of Chicago Press, 1978), 135-55.

[61]Edward Collins Vacek, "Love for God: Is It Obligatory?," in *Annual of the Society of Christian Ethics* (Chicago: Society of Christian Ethics, 1996), 203-21; "The Eclipse of Love for God," *America* (9 Mar 1996), 13-16.

[62]Klaus Demmer, "La Competenza normativa del magistero ecclesiastico in morale," in *Fede Cristiana e Agire Morale*, Klaus Demmer and Bruno Schueller, eds. (Assisi: Cittadella Editrice, 1980), 144-69; J. Fuchs, "Teaching Morality: The Tension between Bishops and Theologians within the Church," in *Christian Ethics in a Secular Arena* (Washington, D.C.: Georgetown University Press, 1984), 131-53; Gerard Hughes, *Authority in Morals* (London: Sheed and Ward, 1978); R. McCormick, "Bishops as Teachers and Jesuits as Listeners," *Studies in the Spirituality of Jesuits* 18.3 (1986). Similarly, see the questions raised in James Torrens, "A New Form of Papal Teaching," *America* (3 April 1999), 19-20; Hermann J. Pottmeyer, "Fallible Infallibility? A New Form of Papal Teaching," *Stimmen der Zeit* 4 (April, 1999): 233-42.

[63]See my "Catholic Moral Theology, Ignatian Spirituality, and Virtue Ethics: Strange Bedfellows," *Supplement to the Way: Spirituality and Ethics* 88 (1997): 36-45. In the same issue, Jean Porter claims that moral theology ought to precede ascetical theology; see her "Virtue Ethics and Its Significance for Spirituality," 26-35.

[64]William Spohn, "Passions and Principles," *Theological Studies* 52 (1991): 69-87; "The Return of Virtue Ethics," *Theological Studies* 53 (1992): 60-75; "Spirituality and Ethics: Exploring the Connections," *Theological Studies* 58 (1997): 109-23.

[65]Joseph Kotva, *The Christian Case for Virtue Ethics* (Washington, D.C.: Georgetown University, 1996).

[66]Paul Lauritzen, "The Self and Its Discontents," *Journal of Religious Ethics* 22 (1994): 189-210, at 206.

[67]James Keenan, "Proposing Cardinal Virtues," *Theological Studies* 56.4 (1995): 709-29.

[68]Paul Ricoeur, "Love and Justice," in Werner G. Jeanrond and Jennifer L. Rike, eds., *Radical Pluralism and Truth: David Tracy and the Hermeneutics of Religion* (New York: Crossroad, 1991), 195.

[69]Bernard Williams, "Justice as a Virtue," in *Essays on Aristotle's Ethics*, ed. Amelia Oksenberg Rorty (Berkeley: University of California Press, 1980), 189-99. See also Seamus Murphy, "The Many Ways of Justice," *Studies in the Spirituality of the Jesuits* 26.2 (1994): 1-40.

[70]See a similar insight in Spohn, "The Return," 72. In several questions dealing with charity, Aquinas argues that we have greater obligations to those with whom we enjoy specific relationships; see II. II. 31.3 and 32.9.

[71]Reinhold Niebuhr, *Love and Justice: Selections from the Shorter Writings of Reinhold Niebuhr*, ed. D. B. Robertson (Louisville: Westminster, 1957); on a similar insight, see Karen Lebacqz, *Justice in an Unjust World* (Minneapolis: Augsburg Publishing House, 1987); José Miranda, *Marx and the Bible* (Maryknoll: Orbis, 1974).

[72]Carol Gilligan, *In a Different Voice: Psychological Theory and Women's Development* (Cambridge: Harvard University, 1982).

[73]Paul Ramsey, *The Patient as Person: Explorations in Medical Ethics* (New Haven: Yale University, 1970); *The Essential Paul Ramsey: A Collection*, ed. William Werpehowski and Stephen Crocco (New Haven: Yale University, 1994).

[74]Gilbert Meilaender, *Friendship: A Study in Theological Ethics* (Notre Dame: University of Notre Dame Press, 1981).

[75]Paul Wadell, *Friendship and the Moral Life* (Notre Dame: University of Notre Dame Press, 1989).

[76]George Fletcher, *Loyalty: An Essay on the Morality of Relationships* (New York: Oxford University Press, 1993).

[77]Margaret Farley, "An Ethic for Same Sex Relations," in *A Challenge To Love*, ed. Robert Nugent (New York: Crossroad, 1986), 93-106; *Personal Commitments: Beginning, Keeping, Changing* (San Francisco: Harper and Row, 1990).

[78]William Werpehowski, "The Professions: Vocations to Justice and Love," in Francis A. Eigo, O.S.A., ed., *The Professions in Ethical Context* (Villanova: Villanova UP, 1986), 1-24.

[79]Ricoeur, "Love and Justice," 196.

[80]Ibid, 197.

[81]Feminist therapists use the term self care in professional ethics. See L. S. Brown, "Ethical Issues in Feminist Therapy: Selected Topics," *Psychology of Women Quarterly* 15 (1991): 324-33; Katherine M. Clarke, "Lessons from Feminist Therapy for Ministerial Ethics," *Journal of Pastoral Care* 48 (1994): 233-42. See another example: Marc Lappe, "Virtue and Public Health," in Earl Shelp, ed., *Virtue and Medicine* (Dordrecht: D. Reidel Publishing, 1985), 289-303.

[82]The concern for self care runs throughout the *Summa* from I. 5. 1c and 48.1, which concern the insight that all nature seeks its own perfection, to I. II 27.3, that insists that it is natural to prefer oneself over others, and 29.4, that it is impossible to hate oneself. In II.II, Aquinas argues that, though inordinate self love is the source of sin (25.4, 28.4.ad1), self love

belongs to the order of charity and is prior to neighbor love (25.12, 26.4). He adds that from charity comes peace that aims at ending conflict, not only with others, but also within oneself (29.1).

[83]Besides *The Evolution of Altruism,* see his "Expressive Individualism and True Self-Love: A Thomistic Perspective," *Journal of Religion* 71.3 (1991): 384-99.

[84]Vacek, *Love, Human and Divine,* 239-73.

[85]Joseph Burroughs, *Prudence Integrating the Moral Virtues According to Saint Thomas Aquinas* (Washington, D.C.: Catholic University, 1955).

[86]See Daniel Mark Nelson, "Karl Rahner's Existential Ethics: A Critique Based on St. Thomas's Understanding of Prudence," *The Thomist* 51 (1987): 461-79; *The Priority of Prudence* (University Park: Pennsylvania State University, 1992).

[87]The finest collection on the topic remains Ignacio Ellacuría and Jon Sobrino, eds., *Mysterium Liberationis: Fundamental Concepts of Liberation Theology* (Maryknoll, N.Y.: Orbis 1993). The best bibliography in English also remains Thomas Schubeck, "Ethics and Liberation Theology," *Theological Studies* 56 (March, 1995): 107-22.

[88]Gustavo Gutierrez, "Option for the Poor," *Mysterium Liberationis,* 235-50.

[89]Pamela Cooper-White, *The Cry of Tamar: Violence against Women and the Church's Response* (Minneapolis: Augsburg/Fortress, 1995); Elisabeth Schüssler Fiorenza and M. Shawn Copeland, eds., *Violence Against Women* (Maryknoll: Orbis, 1994); Myra Burnett, "Suffering and Sanctification: The Religious Context of Battered Women," *Pastoral Psychology* 44 (1996): 145-49; Carol Schlueter, "Creating a New Reality: No More Domestic Violence," *Currents in Theology and Mission* 23 (August, 1996): 254-64; Marc Cwik, "Peace in the Home? The Response of Rabbis to Wife Abuse within Judaism," *Journal of Psychology and Judaism* 20 (1996): 273-348; 21 (1997): 1-82; Marie Fortune, "Picking Up the Broken Pieces: Responding to Domestic Violence," *Church and Society* 85 (1995): 36-47; Alberta Wood and Maureen McHugh, "Women Battering: The Response of the Clergy," *Pastoral Psychology* 42 (1994): 185-96; Jim Bowman, "Is Male Headship Linked to Spousal Abuse?," *Christianity Today* 38 (20 June 1994), 62; Linda Midgett, "Silent Screams: Do Evangelicals Hear the Cries of Battered Women?," *Daughters of Sarah* 20 (1994), 43-45; Lutheran World Federation Council, "Resolution on Violence Against Women," *LWF Documentation* 33 (1993): 120-21.

[90]Feminist theologians have begun to make for us a connection with liberation theology: Maria Pilar Aquino, "Women's Contribution to Theology in Liberation," in *Readings in Moral Theology No. 9: Feminist Ethics and the Catholic Moral Tradition* (New York: Paulist Press, 1996), 90-119; Ada María Isasi-Díaz, "Defining our *Proyecto Historico: Mujerista* Strategies for Liberation," ibid., 120-35.

[91]See the writings of Susan B. Sorenson: "Violence and injury in marital arguments: Risk Patterns and Gender Differences," *American Journal of Public Health* 86 (1996): 35-40; "Violence Against Women: Examining Ethnic Differences and Commonalities," *Evaluation Review* 20 (1996): 123-45; "Physical, Sexual and Emotional Abuse by Male Intimates: Experiences of Women in Japan," *Violence and Victims* 9 (1994): 63-77.

Sexual Morality in the New Millennium

Christine E. Gudorf

If present trends continue, there are at least three independent variables that will have a great impact on sexuality and sexual morality and to which the Churches should respond in the new millennium. They are: 1) the confluence of population, consumption, and environment; 2) the AIDS pandemic; and 3) the erosion of dimorphism as the basic paradigm for human sexuality. I will deal in turn with at least some of the aspects of each.

I. Population, Consumption, and Environment

When many of us first became aware of the "population crisis," it was the sixties, and the big question was how long the world's growing population could be fed. For some time now, the shape of the population question has been radically different. For one, it is well understood that the key issue is not whether we can continue to extract sufficient food or even energy from the earth, but, rather, what are the long term effects of human extraction of resources, that is, what is the cost to the biosphere of farming, mining, smelting, manufacturing, energy production, construction, and lumbering — the impact on our air, earth temperature, surface water, aquifers, oceans, soil, plants, and animals? The costs of human activities expand with the scale of such activities, and the scale rises, at different rates in different parts of the world, with population levels. North Americans use more than twice as much fresh water per person as Europeans, produce two and a half times as many tons of carbon dioxide emissions, and use almost two and a half times as much energy.[1] Compared with Africa, North

29

America uses twenty-four times more energy per person, almost three times as much water, and produces eighteen times the amount of carbon dioxide emissions.[2] A child born in the United States will cause about thirty times the total environmental damage as a child born in a nation of the Third World, of which garbage production (radioactive, chemical, construction, and simple household types) is a significant part.

By the late eighties, it had become clear that the only way to make figures for population, or consumption, or environmental health meaningful was to relate them to one another. We cannot know what the carrying capacity of the earth — what size human population can be sustained — until we figure in both the consumption levels of that human population and then the environmental impact of that size population at that level of consumption. One of the most common models for gauging the environmental impact of population and consumption on the environment is the IPAT model of Ehrlich and Ehrlich: $I = PxAxT$, that is, Environmental Impact = (Population size)x(Affluence level)x(Technology).[3] At present levels of consumption, mid range estimates of the carrying capacity of the earth run from seven to twelve billion persons; conservative estimates of three to five billion were surpassed in the late seventies and eighties.

We can legitimately have different moral responses to aspects of the environmental crisis. Many deep ecologists propose that no one species should have any priority over other species, so that the third to half of modern species which have not yet become extinct through human activities have a veto power over human projects.[4] The more populist position seems to be compromised between the needs of humans and those of other species. But, there are also dangerous macro trends, such as global warming, about which there can be less dispute. Oceans all over the world have become warmer in the last twenty years at the same time that the average land temperatures have dropped about one degree.[5] This warming trend has already put intense pressure on species in many parts of the world. In the last five years, scientists who used to be divided over the theory of global warming have reached general agreement that carbon dioxide emissions are at least one significant cause of global warming which is not only destroying species' habitats, but aggravating in many parts of the world already existing problems from overpopulation, such as desertification and dropping water tables. Rising temperatures have already increased the spread of dry season fires throughout the world which add to the carbon dioxide emissions level. On macro trends, such as global warming, the debate that remains is how fast we need to act to keep how much life sustainable.

As of a few months ago, the earth held more than six billion humans. Population control measures in the last thirty years have reduced the number of children per woman in the developing world from more than 6 to 3.3.[6] But, the population of most developing nations tends to be so young (one third under 15) that, even if the world as a whole had already reached replacement level (2.1 children per couple), the population of the world would still increase to almost twelve billion before it began to stabilize.[7] And, the world is not even close to that 2.1 replacement rate. We will almost certainly reach or surpass the most optimistic estimates of the earth's carrying capacity — twelve to fifteen billion humans.

Justice requires that we deal with consumption levels in two different ways. On the one hand, developing nations must be allowed to increase consumption levels because their level of poverty is morally unacceptable. Seventy percent of the population of Latin America, and an even higher proportion of Africa, lives in poverty. Catholic social teaching has long been clear that the poorest populations in the world need to consume *more* food, energy, housing, medicines, immunizations, books and newspapers, technology — all those things that alleviate poverty and misery and support human dignity.[8] As recent industrialization in China, Korea, and Taiwan has raised the standard of living of the poor majorities, it has also increased pollution of air, water, and soil. Similar increase in pollution will be unavoidable for other developing nations as well, though they should not be exempt from conservation measures. The earth cannot survive the damage that will accompany development in these nations unless those rich nations which have been disproportionately supplying the vast majority of the pollutants cut back significantly both on per person consumption and on their own levels of population.

Basic human morality dictates that the most affluent twenty percent of the world should not continue to consume eighty percent of the world's clean air, water, energy, and soil. We in the rich nations must not only begin serious reduction in consumption, but, to the extent that our per person consumption remains in excess of that of others, we must further reduce our population growth rate and open our doors to excess population from the most stressed areas of the world.

The implications of this for sexual morality are critical. If Americans and other privileged groups are not to become largely celibate, with licenses to marry and procreate as the new prizes in state lotteries, sex must be normatively contraceptive. We *must* separate sexual activity and reproduction. This does not mean that sex must become "merely" recreational or that reproduction must become technologized or mechanized production.

We must abandon both the "modern scientific" view of the natural as chaotic material to be ordered, controlled, and given purpose by human reason, as well as the traditional Catholic interpretation, which has been to identify patterns in nature as representing the will of the Creator to be simply transcribed into moral law for humans. Discerning Natural Law requires very critical discernments of processes, interactions, and systems; simplistic analyses of individual actions are not sufficient. We can no longer assume that whatever seems to happen "naturally" is good; behavior that has long been assumed to be natural in the past — the identification of procreation as both an unambiguous good and as the end of sex — is now killing, and may finally destroy, all of God's creation. Rather, we should assume that the destruction of the entire biosphere through over reproduction is contrary to the will of the God of life and is certainly contrary to God's command of human stewardship of the earth.

The Catholic Church has taught that all persons have the right to marry, that celibacy is a gift, that marriage entails an openness to having children who can be prevented only through the use of sexual abstinence. This is a formula for planetary death. Even if it *were* possible to convince people the world over that the answer to the population/consumption/environment crisis was that married people must use sexual abstinence to prevent having more than one child — a message which has been less than persuasive over five decades — the global results would be disastrous. Most women are married, or otherwise coupled, for the majority of their fertilized years, an average of more than thirty years. Abstinence in the fertile period would mean approximately nine to fifteen days of abstinence per month *in addition to* the four to twelve days of sexual abstinence for those whose religious, cultural, or personal traditions forbid sex during or immediately after menstruation. For the fifteen to twenty-five percent of women with irregular menstrual cycles, safe use of natural family planning may restrict sex on all but three or four days a month. For couples in which one or both travel on business, are in the military, or have illnesses which can also restrict sex, the irregularity of marital sex under natural family planning can put severe strain on the marital bond itself.

Even when couples are able to restrict sex to one or two weeks every month for month after month, year after year, is it really reasonable to imagine that their willpower would be strong enough to endure thirty years of intimate living? Is the ovulatory schedule of the wife really a more humanly valuable indicator of when sex is appropriate between spouses than is the need to physically share mourning for the loss of a child or parent, celebration of an anniversary, or affirmation of one's contrition and forgiveness of the spouse? The Jesus who insisted that the Sabbath was made for humans, and not humans for the Sabbath, would, I think, reject the priority of the vaginal thermometer over spousal need to express love.

Natural family planning can be as effective as most mechanical or chemical methods when it is implemented correctly. But, there is a lot more incentive to fall off the natural family planning method than there is with pills or diaphragms. Using pills or diaphragms usually attaches minor inconvenience or delay to occasions of marital sex; natural family planning *eliminates* occasions of marital sex. Loving, committed couples who follow natural family planning for thirty years and have had sex only once every six years in the fertile period should be commended for their self control — but, they still may have five children. And, at what cost to their relationship have they so frequently resisted their desire for each other?

Within the Catholic community, the debate that began in the 1960s over contraception and the role of sex in marriage was the field in which many lay persons first learned to express their marital sexual experience in theological terms, as religious experience, as sacramental, and as an ongoing symbol of the mutual self giving which lies at the core of marriage. Natural family planning may well be the best method for spacing children; it is without a doubt the safest. It may be valuable as a supportive discipline in the spiritual lives of couples, as is often claimed. As a method of preventing conception for thirty years per woman, it simply cannot be relied upon to produce a 1 to 1.5 children per woman fertility rate for six to fifteen billion people.

In the Catholic community, the issue of contraception was originally raised in a rights context: did couples have a moral right to limit the number of their children? The implication was that having fewer children was a personal preference; such a preference has been regularly criticized by many in the Church as selfish, materialist, and antilife, as rejecting the gift of God's bounty. Today, the Church must recognize that it is large families that are selfish and antilife and require moral justification. Contraception is not only, or even primarily, an individual right; it is a social obligation.

Other than hoping that natural family planning will suddenly inspire billions with a miraculous newfound commitment to regular monthly abstinence, we have two options as a world community. We can either deny a universal human right to marriage and sex, or we can retain the right to marriage and sex, but severely limit procreation through use of artificial contraception. Both in practical and in doctrinal terms, it seems to me that there is no contest here.

Sexual relationship is a central aspect of the sociality of humans. Celibacy *is* a real possibility for humans; the real questions are how desirable is it for whole societies, what degree of coercion would be required to enforce it, and at what social cost? The particular meanings of sexual relationship differ in every age and culture and, as we shall see, are under tremendous transformation in post-modernity. While there can be little doubt that sexual pairing has been a foundation of human society in terms of its social structure, the organization of work and shelter, and the distribution of social resources, neither procreation nor sexual pleasure has ever exhausted the meaning of sexual pairing. Sexual pairing has been considered so fundamental to human beings that the Catholic Church has taught that the dignity of the human person entails the right to decide for oneself whether or not to marry and whom to marry.[9] No person and no society has the right to make that decision for one. One might even argue that to deny humans a right to marry would be to move backward in evolutionary terms to the societies of ants and bees in which reproduction is reserved for the few and the rest designated as workers. What meaning could human rights have in a community made up largely of drones?

Contraceptive sex as normative is much more achievable than restricting marriage and sex and much less morally problematic because less coercive. The best proof of this is that sixty-seven nations of the world have already reached birth rates at or below replacement levels by voluntary means.[10] Many couples within these nations have chosen to have one or no children. Separating sex and procreation can have real social benefits for the budgets of poorer nations and families, for family health, and even for care of children. Wanted, planned children fare better than do "accidental" children.[11]

At the same time, however, there is a great danger in childlessness for societies like ours which have tended to understand children as extensions of their parents. Parents have understood themselves to have an interest in the society's future beyond their own lives because they see their children and their children's children as their own immortality. We must find new ways to connect nonparents with those who will live into the future. Decreasing the number of parents should be linked to new initiatives at sharing our connections and commitments to children.

In my home state of Florida, as in parts of California, many of the retirement developments are incorporating into towns in order to avoid paying for local schools. Seniors argue that, since their developments allow no children to live within their boundaries, they should not have to pay for schools for children. With the baby boomer generation, the biggest single group of Americans and fast heading for senior status, a widespread trend in this direction poses high risks for the welfare of children. We must find ways to link adult nonparents to children so as to enrich both the childless with hope in, and commitment to, the future and children with broader exposure to the wisdom and resources of age.

The likelihood is very great that we will have contraceptive coercion within the next two to three generations, at least in most of the earth. Nations in Asia have been using coercion in contraception for more than thirty years. The Chinese did not introduce coercive contraception; they were simply more public, more just, and more successful with their programs.[12] Coerced contraception of the poor and minorities has long histories in such nations as India, Bangladesh, and Indonesia, as well as Kenya, Nigeria, and even Brazil and Colombia.[13]

Nor is sterilization abuse limited to these nations. It has occurred within minorities in the United States for both eugenic and racially motivated population control purposes. We have a history of "Mississippi appendectomies," as well as sterilizations of young black women without their consent in the rural South, sterilizations of the institutionalized mentally ill and prison inmates, and hysterectomies to sterilize Northern "welfare mothers" at delivery to provide surgical practice for residents in city hospitals.[14] Large proportions of both Puerto Rican women since the sixties and Native American women since the seventies have been sterilized through government programs; an investigation in 1976 by the U.S. General Accounting Office found that 3,000 Native American women had been sterilized in the previous four years without adequate consent forms.[15] All of these practices have been justified as keeping down the welfare rolls.[16] Today, poor women are coerced into permanent sterilization by the lack of Medicaid funding for abortion since 1977, by the failure of the legal minimum wage to raise working families out of abject poverty, and by the two year limit on aid to mothers of dependent children, which send women into the workforce at minimum wage jobs without providing affordable daycare. Americans need to look at these numbers before we focus on contraceptive coercion in other nations.

In India, women, and even men, were rounded up, village by village, by the army and sterilized by teams of doctors in the late seventies. Bangladeshi policy in the floods of 1984, when eighty percent of the population relied on disaster relief to eat, was to provide relief food only to women who — regardless of their age or marital status — had proof of sterilization.[17] In both these nations, as well as in many others, the payment of one to two months' wages to women who are sterilized targets the poor whose sterilization rates soar in the last months before harvests and drop with harvesting.

In fact, for women in much of the world, there is no such thing as reproductive freedom even when their *nations* are not coercive about reproduction. Family planning workers around the globe report that women are often beaten and even killed when they suggest the use of contraception to husbands or when husbands or families discover that they are using contraception. Even more common is women's lack of freedom around sexuality itself.[18] Most women in the world are not assumed to ever have the right to say "no" to a husband who wants sex. Religion often reinforces culture on this issue. Christian women have had Saint Paul quoted to them:

> Because of cases of sexual immorality, each man should have his own wife and each woman her own husband. The husband should give to his wife her conjugal rights, and likewise the wife to her husband. For the wife does not have authority over her own body, but the husband does; likewise the husband does not have authority over his own body, but the wife does. Do not deprive one another except perhaps by agreement for a set time, to devote yourselves to prayer, and then come together again, so that Satan may not tempt you because of your lack of self-control (I Cor 7:3-5).

While this teaching seemingly has the virtue of mutuality, Church tradition from the Fathers of the Church through Thomas Aquinas was clear that, while sexual rights were mutual, only men utilized them. The supposed modesty and natural subservience of women — that is, their dependency and powerlessness — was understood to prevent them from claiming conjugal rights.[19] The result of Saint Paul's teaching within a culture of male dominance — exemplified by Church teachings on the headship of husbands and the submission of wives — was to reinforce that dominance by forbidding women control of their own bodies. In the Catholic tradition, the only Pope to explicitly disavow male headship in the family has been John Paul II,[20] though there has been little emphasis given this revolutionary stance. Decades before, Pope Pius XII had written:

> And do you, o brides, lift up your hearts. Do not be content merely to accept, and — one might almost say — to tolerate this authority of your husband, to whom God has subjected you according to the dispositions of nature and of grace; in your sincere submission you must love that authority and love it with the same respectful love you bear toward the authority of Our Lord Himself, from whom all authority flows.[21]

John XXIII implied much the same about sex roles in marriage and family when he wrote in his first encyclical, *Ad Petri Cathedram*: "Within the family, the father stands in God's place. He must lead and guide the rest by his authority and the example of his good life."[22]

In Islam, male control of women's sexual bodies was made clear. The Quran quotes Allah as saying to men: "Your women are a field for you; so plow your field as you wish, and forward for your souls; and fear Allah and know that you shall meet him" (Quran II: 223). Though the Hebrew Scriptures depict women's sexuality as very much under male control, developed Judaic Law is distinct in not presuming husbands' control of women's sexuality. This occurred primarily because sex was understood to involve risk to women's life through childbearing and, therefore, required female consent. Judaism also made sexual satisfaction of wives a responsibility of husbands.[23] But, because Judaism assumes a universal responsibility of Jewish males to marry and reproduce, it has historically encouraged men to divorce both barren women and women who refused sex. Divorced women lived under a heavy social and economic onus through most periods of Jewish history.

Buddhism's distinct preference for celibate monastics over married spouses has led to very few references to marital sex in its canonical texts, commentaries, and contemporary studies.[24] Buddhism has no specific teaching on marital sex, but has adapted to prevailing cultural norms, most of which have been patriarchal. There are few, if any, Buddhist societies in which women exercise clear sexual control or responsibility in sex, and the Buddhist doctrine of *Karma* has frequently been used to justify female powerlessness. It is assumed that, since bad *Karma* from a past life is the reason that an individual is reborn as both a woman and into particular situations of sexual victimization, there is justice in her powerless plight.[25]

To move human society toward voluntary contraceptive sex as normative and reproduction as rare and planned will thus require a vast amount of social change. Where sex is still understood as solely or primarily for purposes of reproduction or where it is understood as an unlimited prerogative of men, the whole meaning and symbolism of sex must change if men are to collaborate with women in the practice of contraception. World religions must not only change their teachings on sex and reproduction, rejecting traditional associations of birth with communal life and reinterpreting stewardship of the earth as requiring birth limitation; but, they must also change their teachings on gender roles, so that women's participation in birth limitation — as well as birthgiving — is voluntary and not coerced. The present danger is that women will move from being coerced into sex and motherhood to being coerced into sex and sterility.

In the Catholic tradition, we have developed some steps in the necessary shift from women's coercion to women's empowerment. In the Western European and the United States Catholic tradition, the general base of support for women's empowerment is an increasingly lay Catholic spirituality which interprets human experience to include the divine as embedded within the life experiences of the laity.[26] Experience of divine presence is not limited to solitary prayer or meditation, but is experienced in parenting, in intimate friendship, in marital sex, in art, music, and nature, in other forms of creativity, and, if we are very lucky, in the work that we do to sustain our lives. Recognition of the presence of the Spirit of God in these areas of our lives makes us less dependent on past religious teachings as the path to fulfilling God's will for us, more open to discerning the messages that God may be sending through ongoing history and experience, and more committed to integrating those into inherited teaching. Women and men who experience their marital sexual relationship as sacramental, for example, ask more critical questions of the Catholic teaching that sexual abstinence is both a good in itself and the only moral means to population limitation.

Nowhere is this reliance on experience more true than it is in justice and charity, where the obligations due others are so contextual. Issues of poverty, environment, and reproduction do correspond to general, unchanging universal principles, but specific moral action on such issues must also respond to particular contexts in order to be truly just or loving. This is the reason that Catholic social teaching is so very contextual and uses so much more social analysis than do other aspects of teaching.[27]

Within official Catholic teaching as well, there has been significant movement in this direction in the last forty years, though there is still a great distance to be traversed. We no longer find in papal teaching the glorification of large families that was typical, for example, under Pius XII, who said:

> A cradle consecrates the mother; more cradles sanctify her, and glorify her in the eyes of her husband, her children, the Church and the nation. Those mothers who are filled with regret when another child seeks the nourishment of life at their breast are foolishly unhappy: they do not know of what stuff they are made. Complaint at the blessing of God which surrounds and increases the family hearth is the enemy of domestic happiness. The heroism of motherhood is the pride and glory of the Christian wife.[28]

By the time of Paul VI, instead of explicitly urging couples to have large families, we find more guarded language. *Gaudium et Spes* says frankly, "Marriage, to be sure, is not instituted solely for procreation,"[29] and refers to couples making responsible decisions about family (presumably about size), but then adds: "those merit special mention who with wise and common deliberation, and with a gallant heart, undertake to bring up suitably even a relatively large family."[30] Clearly, in 1965 the bishops understood the population debate to be about family, and not biospheric, impoverishment.

In the context of development of poor nations, Paul VI wrote:

> Finally, it is for the parents to decide, with full knowledge of the matter, on the number of their children, taking into account their responsibilities to God, themselves, the children they have already brought into the world, and the community to which they belong. In all this they must follow the demands of their own conscience enlightened by God's law authentically interpreted, and sustained by confidence in him.[31]

John Paul II has often spoken at length, acknowledging the ecological crisis without including population concerns as relevant, as he did in his 1990 World Peace Day message (issued December 8, 1989) which pointed only to overconsumption by the rich and irresponsible use of science and technology as causes of environmental damage.[32] In other texts and messages he has responded to concerns about population pressures on the environment as he did in his 1995 encyclical, *Evangelium Vitae*:

> Certainly public authorities have a responsibility to "intervene to orient the demography of the population" (*Catechism of the Catholic Church*). But such interventions must always take into account and respect the primary and inalienable responsibility of married couples and families, and cannot employ methods which fail to respect the person and fundamental human rights, beginning with the right to life of every innocent human being. It is therefore morally unacceptable to encourage, let alone impose, the use of methods such as contraception, sterilization and abortion in order to regulate births. The ways of resolving the population problem are quite different. Governments and the various international agencies must above all strive to create economic, social, public health and cultural conditions which will enable married couples to make their choices about procreation in full freedom and with full responsibility.[33]

If world population were half as large, I would take my stand by the Pope's side, not because I reject voluntary adoption of contraception, sterilization, or even as a backup method of contraception, abortion, but because I would much prefer to see the people of the poor nations of the world have the same two hundred and fifty years of freedom to voluntarily ride the demographic transition from large to small families as did the people of the developed nations. I, too, am suspicious of First World motives in pressing

injectibles, implantables, pills, condoms, and IUDs on clinics in
the Third World that have no aspirin, antibiotics, children's immunizations, rehydration salts, or drugs to treat TB, much less
HIV, all in the name of ecology, with no parallel efforts at controlling consumption in our own rich nations.[34] I, too, would much
prefer to see an emphasis on controlling technology and ending
poverty through justice as the paths to environmental preservation.

But, our world does not have three billion people; it has six and
very soon will have more than twelve billion, probably even fifteen
billion, many of whom are trying desperately to increase their consumption rates to combat endemic poverty. China's economy grew
tenfold between 1953 and 1989, but its energy consumption —
and its carbon dioxide production — grew eighteen times during
those same years.[35] We cannot have just development for today's
poor, their children, and grandchildren without killing the earth,
unless we have less consumption among the rich and birth fewer
people among both rich and poor.

While the Christian tradition is very clear on the point that life
is not the ultimate value and cannot take priority over basic human
dignity and integrity, the possibility for sustaining, not only human
life, but all life on earth, does seem to me to trump almost all other
values. It does not supersede justice, but it may privilege some
forms of justice over others. As I mentioned, if the world population were a fraction of what it is, then the poor nations of the world
should have the same two hundred fifty plus years to undergo the
demographic transition that the rich nations enjoyed. Full and
equal justice would also allow the poor nations of the world the
same obliviousness to environmental consequences in their choice
of industrial technologies as the rich nations of the world enjoyed
when they were industrializing. But, this kind of justice is not possible. Moral responsibility demands that each one of us make our
decisions with a view to the consequences of those decisions *within
our own context* and not within some past historical context.
Catholic social teaching has repeatedly recognized this. For example, John Paul II wrote:

> The newly industrialized States cannot, for example, be asked to
> apply restrictive environmental standards to their emerging indus-
> tries unless the industrialized States first apply them within their
> own boundaries. At the same time, countries in the process of
> industrialization are not morally free to repeat the errors made
> in the past by others, and recklessly continue to damage the envi-
> ronment through industrial pollutants, radical deforestation or
> unlimited exploitation of non-renewable resources.[36]

It is not difficult for most of us to accept that the freedom to
pollute is not absolute, but is limited by the needs of others. The

freedom to reproduce is a very different kind of freedom, but it can be analogous. Human society — in particular the Church — has always placed some limitations on the ability to reproduce, especially by insisting that reproduction take place within the context of marriage. The Catholic Church was responsible for centuries of coercion on this matter, when unwed mothers throughout Europe were not only deprived of their children, but sentenced to terms of a year or more of imprisonment in foundling hospitals as wetnurses to unrelated infants.[37] The question that looms before us today is how we can best preserve the right of persons to marry and reproduce without reproducing the earth to death. We need to move beyond understanding the right to marry and reproduce in libertarian terms and reconfigure them within more communitarian approaches that will allow us to safeguard the life, dignity, and integrity of the planet.

II. Sexual Morality and the AIDS Pandemic

To many in the developed world, the idea that AIDS will have a major effect on understandings of sexual morality in the new millennium may seem passé. But, the vast majority of adults today were born into the age of AIDS.

We have no reason to doubt that HIV positive will be with us for the foreseeable future, raising the risks to life and health from fulfilling the command to love the neighbor. How *does* AIDS impact the way we relate to others? In particular, how do — and should — Christians understand the commandment of neighbor love in the context of AIDS? Even more particularly, how does the AIDS pandemic impact the love imperative within marriage?

I have a strong sense, from teaching sexuality courses in both a private university in the Midwest and a public university in Miami, that many sexually active heterosexual young people have developed a response to the threat of AIDS. They have not chosen abstinence; many have not even opted for condom use. They may have fewer partners than they did before AIDS, but anecdotal suggestions to this effect have not been born out in any statistics I have seen. This is in contrast to the homosexual population which dramatically reduced a variety of risky behaviors following the advent of HIV, though with some relapse among young gays today. Many young heterosexuals seem to have decided that the best line of defense against HIV and other STDs is to stick to your own kind. Stick to members of your own class, own race, or ethnic group, especially to those people who are known to your friends.

HIV is not the only lurking threat that pressures young people to choose ingroup partners. Especially for women today there is

heightened awareness of sexual violence. Choosing a sexual partner from a pool of people known to your friends is assumed to also
help protect you from the likelihood of date rape or battery, even
from men who might stalk or kill you at the end of the relationship.

Instead of swearing off men and sex altogether, many young
women try to get as much information about a potential partner's
history and connections as they can before they open up their bodies and hand over keys to their apartments. They assume that these
informal information networks are effective, not only on issues of
emotional and physical safety, but also against the threat of viral
infection. They do not seem to have done any assessment of the
effectiveness of this form of screening either for violence or for disease prevention.

By contrast, health workers in areas of the developing world
where HIV death rates are highest report no clear patterns to self
protection, but, rather, a kind of fatalism. People may even deny
that sexual contact is the method of transmission. So many people,
especially children and young adults, are dying that it seems to
many that AIDS just takes whom it wants, regardless of what individuals do, period. I suggest that both of these responses are
morally defective. Fatalism attracts the morally lazy; it allows them
to throw up their hands and deny that there are any effective methods of protection. Fatalism characterizes those whose self
understanding is of themselves as victims who do not feel worthy
of efforts at self preservation. Fatalism is also attractive to victimiz-
ers, unwilling to give up the power they exercise over others in
exposing them to risk.

But, confining oneself to a small pool of partners known to
one's intimates is also morally problematic at two levels. First, it is
too restrictive. It is the equivalent of not leaving one's home for
fear of muggings, not riding in cars or airplanes for fear of crashes,
and other paranoid behaviors. God gives us life and wants us to live
it fully; that involves taking those precautions which can prevent
untimely death and which do not unduly restrict our ability to live
life fully. To refuse to know new neighbors or coworkers or parish-
ioners because they are not known to one's friends is to seriously
restrict God's gift of sociality which is our chief mechanism for
growing and developing as persons. Such restrictions can keep us,
not only from appreciating diversity, but can make us prejudiced
bigots, more easily influenced towards violence based on fear.

But, the other problem with restricting ourselves to the circle of
those already known to our friends is that it does not work. It does
not protect us from any of the dangers from which we desire protection. Domestic batterers, for example, seldom beat their
mothers and sisters, and most did not beat their dates; many do

not immediately begin beating their wives on their wedding day. Men who stalk their girlfriends or kill their wives are often described by their neighbors and coworkers, even many of their families and former girlfriends, as gentle, caring people. In terms of protection from HIV, this type of screening is even less effective since close friends might know that a person had a *habit* of buying sex, injecting drugs, bisexuality, or a medical history of hemophilia, but probably *would not* know of single experiments, drunken episodes, or vacation flings that resulted in an HIV infection which might or might not be known even to the person himself or herself.

A central issue for the Churches in this situation is the way to teach the relationship between the obligation to preserve one's life and the obligation to love the neighbor. Does the one obligation have any permanent priority over the other, regardless of who the neighbor is? Or, does the type of relationship affect the level of risk to self preservation one should accept?

Is having sex with our HIV positive spouse something we should do out of marital obligation — what used to be called the marital debt, based on the Pauline passage quoted earlier? For Thomas Aquinas, the marital debt took precedence over self preservation; this is the reason Thomas suggested that, even with a leprous husband, a woman must submit to sex, though not to cohabitation.[38] The rationale here, which may have been less than convincing then, but certainly is unconvincing now, was that a major function of sex was to prevent sin, and a man's sinful recourse to adultery or masturbation would be a far more serious event than a woman's becoming leprous from satisfying his lust would be.

On the other hand, if having sex with your HIV positive spouse is *not* required by the marital debt, is it then a superogatory act, above and beyond what can be demanded of one? Is it something only saints could do and not a part of the ordinary habit of virtue?

There are a variety of situations in which the risk of HIV is often assessed in conjunction with different levels of trust in, and commitment to, the other person. A spouse has voluntarily promised a higher level of commitment and loyalty to this particular other person than is offered and expected between most neighbors, coworkers, casual daters, teachers and students, or health care workers and patients. In these other situations, the commitment is usually less personal, less voluntary, or less committed, and, therefore, the obligation to risk self in these relationships is lower. But, how much lower? Should the Church urge young people to make proposals and acceptances of marriage contingent on a doctor's exam and a battery of lab test for STDs? Or, should a couple who is ready to marry have established a level of knowledge and trust that makes such a condition unnecessary, even insulting? After marriage, should anniversary celebrations include, not only champagne, but STD tests?

It seems to me that the professions, especially the secular health care profession, have done a much better job than the Churches have of working through this question. The health professions have held the obligations to neighbor love and to self preservation in a creative tension as they have decided, in a wide range of types of situations, what level of risk health care professionals should accept in treating HIV positive, or possible HIV positive, patients. The professional standard begins with the assumption that health care cannot be denied to HIV positive persons or those suspected of being HIV positive. It insists that universal precautions should always be employed to protect workers. It recognizes that individual workers have a right to refuse even this (lowered) level of risk, but are not, then, living up to either peer group or social expectations of health care professionals and that satisfaction of the needs of the patient population may, therefore, dictate arbitrary placement and use of these refusing personnel. On the other hand, those health care workers who, in emergency situations where protective gear is not available, risk themselves in order to treat HIV positive, or suspected HIV positive, patients are regarded as acting above and beyond the call of duty. The still open area of dispute is about HIV positive health care workers, their place in the health care system, the liability of their employers, and appropriate limitations, if any, on their practice of health care.

The field of education lags behind health care, though it is much improved from the early days when HIV positive children, like Brian White, were hounded from the schools. The largest obstacle to progress in the way education treats HIV positive is the absence of agreement around universal precautions in education. Elementary, and some secondary, teachers do not want to think of each child as a possible HIV positive carrier and have no idea the way their behavior, or the educational system itself, could or should change if they did. But, without universal precautions, any demand for nondiscrimination against possible HIV positive persons will founder on the rocks of self preservation and the need to protect other children.

We have nothing like health care's level of clarity in the Churches. I suspect that there would be general agreement among Christian theologians that medical personnel who demand transfers rather than have any contact with HIV positive patients have less than ideal understandings of Christian love. But, I know of no pastoral attempts in the Church to deal with fears of HIV and avoidance behaviors, no attempts to bring to bear the rich heritage of Christian saints who risked their lives and health in the care of plague and other epidemic victims. Furthermore, it seems to me that even what theological consensus might be developing disappears when HIV is at issue in marital/sexual relationships. There are two ironies in the lack of consensus around HIV in marital sex. The first is that, unlike education where there is uncertainly as to the forms universal precautions should take, double condoms are the obvious universal precaution in marital sex. The second irony is that there is an historical theological tradition which dealt with sexual obligations of spouses in situations of risk. The risk of contracting a contagious disease through sex was always present in Christian societies afflicted not only with leprosy, tuberculosis, and syphilis, but also with recurrent outbreaks of typhoid, plague, smallpox, and other epidemics. Until the twentieth century, the risk of death or permanently impaired health from childbearing always hung over sex for women. Cemeteries all over the world attest to the death toll that childbearing took on women. It was by far the most common cause of female death before old age. Only war ever raised men's death rate to that of women.

And, yet, despite the fact that the Christian theological tradition, for almost two thousand years, has reflected on the question of how much risk spouses should assume in marital sex, the fruit of that reflection is not taught today. I suggest that it is not taught because it is not satisfying; it does not "fit" our understanding of marriage in the new millennium.

Traditional reflection on the tension between self preservation and marital obligations in situations of risky sex is marked, not only by assumptions that sex is for reproduction and avoidance of sin, but also by a long history of Christian patriarchy which has been a major source of the traditional Christian understanding of love as self sacrificial. Today, we in the West are imbued with assumptions of secular human rights theory and its individualism which push us to question all demands for self sacrifice.

As noted earlier, Christian sexual theology began with an understanding of marriage as conferring on the spouses ownership of each other's bodies. Though often touted as a wonderful example of equality and mutuality, this formulation is extremely problematic. It is irreconcilable with any human rights standard. There is simply no way that bodies can be legitimately given away by their "owners" because the body *is* in many critical ways the self. While Saint Paul's intentions may have been good, his use of legal language of ownership undermines his intentions. Persons and bodies cannot be owned; to speak of them in this way is to objectify them

and set them up for abuse. The only positive way to interpret these
verses would be to say that, in marriage, spouses who love one another offer, time and again, the service of their bodyselves to their
spouses as symbols of their love. The bodyself of the spouse is not,
then, a thing, a permanent gift to the spouse, but is, rather, an
agent acting out love in the form of personal service. Whether I
use my body to pleasure my husband in sex, to bring him relief
with a backrub, or to give him some extra sleep by taking his turn
to get the kids off in the morning, I have given him the temporary
benefit of my body without conferring upon him any ownership rights over it. Real gifts are gratuitous; they have no strings
at all. They not only do not have strings from the giver to the
receiver, but neither do they have strings from the receiver to the
giver.

How did Jesus' emphasis on love as service get transformed into
marital love as ownership of the other? Earlier patriarchal assumptions that men own and control women (and children and lesser
men as well) were carried over into early Christianity. As Elisabeth
Schüssler Fiorenza has explained so well,[39] patterns of coequal discipleship among Jesus' early followers were blended with
patriarchal patterns of social relations in the wider society to produce a love patriarchalism which Church leaders assumed
ameliorated the potential for abuse in secular patriarchalism without altering its fundamental power relations. The equality of Gal
3:28 and I Cor 7:4 and the hierarchy of the Roman household
code in Col 3:18-4:1 were fused and perhaps best illustrated in the
more "Christian" version of the Roman household code in Eph
5:22-6:9. In these verses, the inequality of power that prevails in
the world between men and women, masters and slaves, and fathers and children is confirmed and accepted, but the more
powerful are admonished not to abuse the less powerful, and the
less powerful are urged to respect and obey, "knowing that he who
is both their Master and yours is in heaven, and that there is no
partiality with him" (Eph 6:9).

It was to this model of social relations that the theological concept of sacrifice was wedded. Jesus' suffering and death was
understood as the sacrifice which earned universal human salvation. Given the example of the early martyrs, the Church
broadened Jesus' salvific suffering so that innocent suffering in
general (human imitation of the sacrifice of Jesus) became salvific.
Christians were then called to imitate, by opting for self sacrifice,
the example of Jesus who died to save humanity from its sins. How
did this fit the love patriarchal model of marriage? Because sacrifice was understood to be appropriate to one's social role — that
is, to where one stood in the power hierarchy. Less powerful men's

sacrifice has generally been understood to consist of their labor and the responsibility they bear for economic maintenance and protection of the home. Cobb and Sennett, in their study of men in the working class, wrote of a grandson of an immigrant with five children of his own:

> Bertin feels that his experience — his hopes, his failures, even his failures — has in itself no power to gain his children's respect. He has, however, one claim on them: the fact that he is sacrificing himself, his time, his effort, for them. He has still his power to act as an agent for others, to give his wife and children the material means to move away from him. That stewardship he can indeed control. He is acting as a free man when he thinks of himself as choosing to sacrifice. Having been so repeatedly denied by the social order outside himself, now he will usurp the initiative, he will do the denying, the sacrifice of himself will become a voluntary act ... The outer face of this process is a great harshness on the part of the father; the inner face is one of self-contempt, the plea that the children not become the same as he.[40]

More powerful men's sacrifice — that of élite men — has consisted of their exercise of power in the form of responsibility, which, of course, can be burdensome, but also has many rewards. Women's sacrifice has been understood in terms of personal service and submission; that is, much of women's sacrifice has consisted in accepting their lack of power.[41]

The Christological images underlying these understandings of men's and women's love have not been the same. Men are called to imitate, not only the love of Jesus, who died on the cross for all humans, but also the love of Jesus who reigns at the right hand of his Father in heaven. The higher the social status of a man, the less his love resembles that of Jesus crucified, and the more it resembles that of Jesus crowned.[42] At the lower ranks of men, men's lives in many societies are defined by the sacrifice involved in their work. They have been taught to interpret such sacrifice as for the benefit of their families and to understand it as entitling them to rule those families. But, women in Christian tradition have had few opportunities to imitate the sacrifice of the crowned Jesus by ruling; their entire lives are deemed appropriate for sacrifice, and that sacrifice has often been the sacrifice of selfhood. Thus, what may appear on the surface as an identical call to men and women to imitate the sacrifice of Jesus has actually called men and women to positions of ruler and ruled within society and family.

In the same way, contemporary ideas that reflect equality and mutuality of the sexes often end up victimizing women because they presume an equality of social relations which does not exist. Ironically, in the context of AIDS the power relations of patriarchy are reinforced by the biology of virus transfer. While theoretically both men and women transfer HIV to each other, the rates of transfer are not at all equal for both biological and sociological reasons.

The most common direction of heterosexual transfer is from males to females. There are a number of reasons for this, among them: (1) the greater number of First World males infected from needle sharing, (2) the greater powerlessness of women to demand protective measures, (3) the fact that transfer requires the exposure of infected body fluids (blood, semen) to a tear in the skin of another person, such as those that follow from childbirth, female circumcisions, or penile movement in the vagina or anus.[43] This is the reason the difference in transmission rates is many times higher from male to female than it is from female to male. Female sex workers with large numbers of partners are one major source of transfer, but females in general are more likely to get than to give HIV positive and to give HIV to their children than to their sexual partners.

The greater ability of men to infect women is further supported by social inequality in gender relations. Men normally control heterosexual sex. As Brock and Thistlewaite suggest of sex in the Freudian tradition, it cannot even be sex unless men control it:

> This aggressive, dissociated sexuality was espoused by one of the major definers of modern sexuality in the West, Sigmund Freud. Freud viewed sexual relations as fixed, immutable, and ordered by unequal power. In fact, sexual relations that do not involve an aggressive, perhaps even violent, attack on a female's gatekeeper function are less satisfying, since a man "always feels his sexual activity hampered by his respect for the woman and only develops full sexual potency when he finds himself in the presence of a lower type of sexual object."[44]

They are much more likely to decide, whether with wives or with prostitutes, whether or not sex will occur and whether or not a condom will be worn. This is still, despite the women's movement, the prevalent pattern in the developed world; in the underdeveloped world, male control of sex is virtually an undisputed right.[45]

The understanding of marriage taught by the Churches should include neither the notion of marital debt as in the ownership of each other's bodies, nor the avoidance of sin as the primary purpose of sex. It was historically the combination of these two teachings that obliged spouses to risk their lives when the infected spouse desired sex. The much touted shift from contract to covenant model of marriage has resulted in an understanding of marriage which, while often over romantic and sentimental, is appropriately based in love aimed at intimate communion of the spouses.[46] In this model, love for the spouse causes one to desire sexual communion with the spouse, not only as an expression of emotional and spiritual union, but also as a way of feeding and growing that spiritual and emotional union. While this model understands one fruit of this communion as sensitivity to the needs and desires of the spouse, so that one may acquiesce to sex, at least initially, out of desire to satisfy the spouse, this is not so much a sacrificial act as it is a sacrificial moment in a mutually rewarding act within a mutually rewarding relationship.[47]

One of the implications in the shift from a model of contract, obligation, and sacrifice to one of mutually rewarding intimacy is that the contract model can more easily accommodate juridical demands in the form of universal rules. With the intimacy model, it is more difficult to set universal demands, for the degree of moral obligation seems to be pegged to the level of intimate communion achieved within the relationship. The more communion I have achieved with my spouse, the more I know and understand what helps and hurts him and can anticipate his needs, the better I know the way to love him well. If the level of trust and disclosure between us is low, I will not only be less motivated to take risks for him, but will be less sure about the good to be achieved for him by my taking particular risks.

For example, the degree of obligation to risk one's life in sex with an HIV positive partner (assuming the use of condoms) often varies depending on the way the spouse contracted HIV. If HIV was contracted in routine adulterous sex, the uninfected spouse might well feel less inclined and less obliged to respond to requests for sex. On the other hand, a spouse whose partner contracted HIV positive in a laboratory accident or in a blood transfusion might well be initially so spontaneously moved to physical communion with that spouse by his/her tragedy as to barely even consider the risk to self (though, one would hope, not so moved as to neglect universal precautions which make the risk to self acceptable). Later, the habit of physical communion may well be so ingrained that the sexual relationship continues without great soul searching, but with condoms. These different scenarios, of course, occur in relationships which are qualitatively different. And, this is the point — the more that intimate communion has become habitual for a couple, the greater will be the willingness of a spouse to take risks by making her/himself vulnerable. This willingness to make oneself vulnerable is, of course, a central aspect of love.

So, if it is the quality of the marital relationship which does and should influence willingness to expose oneself to HIV or any other threat carried by the partner, then the Church, or any other external entity, could not set minimal universal standards, but would instead need to teach this proportionality between spousal communion and willingness to risk. Thus, it might be appropriate for a counselor to suggest, or for a couple themselves to initiate, STD testing before marriage if one or both fiancés were known to have been sexually active or involved in IV drug use or other risky behavior. Testing under such circumstances might well serve as a signal of their mutual openness to, and concern for, each other. Testing might serve this same purpose for married couples who have persevered through separations or affairs. But, routine demands for premarital STD testing either by Church representatives or by one spouse of the other could have the opposite effect of destroying trust and causing resentment instead of reassurance. However, it would be appropriate for state licensing requirements to include STD tests if tests for the most serious STDs became less expensive.

III. The Collapse of the Sexual Dimorphism Paradigm

One of the most distinctly postmodern aspects of sexuality at the turn of the millennium is the erosion of the sexual dimorphism paradigm. For as far back as we can trace in human history, sexual dimorphism — the division into male and female — has been the paradigm for interpreting human sexuality. All other aspects of sexuality were understood to rest upon this division, understood as clear, universal, and completely determinative.

In the second half of the twentieth century, this paradigm began to erode. The first aspect of sexuality to be separated from dimorphism involved recognition of what came to be called sexual orientation. Until the mid twentieth century, maleness was understood to entail sexual attraction to females, and femaleness, sexual attraction to males. Before the modern period, in the West exceptions to this pattern had been treated in terms of deliberate sin and, in the early twentieth century, were understood either in terms of sin or, among those uncomfortable with assigning moral blame, in terms of psychological illness. By the seventies, sexual attraction was no longer assumed by scientists or social scientists to be determined by one's sex; homosexuals, heterosexuals, and bisexuals were understood to be responding to some aspect of identity which was initially assumed to have been conditioned or learned, but which has come increasingly to be understood in the West as including both genetic predispositions as well as conditioned responses.

At the same time, an increasing number of crosscultural studies involving sexuality and gender, beginning with Margaret Mead in 1935,[48] began to indicate that sex, understood as maleness or femaleness, did not determine gender, which increasingly came to be seen as society's interpretation of sex which was then socialized into its members. The evidence for this seemed irrefutable. As we came to know more and more cultures, we realized that the behaviors and traits expected of males (masculinity) and females (femininity) were not at all universal, but, rather, that every society seemed to have somewhat different expectations of the same sex. Furthermore, these expectations differed a great deal, not only from society to society, but also from class to class and from one historical period to another within the same society.

And so, what had originally been a concept of sexuality more or less exhausted by the elaboration of dimorphism came to be separated, not only into sex and sexual orientation, but now sex, sexual orientation, and gender. Sex came to be restricted to biological maleness or femaleness and understood as innate, while gender was understood to be socially constructed and sexual orientation was assumed to be at least partially socially constructed as well.

But, by the nineties, these distinctions of the seventies also began to erode. Attacks on what remained of an all encompassing concept of sexual dimorphism actually accelerated and came from a variety of sources. Biologists were among the most damaging. As biologists examined the concept of sex, they found there were six physiological traits, not one, which affected what has been known as maleness or femaleness: chromosomal sex, gonadal sex, hormonal sex, sex of the brain, sex of the reproductive tract, and sex of the genitalia.

Historically, human society determined sex based on the sex of the genitalia, which is still by far the predominant method of determining sex around the world. While the appearance of the external genitalia at birth normally falls into a dimorphic pattern historically called male and female, all peoples of the world have also recognized exceptions called hermaphrodites. True hermaphroditism is very rare. A true hermaphrodite is a person who has the reproductive tracts of both males and females. Most hermaphrodites will have a female ovary on one side and a male testis on the other, along with a female uterus. But, most people called hermaphrodites are really pseudohermaphrodites; they have the reproductive tract of their chromosomal pattern, but their external genitalia do not "match" the reproductive tract. The two most common causes of pseudohermaphroditism, among more than seventy, are androgen insensitivity syndrome and adrenogenital syndrome, which respectively cause the male body to ignore the normal release of male hormones or the female fetus to respond to external sources of androgens. Different cultures have treated hermaphroditism variously, from killing children with signs of hermaphroditism to making special élite roles in the society for such individuals.

In the developed nations of the West in the twentieth century, chromosomal testing began to replace observation of external genitalia as the method of determining the sex of newborns. But, even in the developed world where it is predominantly used, chromosomal testing has never been consistently definitive, either. Children whose genitalia at birth or during childhood had been ambiguous or did not match their chromosomal sex were, and still are, often surgically altered, not to conform with their chromosomal sex, but in the direction of the gender in which the child had thus far been socialized — which was, of course, that indicated by external genitalia. Thus, sometimes human societies use external genitalia as the definitive criterion for assigning sexuality and sometimes chromosomal sex as the definitive criterion.

Even chromosomal sex itself is not completely dimorphic. While the vast majority of people are either XX or XY, there are a significant number of persons who are XXY, XXX, XO, or XYY. For example, Klinefelter's syndrome, the XXY chromosomal pattern, occurs once in every five hundred live male births,[49] and Turner's syndrome, the XO chromosomal pattern, occurs in every twentyfive hundred live female births.[50]

Male and female hormones in the blood are yet another possible determinant of sex. Not only do hormones or their lack affect development of the gonads, external genitalia, and secondary sexual characteristics, but they also affect the sex of the brain. Some patterns of brain development are predominantly associated with males and others with females as a result of the action of hormones on the fetal brain and later, though with this, as in all the other determinants, there are other significant numbers of persons who do not fit the general pattern for those with their chromosomal sex. One aspect of brain sex involves prenatal hormone programming which determines the pattern of function of the hypothalamus and pituitary gland during and after puberty; it is the reason girls have cyclic sex hormone production and menstrual levels and boys have a relatively constant level of sex hormone production.

When we place all the persons with these nonnormative physiological sexual conditions together, we have a very significant number of persons for whom these varied determinants of sex are not completely aligned. They will conform to a male or female pattern in 2, 3, 4, or 5 of the six determinants, but not in the others.

In addition to lack of alignment among the physiological determinants of sex, there are also many cases of lack of alignment between physiological sex and psychosexual sex. This kind of lack of alignment ranges from mild, as in tomboyish girls, to the extreme of transsexuals, whose self identity is at odds with their predominant, usually chromosomal, physiological sex. As adults, many transsexuals are surgically reassigned a different sex from the chromosomal sex with which they were born. Surgical reassignment of transsexuals occurs in adulthood as the culmination of a long process of evaluation. Surgical sexual reassignment occurs, then, in our society both for adults who experience themselves as the other sex as well as for children who are discovered to have been socialized in the sex which does not match their chromosomal sex.

Yet another group in our society which challenges any neat assignment of all people into the dimorphic division of male and female is transgendered persons. These are persons who accept the sex of their bodies in a biological sense. Those who have a penis want a penis, and those who have a uterus want a uterus. But, they do not accept the roles which are socially assigned to those bodies. Some persons who biologically father children want to mother their children dressed as traditional "feminine" women, speaking and acting as women and carrying out more or less traditional women's roles. Some of these transgendered persons have remained married to their spouses of the other sex; their children have two mothers and two fathers who happen to be of different physiological types.

Thus, in our society, sex, at both a biological and a psychological level, not to mention the level of social sexual activity, has become much more complex than the dimorphic model ever allowed. Many will undoubtedly say, and probably already have, that this is just the degenerative West; what can you expect? But, the challenge of dimorphism is not at all limited to the West or to modern societies.

Dimorphism is a paradigm for interpreting sexuality. No paradigm completely explains all the data, and sexual dimorphism never completely explained human experience of sexuality, as we saw with hermaphroditism which has always been known. But, a successful paradigm explains the vast majority of the data in any given area. Sexual dimorphism was the paradigm for interpreting sexuality in every human community we know, but different human communities had different ways of interpreting those cases which the dimorphic paradigm could not. Sexual anomalies in one society might be eliminated as "mistakes" by infanticide, while in another moral fault might be attributed to the parents or even, in karmic cultures, to the individual him/herself. But, in a variety of societies where the general dimorphic character of sex was preserved, exceptions were recognized, accepted, and even assigned special social roles. These roles are distinguished as third-gender or third-sex roles, as anthropologist of sexuality, Gilbert Herdt, explains:

> Through the long course of generations and with sufficient histori-
> cal time, the necessary presence of individuals who desire to be
> different and serve in third-gender and third-sex roles enables us to
> understand how a community might provide for these alternative
> sexual lifeways. For the third-gender, as in the case of women who
> dress in men's clothes, we are dealing with biologically normative
> individuals who only change their role. That is, they learn the
> knowledge and social performance of the other gender. However,
> in the case of third-sexes, we are dealing with individuals who are bi-
> ologically hermaphroditic or who make themselves that way
> through cultural means, such as castration. Examples of third-sexes
> are the famed sexual eunuchs of the Byzantine Empire or classical
> Arabia; the Hejiras of India who are either biologically hermaphro-
> ditic at birth or who undergo a castration rite in late adolescence;
> and the modern transsexual....[51]

Herdt describes the geography of historic third-sex and third-gender roles as including Europe and the New World, the Middle East, insular Southeast Asia, and a sparse, but wide ranging, distribution in Africa.[52] Our knowledge of this phenomenon is based primarily upon the two-spirit person (formerly called *berdache*) among North American Natives, the cross dressing women of Europe from the fourteenth to the early twentieth centuries, and Polynesian forms of gender transformation. In all of these, the culture in question not only constructed a role for the person, but also elaborated a mythology and social ritual which supported the development of the person taking on the role. For example, Herdt cites the Mojave initiation of the two-spirit people at age ten and the Navajo fertility magic controlled by the two-spirit person.[53] Recruitment into the role might come through personal feelings of being different, a vision quest, desires of one's family, or the decisions of religious groups. Studies by Blackwood and Williams have found the two-spirit role widespread and well accepted in more than one hundred North American Native tribes.[54] In all of these tribes, men took on the role, while, in about one third, women also took on the two-spirit role.

One reason for the building pressure on the concept of sexual dimorphism today is that, once we are confronted with the variety of ways that different cultures have "explained away" the sexual facts and experience which could not be subsumed under dimorphism, the exceptions and denials begin to take on growing significance and ultimately bring the paradigm itself into question. There can be no doubt that this is happening all over the world, but most explicitly in the postmodern West. Youth culture since the sixties has had a strong unisex emphasis, and many men and women socialized in the sixties continue this emphasis into late middle age. They rejected the dimorphic division that exaggerated the differences between men and women by making them dress and behave very differently. In many parts of the developed world, men now wear long hair and ponytails almost as often as women, and women as well as men have burr haircuts. Among music and film stars and models, these trends are even more dominant. Much of women's clothing and virtually all casual wear, including shoes, are indistinguishable from men's. More men are carrying "bags" which used to be called purses. Men now wear jewelry that used to be only for females, from earrings to bracelets and necklaces.

There can be little doubt that labor specialization, along with the class system that is caused by the conjunction of property ownership and labor specialization, is replacing sex as the principal source of social differentiation. Men and women who enter the same field of labor increasingly have the same education, training, and employment. In leisure and recreation, women have moved into sports from the pee wee to professional level. Men are agitating for child custody in divorce cases. Increasingly in the West, sex is losing its place as the most basic form of differentiation. In general social relations, we can see two distinct patterns at social events. In much of the world, and in rural areas even within the developed world, the social circles at community celebrations and extended family parties are sex based. The men talk about farming, hunting, sports, politics, and other predominantly male interests, and the women talk about children, husbands, cooking, craft projects, and other shared work and interest. There are areas of overlap and occasional sexually integrated conversations. But, the lives of men and women in traditional societies have run on parallel tracks for the most part, not the same track. Increasingly, this is not the case at urban gatherings in late modern society, where the circles of conversation are more likely to be circles of lawyers, runners, movie critics, those interested in technology stocks, or those trying to find a good, affordable, daycare center — quite regardless of their sex. This is the way having good friends of the opposite sex has become so discussed in the last generation: it simply was not a real possibility for the vast majority of the population until recently, because men and women were socialized into such different interests and roles.

Sexual dimorphism is under attack on multiple fronts. Even the vast difference between sex and gender is now in question. The late twentieth century distinction between sex and gender was that sex refers to one's biological givenness and gender to the role that persons of one sex were socialized to play in society. But today, it is clear that sex is not a given; persons' sexuality is a sign to them, either directly in the case of surgically altered children and adults, or more indirectly, depending on which of the six aspects of physiological sex a given group or society decides to make determinative. Whichever, human beings are deciding what sex is and the way it is to be interpreted, just as human culture does with gender. Both are socially constructed. Once the division of sexuality into two divisions called male and female is recognized as socially constructed, there can be no reason for some persons, groups, and societies not to construct other sexual systems. Some parts of youth culture in the West seem to be about constructing a trimorphic division consisting of male, female, and ambiguously sexed person, and other parts of the culture seem determined not to recognize any rigid sexual division at all, but, instead, to view sexuality as a spectrum — from traditionally male on the one end to traditionally female on the other — on which individuals can place and, therefore, define themselves.

How does the end of sexual dimorphism challenge sexual morality in the millennium ahead? In a variety of ways. The easier questions are the practical ones we already see in the parishes. These are questions regarding who can marry and what counts as sexual sin. If marriage must include a male and a female, how are we to interpret the sex of those who present themselves for marriage? On the basis of self presentation — they are what they say they are? Should priests marry couples in which both are chromosomal males, but one was reassigned and then reared as female following a circumcision accident on the day of birth? Is there no problem marrying a chromosomal male and female both of whom present themselves as females intending to be joint mothers of their children? Is gender really irrelevant? Which of the determinants of sex should the Church use?

The most traditional of the determinants would be external genitalia, but the use of hormones and surgery to alter external genitalia mitigates against assumptions of its "naturalness" and may encourage a shift towards chromosomal sex. Such a shift would increase the burdens on the already burdened: children sexually reassigned following genetic disorders or surgical mishaps or transsexuals. In the same vein, is it homosexual sin for the chromosomally male person reared as a female to choose a male love object? For the male-to-female transsexual?

We have come to the point where there is no hard and fast legal or scientific definition of sex, and it is not the task of the Church to define sex. Pastoral practice needs practical solutions, and the practical solution here is to do the counseling and testing of all couples and marry those who seem sufficiently matured and sufficiently well prepared to take on the responsibilities of a lifetime commitment of love to another. We obviously need to expand the sexuality section of the readiness instruments we give the engaged and the level of sexual counseling. Frankly, the greatest pastoral dangers we face come, not from the way the Church applies its legal rules on marriage and homosexuality, but from how well we expand sexual education within our Churches and schools in order that the sexual naïveté of more sheltered Catholic youth does not lead them unsuspecting into complex sexual relationships they cannot handle. Most pastors have counseled naïve, unsuspecting young women married to men denying their homosexual desire and wanting to be "normal." But today, the varieties of unconventional situations are much broader than this. To deal with them responsibly, we will have to find ways as Churches, as a society, to encourage both sufficient openness so that persons are neither deceived nor coerced as they choose relationships and sufficient tolerant respect so that less conventional persons are not punished. In the end, I suspect that it is this issue which will eventually put the final nails in the coffin of the premarital sex ban.

In some ways, the really hard questions come, not at the pastoral level, but at the conceptual level, from rethinking the meaning of sexuality. When maleness and femaleness no longer determine the basic shape of our traits, abilities, interests, and vocations, we must abandon the idea of sexual complementarity which has been foundational in Christianity. Complementarity among humans is still real and necessary, but it is broader and more social, not sexual. We become human and whole only by interacting with a variety of different persons throughout our lives. There is no "opposite" sex. Adam and Eve were complementary because they socially interacted, not because they were male and female. Only in reproductive terms is sexual complementarity real. And, as we have seen, the world can no longer afford to read sexuality through the lens of human reproduction, as we have done and still continue to do; for example, the Catholic requirement that males, in order to marry, must be capable of penile-vaginal intercourse and, therefore, erection. Once procreation is no longer or possible in marriage, what is there that makes penile-vaginal intercourse "real" sex? For many of the disabled and for the elderly, other forms of sexual bonding and pleasuring are just as real and just as desirable.[55]

The growing anonymity and impersonality of mobile, super specialized, postmodern society produce people with tremendous interpersonal needs: needs for intimacy and connection, for self reflection and support in identity formation, and for challenge and validation. Fewer and fewer of us will parent fewer and fewer children in the future. This does not mean less sex is in order. Our society will need replacements for the intimate, trusting, personal, bodily connection to another that parenting children has provided for humans since time immemorial.

What this means is that, paradoxically, the concept of sexuality is becoming less and less important in our world at the same time that intimate relationship, which most of us experience as sexual relationship, is becoming more and more important. Our sex explains and defines less and less about us and defines less and less of what we do and the way we act in society at the same time that our need for the kind of emotionally and physically intimate relationship we have associated with sexuality is increasing.

Conclusion

There are, I think, some ways in which these trends link. All of them point to the fact that Christianity needs to go back to its sources and reinterpret them. We need to recapture our God as the God of Life, the God who both gives and sustains life and who demands the same of us. We need to reinterpret Gen 1, understanding that the goal of the divine command was to fill the earth with the living, not that we continue multiplying until we killed the earth. When we read the dominion God gave humans over all living creatures (Gen 1:28), we need to link that dominion with the steward of Jesus' parables (Lk 16) who was called by the Master to give an account of his stewardship. Similarly, the stories of the creation of Adam and Eve need not be interpreted in terms of sexual complementarity, as if these two exhaust all human diversity. After all, many other human differentiations (race, language, culture, mode of production, et cetera) unfolded out of original creation and were not fully developed from the beginning. Why should we not understand sexuality as encompassing multiple spectra of traits and behaviors and taking different forms under different conditions of human life?

What is it that ties together the moral challenges from the environment, HIV/AIDS, and the collapse of sexual dimorphism? More than anything else, I think, it is human desire that our world be simple, not complex; that our moral imperatives be universal and absolute, not contextual; and that the will of our God be unchanging, not dynamic and responsive. But, if God be living, then God's will for specific situations reflects the changes in those situations. If God is the God of Life, then God's will continues to be that creation live. And, that means that, because our world, like its Creator, is complex and unfolding, our moral imperatives are also complex and unfolding.

NOTES

[1]"Population and Resources Supplement," *National Geographic Magazine* (October, 1998).

[2]Ibid.

[3]P. R. Ehrlich and A. H. Ehrlich, *The Population Explosion* (New York: Simon and Schuster, 1991).

[4]Arne Naess, "The Shallow and the Deep, Long-Range Ecology Movement," in Louis P. Pojman, ed., *Environmental Ethics* (Boston: Jones and Bartlett, 1994), 102-04.

[5]Christopher Flavin, "The Heat Is On: The Greenhouse Effect," *Environmental Ethics*, 371-78.

[6]"Population and Resources Supplement," *National Geographic Magazine.*

[7]Ibid.

[8]See John XXIII, *Mater et Magistra*; Paul VI, *Populorum Pogressio*; John Paul II, *Sollicitudo Rei Socialis*, in David J. O'Brien and Thomas A. Shannon, eds., *Catholic Social Thought: The Documentary Heritage* (Maryknoll, NY: Orbis, 1992).

[9]Pius XI, *Casti Connubii* #6, in *Seven Great Encyclicals* (New York: Paulist, 1963), 78-79.

[10]"Population and Resources Supplement," *National Geographic Magazine.*

[11]The technical background papers for the International Conference on Better Health for Women and Children through Family Planning showed in country after country that both infant and child mortality decreased when contraception was used and drastically decreased when it delayed initial childbearing beyond the teen years and caused births to be more than two years apart (John Hobcraft, *Does Family Planning Save Children's Lives?* (Population Council, August, 1987), 46-49). However, Betsy Hartmann explains that statistics on the Matlab project in Bangladesh illustrate that neither infant nor maternal mortality declines solely as a result of contraception. In virtually every case where the decline occurs following contraception, the reason is that provision of contraception occurred within a provision of broader programs of healthcare, including prenatal and infant care (Betsy Hartmann, *Reproductive Rights and Wrongs* (Cambridge, MA: South End Press, 1995), 238-40).

[12]This is not to defend the human rights violations that were clearly allowed to occur under the policy (i.e., forced abortions). It is to say that China has made the distinction only between rural and urban populations; unlike other nations, it did not impose upon the poor majority a policy from which the middle classes or élites were exempt. See Daniel C. Maguire and Larry L. Rasmussen, *Ethics for a Small Planet* (Albany: State University of New York, 1998), 10-15.

[13]Hartmann, 251-55, 226-40, 73-89.

[14]Ibid., 254-55.

[15]Ibid., 255, quoting Rosalind Petchevsky, "Reproduction, Ethics and Public Policy: The Federal Sterilization Regulations," *Hastings Center Reports*, October, 1979.

[16]Rosalind Petchevsky, "'Reproductive Choice' in the Contemporary United States: A Social Analysis of Female Sterilization," in Karen L.

Michaelson, ed., *And the Poor Get Children: Radical Perspectives on Population Dynamics* (New York: Monthly Review Press, 1982).

[17]Betsy Hartmann, *op. cit.*

[18]Ibid., 47-52.

[19]Thomas Aquinas, *Summa Theologiae Suppl.* 64, 2; 64, 5 ad 2; Eleanor McLaughlin, "Equality of Souls, Inequality of Sexes: Woman in Medieval Theology," in Rosemary R. Ruether, ed., *Religion and Sexism* (New York: Simon and Schuster, 1974), 226.

[20]John Paul II, *On the Dignity and Vocation of Women* (Washington, D.C.: U. S. Catholic Conference, 1989), 244-6.

[21]Pius XII, "Address to Newlyweds," in *Papal Teachings: Woman in the Modern World* (Boston: Daughters of St. Paul, 1959), 68.

[22]*Actae Apostolicae Sedis* 51 (1959): 509.

[23]Vernon Reynolds and Ralph Tanner, *The Social Ecology of Religion* (New York: Oxford, 1995), 156.

[24]Ibid., 155.

[25]Rita Nakashima Brock and Susan Thistlethwaite, *Casting Stones: Prostitution and Liberation in Asia and the United States* (Philadelphia: Fortress, 1996), 235-67.

[26]Charles Gallagher et al., *Embodied in Love: Sacramental Spirituality and Sexual Intimacy* (New York: Crossroad, 1986).

[27]Christine E. Gudorf, *Christian Social Teaching on Liberation Themes* (Washington, D.C.: University Press of America, 1980), Chapter Two.

[28]Pius XII, *Papal Teachings*, 82-83.

[29]*Gaudium et Spes*, #50, *Catholic Social Thought*, 199.

[30]Ibid.

[31]Paul VI, *Populorum Progressio*, #37, *Catholic Social Thought*, 249.

[32]John Paul II, *The Ecological Crisis: A Common Responsibility* (Washington, D.C.: U.S. Catholic Conference, 1990), #7, 13.

[33]John Paul II, *The Gospel of Life: Evangelium Vitae: On the Value and Inviolability of Human Life* (Washington, D.C.: U.S. Catholic Conference, 1995), 161-62.

[34]Testimony of hundreds of doctors, nurses, and clinic and hospital administrators in the Third World at the NGO Forum of the UNCPD in Cairo, September, 1994.

[35]"Population and Resources Supplement," *National Geographic Magazine.*

[36]John Paul II, *The Ecological Crisis: A Common Responsibility*, IV:10.

[37]David I. Kertzer, *Sacrificed for Honor:Italian Infant Abandonment and the Politics of Reproductive Control* (Boston: Beacon Press, 1993).

[38]Thomas Aquinas, *Summa Theologiae Suppl.* 64, 1 and 4.

[39]Elisabeth Schüssler Fiorenza, *In Memory of Her* (New York: Crossroad, 1984).

[40]Jonathan Cobb and Richard Sennett, *The Hidden Injuries of Class* (New York: Vintage Press, 1973), 122.

[41]See Gudorf, "Parenting, Mutual Love and Sacrifice," in Barbara Andolsen et al., *Women's Consciousness, Women's Conscience: A Reader in Feminist Ethics* (Minneapolis: Winston-Seabury, 1985), n. 17, 190-91.

[42]Note, for example, the crucified Jesus by Edilberto Merida which graces the cover of Gustavo Gutierrez' *A Theology of Liberation* (Maryknoll,

NY: Orbis, 1973), and a variety of other works in liberation theology. Merida's Jesus is an Indian peasant, with the big feet that suggest barefooted or sandaled workers' feet, the big hands that suggest manual labor, and the distorted facial features that suggest great pain. It is the crucified Jesus with which the Indian poor identify, not the crowned Jesus.

[43]Elizabeth Reid, "Gender, Knowledge and Responsibility," in Jonathan Mann, Daniel J. M. Tarantola, and Thomas W. Netter, eds., *AIDS in the World* (Cambridge, MA: Harvard University Press, 1992), 657-67.

[44]Brock and Thistlewaite, *Casting Stones*, 106, quoting Susan Griffin, *Pornography and Silence: Culture's Revenge Against Nature* (New York: Harper and Row, 1981).

[45]Cheryl Overs, "Commercial Sex Workers:Police or Policies?," in Mann et al., *op. cit.*, 344-45; E. Reid, op. cit.

[46]Charles A. Gallagher et al., *op. cit.*, 21-37.

[47]See my "Parenting, Mutual Love and Sacrifice."

[48]Margaret Mead, *Sex and Temperament in Three Primitive Societies* (New York: W. Morrow & Co., 1935).

[49]William H. Masters, Virginia E. Johnson, and Robert C. Kolodny, *Human Sexuality*, 4th edition (New York: HarperCollins, 1992), 184.

[50]Janell L. Caroll and Paul Root Wolpe, *Sexuality and Gender in Society* (New York: HarperCollins, 1996), 76.

[51]Gilbert Herdt, *Same Sex, Same Cultures* (Boulder, CO: Westview, 1997), 89.

[52]Ibid., 88-89.

[53]Ibid., 90.

[54]Walter Williams, *The Spirit and the Flesh: Sexual Diversity in American Indian Culture* (Boston: Beacon Press, 1986), and Evelyn Blackwood, *The Many Faces of Homosexuality* (New York: Harrington Press, 1986).

[55]Robert Crooks and Karla Baur, *Our Sexuality* (Pacific Grove, CA: Brooks-Cole, 1996), 476-83.

Bioethics in the New Millennium[1]

Kevin Wm. Wildes, S.J.

Free and informed consent has played a central role in the development of bioethics in the last forty years. Informed consent has become crucial to the practice of clinical medicine and medical research. People are routinely asked to consent to treatments or participate in research in a way they once were not. More recently, it has been argued that informed consent needs to become part of the practices of the allocation of health care resources.[2] In view of the importance of free and informed consent for bioethics, I must inform you that I cannot predict the future. Nonetheless, I have been asked to examine the development of bioethics in the new millennium. Bioethics is a relatively new field. Some have dated it to a 1962 story in *Life* magazine (9 November 1962) about a committee in Seattle with the duty of selecting new hemodialysis patients.[3] In this essay, I assume that the past is prologue for bioethics. The trends that have shaped these issues and the field will continue into the new millennium. So, in order to talk about bioethics in the new millennium, I would like to look to the last thirty-five years to gain some insight into the future.

Bioethics has emerged in the last thirty-five to forty years and has become a staple of medicine, research, and public policy.[4] It is a field that has emerged in the headlines of newspapers and television talk shows. One should not think that medicine and ethics discovered each other for the first time in the 1960s. For thousands of years, different religious communities possessed content-full,[5] but differing accounts, of the proper way to practice medicine. Moreover, different cultures showed different approaches to these

matters. To a great extent, these differences were not unexpected.
It was generally understood that different religions and cultures
would give different weightings as to what was important in medicine and so arrive at different conclusions. This recognition of
difference did not necessarily imply a relativism. The ancient
Athenians held that their culture (*paideia*) developed the proper
capacities for moral judgment and discernment (*phronesis*) which
contrasted to the imperfect moral sensibilities of the barbarians.
The Jews understood that faithfulness to the Torah meant that
they possessed understandings richer and more complete than
those of the Gentiles.

Even with the awareness of differences, there was a strong sense
that there was a correct morality. Furthermore, in the Western
world, there was an assumption that correct morality transcended
particular cultures and times and could be known by reason.
Appeals to reason, logos, the Noachite code, or Natural Law were
taken to disclose a commonality of human moral vision. With time,
these hopes found strong expression in Western Christian reflections on Natural Law and public policy.

Rapid developments in medicine, increases in medical costs,
and new biomedical capabilities brought established religious and
cultural traditions to consider the way to meet new challenges. It is
crucial to understand the radical transformation of medicine in
the last forty years. In recent decades, beginning in the 1960s,
medicine has been changed so that it now is able to confront
disease and illness with real options and alternatives. Medicine can
routinely offset systemic diseases and organ failure. For the first
time in its long history, medicine can actually cure people. The development of a scientific model for medicine has allowed it a way
to establish knowledge claims and make predictions. There may
be other forms of healing outside the scientific-medical model, but
the scientific model has an advantage in that it is public and
documentable.

With the development of medical capacities to diagnose and
treat, medical practitioners and patients found themselves with
real choices and options. Much of the moral debate concerning
issues in medicine and biomedical sciences in the 1950s, 60s, and
early 70s took place within, or from, religious visions that frankly
acknowledged their content as particular, albeit normative. Within
such communities, there was a recognition that much was changing and that a new era full of novel medical challenges was
dawning. Each religious community in its own way tried to fashion
a response to these new possibilities and challenges.[6]

The practice of Western medicine was not only tied to religious
traditions; it was also tied to a long tradition of *physician ethics*

dating to the ancient Greeks. One can characterize such ethical codes as guild ethics. However, as the nature of medicine changed from care to cure, medical technologies provided important new possibilities for men and women. There were real choices with real moral costs. These choices led to discussions and debates about what ought to be done. Such discussions were no longer the domain of physicians alone.[7] The emergence of bioethics is not the first time that ethical questions have been asked in medicine. As a field, however, bioethics represents a move beyond "physician ethics" and the ethics of particular religious traditions.

As medicine developed new capacaties for diagnosis and treatment, the paternalism of physician ethics was challenged as was the authority of religious visions of medicine and health care. In addition, the West and America were becoming ever more secularized and more multicultural and morally pluralistic. There were new voices in ethics. Voices that had been silenced before could now be heard. Various individual rights movements were gathering strength. All of this underscored the need to determine the extent to which a general bioethics could be articulated, one that spoke across denominational lines and bound persons as such.

A need for a secular bioethics was especially felt in such countries as the United States, characterized by an officially secular government, by a marked plurality of religious and moral convictions, and by the absence of established religion.[8] The search for a secular bioethics was a natural response to the need to fashion policies that all could endorse. If a secular bioethics could be fashioned to give content-full guidance, it could help citizens of whatever religious persuasion or none to see the moral force and propriety of particular health care policies. The search for a secular bioethics became a search for a secular or civil religion that might bind the sentiments of citizens who were at least nominally divided by religious, cultural, or other moral differences. As we shall see, these aspirations have a consanguinity with those that led to the modern philosophical or Enlightenment project. As the West entered the Modern Age, it was rent by deep religious controversies and bloody wars, of which the Civil War in England and the Thirty Years' War on the Continent were the two most significant. Just as individuals hoped then to discover in reason a content-full understanding of proper conduct and secular moral authority that could be acknowledged across confessional lines, so, too, the hope has been that secular bioethics can provide a content-full morality to guide public policy decisions and to give them a secular moral authority.

The search for a secular bioethics thus appears unavoidable. As health care is practiced in settings that bring together women and men from different moral views, there is a need to develop an ethics that transcends religious convictions or professional alliances. Indeed, Daniel Callahan has argued that bioethics gained public acceptance by moving beyond theology and religious discourse.[9] The response to the plurality of religious bioethics has been an attempt to establish a particular secular bioethics. But, the difficulty that one faced with religious bioethics, a plurality of moral visions engendering a plurality of religious bioethics, has been recapitulated in secular bioethics. There are now more content-full secular bioethics than there are major established religions or well articulated religious bioethics.

The search for a secular bioethics invites a reassessment of the significance and promise of bioethics. As we will see, a secular bioethics cannot simply be a secular recapitulation of the search for a religious bioethics. The challenge of the future is to understand the way individuals from diverse secular moral and bioethical traditions can recognize some common web of morality and authority, however sparse, that can give guidance and legitimacy for secular health care policy.

Bioethics has developed as a discipline to resolve the moral controversies posed by contemporary medical research, practice, and health care policy in the *secular*, morally pluralistic setting. There are a number of senses which can be given to the notion of secular.[10] In this essay, as I have already indicated, secular will be used to mean a morally neutral framework within which individuals of various moral communities can collaborate.

Because of the very practical nature of bioethics, there is an ongoing tension between agreement on the general universal level and the practical level of moral judgment. There is often a confusion of the arguments that assumes that disagreement on the practical, particular level of judgment entails disagreement on the level of the universal.[11] I will argue that common moral ground, in bioethics, is best explored through an exploration of the morality of common procedures that govern the practice of medicine.

The Emergence of Bioethics: Medical Technology and Moral Pluralism

Multiple forces have shaped the emergence of bioethics. The development of medical technology, which makes possible what was once unthinkable, and the development of moral pluralism, which admits a wide array of often conflicting moral perspectives, have contributed to the displacement of traditional medical ethics. Traditionally, medical ethics has been limited to discussions of the moral conduct of the physician. One of the clearest expressions of this view is found in the Hippocratic tradition when the physician swears to "apply...measures for the benefit of the sick according to *my ability and judgment.*"[12] The orientation of the oath is toward the *physician's* judgment and conduct.[13] However, scientific and technological advances in medicine, such as life prolonging technologies, transplantation techniques requiring noncadaveric organ donations, the development of abortion techniques with extremely low mortality, and the ability to determine prenatally the existence of fetal defects, have led to a greater emphasis on the patient's role in treatment discussions and choices. The development of new medical possibilities through the development of genetic medicine will not only change medical practice, but it will also fuel new ethical debates. Recently, research developments and interests in cloning and embryonic stem cells are symptoms of ongoing scientific development with profound moral implications. Contemporary medical practice and research involve real choices for those men and women who are involved.

The emergence of bioethics as a field of inquiry was facilitated by a number of events. One was the change in medicine that moved medicine from simply being diagnostic and palliative to curative. The development of medical technology, and its wide dissemination, came at a time of great social and cultural change in Western societies. Such changes challenged the traditional medical (physician) ethics as the sole basis of medical ethics. Robert Veatch wrote that "[s]pecial norms...cannot exist for a professional group without collapsing into ethical relativism and particularism."[14]

The moral controversies engendered by health care touch almost every aspect of human life. Questions about contraception, fertility, abortion, consent to treatment, sustaining the lives of those who are terminally ill, and the allocation of funds for health care are the concerns of almost every individual at some point in life. The development of medical technology has changed, and continues to change, the possibilities of human life. Childless couples can now have children. Infertility, which was once a tragedy, is now viewed as a disease in contemporary, developed societies. Birth defects can be diagnosed and, in some cases, treated long before birth. Organs can be transplanted with great success, and pathological conditions can be bypassed such that biological life can be sustained indefinitely.

Medical advances alone, however, do not fully explain the emergence of bioethics. Another crucial element is the moral differences that are found in contemporary secular societies. These differences lead to real moral questions about the way medical technologies should be used. Cultural diversity also challenged an-

other source of medical ethics — theological ethics. There is a
long tradition in Western culture that has seen the interplay of theology and medicine. However, as Western culture has been
deChristianized, so, too, have Western medicine and morality. The
new possibilities in medicine, coupled with social and cultural
movements away from traditional sources of moral guidance, contributed to the development of bioethics.

One can ask, however, what is the reason medicine has a special
place? If modern, secular societies are marked by moral pluralism,
why does medicine become such a focal point of moral controversy? It can be argued that the moral controversies in bioethics
developed in part because health care is a cooperative venture
which potentially brings together an array of moral visions. One
cannot assume that those who participate share a common moral
framework in which to resolve disputes. Health care is set in complex institutional patterns that bring together physicians, patients,
nurses, and an array of health care professionals in ventures which
are sponsored by public and private resources and visions. The
men and women involved in the practice of health care often have
conflicting understandings of the rights and obligations of professionals, patients, and society. The different interests and moral
points of view form the background for the moral controversies of
health care and bioethics in a secular pluralistic society. Because
medical technology can affect so many aspects of human life, and
since health care is a cooperative enterprise, it highlights moral
pluralism in a manner not found in other aspects of life. Men and
women with different moral views can live and work side by side
without engaging in moral controversies. However, in health care
they must collaborate with others, and differing moral views become problematic. Bioethics has emerged as a discipline to resolve
controversies in a secular, morally pluralistic setting. This essay will
now examine: 1) the nature of moral controversies resolutions, 2)
the hope of resolving such controversies by appealing to reason, 3)
common approaches in bioethics to resolve moral controversies,
and 4) the search for moral authority in a pluralistic society.

Closure and Moral Controversies

Moral controversies emerge when men and women differ on either the description or resolution of a moral dilemma. Sometimes
these disputes happen between members of a moral community.
They share common moral commitments, language, and reasoning so as to engage in discussion and argument. However, many
issues in bioethics occur because people do not share the same
moral commitments. For some, the introduction of embryonic

stem cells research represents a serious moral issue for public debate, while, for others, the ban on embryonic stem cells research is the real moral issue. Bioethics seeks to resolve such controversies. However, moral controversies are different from controversies in other intellectual disciplines in that they seem to have an interminable quality.[15] In part, this quality comes about because people frequently hold commitments to different sets of moral values or different views of moral reason. Such foundational disagreements often underlie the moral controversies in health care. One's understanding of moral reason directs the way in which people think about justifying a moral choice (e.g., appeals to rules, principles, virtues, cases) and the values which give content to the reasoning process. As long as men and women share the same understanding or moral reason and moral values, they can, in principle, argue about a moral controversy and reach resolution. However, absent such agreement, the controversy will be intractable. Roman Catholics, for example, may be able to share a common moral tradition which will enable them to analyze such issues as the use of RU-486. They share a common moral tradition which allows them to identify moral issues and possible solutions to those issues. When men and women share enough moral premises in common, they can reach closure by sound argument.[16]

Moral controversies can also be resolved when consensus is achieved.[17] Here, it does not matter whether the claims endorsed by the consensus are true or false. All that matters is that there is agreement. In many controversies in health care, the achievement of consensus has been sufficient for the resolution of moral controversies (e.g., The National Commission, The President's Commission, National Bioethics Advisory Commission).

There are, however, several difficulties with this type of closure. First, there is often a failure to distinguish between consensus and the morally appropriate action. Simply because a consensus existed that hereditary slavery was morally acceptable did not make the practice correct. One's judgment about the moral appropriateness or inappropriateness of an action will depend on the assumptions with which one begins. Consensus simply indicates that people agree, but it does not indicate the depth of the agreement or whether the agreement is right. Second, while consensus may help resolve a particular case where the principals (e.g., physician, patient) reach agreement on what should be done, the adequacy of the consensus may be limited to the particular case. A consensus to limit treatment in one case does not automatically generalize to other cases or into institutional policy. Finally, it is difficult to understand what role consensus should play in the resolution of moral controversies in public policy disputes in health care.[18] In particular, in public policy debates, consensus often does not mean agreement of all parties, but the emergence of a majority able to enforce its moral views.

Another sense of closure is that of "natural death," that is, a controversy dies because interest in the controversy simply goes away.[19] Such closure rarely happens in the moral controversies of bioethics. For example, while the moral controversies which initially surrounded the use of advanced directives have "died," there is continuing controversy about what ought to be allowed in the use of such directives (e.g., feeding and hydration, assisted suicide).[20] Also, the whole area of research ethics, thought by many to be a closed chapter in bioethics, has seen the development of new issues.[21]

There are other ways to close a moral controversy, and these deserve careful examination. Closure can come to a moral controversy by negotiation and appeal to procedures.[22] I will argue that the only resolution of moral controversies, which can be justified by men and women who hold different moral views, is an appeal to a procedural morality; that is, since men and women will speak different moral languages, they will not share enough in common to recognize a content-full closure of a controversy. Yet, they may be able to recognize that there is proper moral authority to close a moral controversy. If one cannot resolve moral controversies by a general consensus, one may decide either to abide by some procedure to produce an answer or to apply procedures that draw authority from the permission of those involved. This is the reason the practice of free and informed consent has come to play such a significant role in health care. If people are at fundamental disagreement about what is proper, they can act together with the moral authority of their limited agreements.

Bioethics has tried to resolve controversies by appeal to sound argument or a set of normative principles or cases. To understand the reason that the only closure possible in a morally pluralistic society is a procedural closure, one must understand the reason that the appeal to arguments, principles, or cases inevitably is limited. The appeal to rationality seems at first to be especially promising. If one is able to provide a definitive rational account of a moral issue, this should resolve all the rational questions advanced by rational individuals. In short, rational individuals could not protest a definitive rational answer to a rational question without declaring their irrationality. Moreover, if one imposes a definitive rational solution on those who rejected it, this imposition would not be untrue to the real nature of those individuals as rational beings. After all, insofar as humans are rational animals, one would realize their true nature by the imposition. The appeal to rationality comes with great promise.

This approach to closure of moral controversies has been central to Western culture since Plato and Socrates. It has deep historical roots in the Natural Law tradition of the West. Roman law, while acknowledging the practices and customs of different cultures, was shaped, under the influences of Cicero, Ulpianus, and Justinian, by a belief in the *jus naturale*, which was known to all animals, and the *jus gentium*, which embodies what reason commands of any rational agent. Gaius speaks of "the law that natural reason establishes among all mankind [and which] is followed by all people alike, and is called *ius gentium* [law of nations or law of the world]" (de Zulueta). This point is repeated in the Institutes of Justinian (Book I.2). Centuries later, William Blackstone picks up this same theme when he writes of one of the purposes of the law as supporting the moral law common to all.[23] More recently, Lord Patrick Devlin argued that the State should "compel a man to act for his own good."[24]

The hope of a common moral culture was realized in the Christianization of the West. The fabric of faith, culture, and State were symbolically woven together in the crowning of Charlemagne on Christmas Day in 800 A.D. by Pope Leo III. This union of throne and altar symbolized the marriage of the moral law and the civil law. The belief that the moral law could be discovered through natural reason and codified in the civil order became embedded in the Christian view of the world. "God" became the keystone of an ordered, rational universe. After the collapse of the Middle Ages' synthesis of faith and reason, the Modern Age attempted to provide rational justification for Judeo-Christian morality without faith in the Judeo-Christian God.[25] Indeed, the hope of developing a rational, content-full moral theory became the hallmark of the Enlightenment and Western culture.[26] The late Modern Age, in the West, is a deChristianized age.[27]

The fundamental conceptual difficulty for the project of resolving moral controversies on the basis of rational argument is that one needs a shared moral view expressed in some set and ranking of moral values, rules, principles, virtues, or narrative in order to give content to the argument. Such standards have been sought (1) in the very content of ethical claims or in intuitions, as self evidently right; (2) in the consequences of actions; (3) in the idea of an unbiased choice made by an ideal rational observer or group of rational contractors; (4) in the idea of rational moral choice itself; or (5) in the nature of reality. None of these strategies can, however, succeed because there is no way uncontroversially to select or discover the right or true moral content in reason, intuitions, consequences, or in the world.

The appeal to intuitions is limited because, for any one intuition which is advanced, a contrary one can be advanced with equal ease. The same can be said with regard to compositions or systems of intuitions. What, for one individual, will appear to be a corrupt or deviant moral intuition can, for another, appear correct, wholesome, and self evident. For some, for example, assisted suicide is a horrible sin while others will think that it is often noble. There is no way to sort out and rank the intuitions without begging the question.

Nor can more success be achieved by appeal to the consequences of one's choices. The appeal to consequences faces the problem of the way to assess and evaluate different consequences. For some, living a while longer after chemotherapy is a better consequence, even with side effects, than is dying. For others, however, living a life unimpaired by treatment is a more important outcome than is extending the quantity of life. To make the judgment, one needs a way to rank the outcomes. A consequentialist will have to build in some presuppositions about the ranking of values in order to evaluate possible outcomes and to know which outcomes are more important and which preferences are to be given priority. One might agree, for example, that the proper goals of political life include liberty, equality, prosperity, and security. Though one may be in agreement with regard to these major goals, one cannot assess consequences until one has decided the way to rank or weigh these goals. Different rankings will give decidedly different outcomes. Each may hold commitments to the same values, but, may rank them in different ways. The problem caused by different rankings will not be solved by an appeal to a preference utilitarianism. One will still need to know the way to rank rational versus impassioned preferences, present versus future preferences. One will need to know God's discount rate for time. Consequentialist accounts are no better advantaged than intuitionist accounts with regard to being able to demonstrate which set of outcomes is to be preferred since such a judgment requires an authoritative means of ranking benefits and harms. We are left in a position that one way of weighing consequences can always be countered by another way of weighing consequences with no way to judge between them except by appeal to our own moral sense.

Others have attempted to develop content-full, authoritative moral conclusions by employing some variety of hypothetical-choice theory. In such theories an Ideal Observer, or set of choosers, needs to be informed of the various possible choices and be impartial in weighting everyone's interests and siding with none of the parties involved. But, if the observer is impartial, how will decisions be made? The observer cannot be so impartial or dispas-

sionate as not to favor certain outcomes over others. Therefore,
despite the guise of impartiality, proponents of hypothetical-
choice theories must build into the observer some particular
moral sense or thin theory of the good in the order of choice. Like
the intuitionist account or the consequentialist account, one needs
a way to rank the choices.

One can see this in John Rawls' *A Theory of Justice.*[28] By imposing
particular constraints on his hypothetical contractors, Rawls builds
in to his contractors a particular moral sense. They must (1) rank
liberty more highly than they do other societal goods;[29] (2) be risk
aversive;[30] (3) not be moved by envy;[31] and (4) be heads of families
or concerned about the members of the next generation.[32] Again,
the problem is that the description of the contractors is one that
presupposes a particular moral point of view. But, one is given no
independent reason(s) which argue for one particular view of the
contractors over any other.

Attempts to discover a concrete view of the good life or of
justice through analysis of the concepts themselves suffer the same
difficulty as hypothetical-choice theories. One must know, in
advance, which sense of rationality, neutrality, or impartiality to use
in choosing among different accounts of the good life, justice, or
morality. There is no content-full moral vision which is not itself
already a particular moral vision. One cannot choose among alternative moral senses or thin theories of the good without already
appealing to a moral sense or thin theory of the good.

Finally, one is not able to resolve moral controversies by appealing to the structure of reality. This model is known as an appeal to
the Natural Law. It assumes that nature is morally normative and
that there is a moral law in the structure of the world and of men
and women (e.g., Finnis). The difficulties here are twofold. First,
in order for the structure of reality to serve as a moral criterion,
nature must be shown to be morally normative. But, in the absence
of some metaphysical account of reality, it will be impossible to
conclude whether the structure of reality is accidental or morally
significant apart from the concerns of particular persons or groups
of persons. This is especially the case with regard to human nature,
which appears in scientific terms to be the outcome of sponta-
neous mutations, selective pressures, genetic drift, constraints set
by laws of physics, chemistry, and biology as well as the effects of
catastrophic events. Human nature is, as such, simply a fact of
reality without direct normative significance.

The second difficulty with appeal to nature is that, even if one
thought that one could find moral significance in human nature,
this would be possible only if one already possessed a canonical understanding of nature. Even if one accepts the normativity of

nature, the structure of reality is open to many descriptions and interpretations. The Natural Law appeal, like others, must build in some particular moral sense which determines which description of nature is to be normative. However, we have no rational way to demonstrate that one description of nature should trump all others. Furthermore, contemporary philosophers like W. V. Quinne have argued that reason can be understood only within a context. Many "reasonable" judgments lose their reasonableness when the context is changed.

In spite of its attractiveness and historical importance, the appeal to reason for content-fully resolving moral disputes has been a failure. Unless men and women share a common understanding of the moral world or moral rationality, they will be unable to resolve moral disputes in a content-full way. Even if men and women could agree on a particular theoretical approach (i.e., an appeal to consequences, or duties, or intuitions), the problem still remains of selecting a particular guiding moral content (e.g., does one rank liberty over equality or equality over liberty; what discount rate for time does one choose?). In order to produce a secular bioethics that can give content-full guidance, one must already have in hand that which one is seeking to discover, namely, a content-full moral vision. A view from nowhere will give no content-full guidance, because it carries with it no particular ranking or account of values. On the other hand, any particular view presupposed what one needs to secure: guiding moral conduct. Generality is purchased at the price of content; content is purchased at the price of generality. This project of justifying a secular bioethics from a single theoretical starting point thus appears impossible. Every argument that will lead to a content-full moral conclusion must start from certain particular assumptions. It is just that they will intractably be at dispute in a secular moral society in which there are communities with different moral visions, moral senses, and moral narratives.

Bioethics: Living in the Hopes of the Past

The limitations of modern, secular moral philosophy have not deterred bioethicists from appeal to reason for content-full solutions to the moral controversies in bioethics. There have been a number of theoretical approaches in bioethics.[33] Each of these approaches encounters two basic difficulties. First, each must build in content to its premises in order to resolve moral dilemmas. Second, each must presume a particular account of the nature of moral reason. For example, Peter Singer defines the most basic element of moral reasoning to be that of a concern for "interests."

However, one might argue that moral reasoning is based on a notion of natural "duties," as Grisez, Boyle, and Finnis do, rather than on a notion of interests. Furthermore, in defining the very concept of "interests," Singer has built in a basic moral commitment. Robert Veatch experiences similar difficulties in his account of the contractual structure of medicine, patient, and society. His argument that medical practice should be understood in terms of hypothetical contracts contrasts sharply to others such as Edmund Pellegrino and David Thomasma who understand the nature of moral reasoning through the concept of virtue. Even if one accepted Veatch's position, there is no compelling reason to think that one should accept his account of the way those contracts would develop. Contractors, with interests different from Veatch's, would make very different bargains.

The foundational problem for any theory of morality is that a theory can resolve moral controversies only to the extent that those involved in the controversy share the same set of moral premises, that is, the extent to which they share the same concept of moral reason and the same set of moral values or intuitions. Absent such similar commitments, the disputes will be interminable. As MacIntyre argues, the interminable nature of moral controversies is based on the lack of a shared conceptual framework and values.

There have been two different attempts in bioethics to avoid the foundational difficulties which have confronted theoretical models. The best known is that of Tom Beauchamp and James Childress who forward the use of middle level principles in resolving moral controversies.[34] Beauchamp and Childress argue that moral controversies can be settled without reaching foundational agreement. They argue that there are enough middle level principles which men and women share to allow the resolution of moral controversies; that is, they hold that there is enough overlap of moral theories that controversies can be resolved by appeal to the middle level principles which are common to different moral theories and viewpoints. These principles are held to be "mid-way" between the general foundations of a moral theory and the particular moral controversy and its hoped for resolution. They argue for four such principles: autonomy, beneficence, nonmaleficence, and justice. These principles are, in their view, an articulation of common morality for health care. They form the most general boundaries of moral commitments and discourse.

There are at least three difficulties with the position they have developed. First, there is an insufficient account of the reason one should accept this list of principles as *the* canonical list of middle level principles. Other principles (e.g., sanctity of life or some principle of human dignity) might be added to the list. Second, it is not entirely clear what the principles mean. While people may speak of "autonomy," they in fact mean very different things. For some, autonomy means the freedom to do whatever one chooses with oneself and consenting others (e.g., assisted suicide) while for others autonomy means the freedom to act within certain moral constraints. For others, it reflects a value assigned to liberty or to acting on one's own authentic values. There is a significant ambiguity in each of the principles which allows them to capture a wide range of interpretations. But, such a range of specifications means that, while people may be using the same words, they may actually be speaking about very different matters.

Beauchamp and Childress do not see this as a problem of "meaning," but of *specification*. The principles are general and need to be specified to the context and situation. This also involves a process of weighing and balancing. Finally, even if the principles shared and their meanings were clearly defined, the way they would be able to address particular moral controversies is not evident, that is, one could easily imagine cases where different principles would seem to address the same controversy. Since there is no theoretical structure to order the principles, there is no definitive appeal by which to sort out the relationship of the different principles one to the other. For example, in discussing the issue of physician assisted suicide, one might appeal to the principle of beneficence in arguing that the physician should assist, while another may appeal to the principle of nonmaleficence in arguing that the physician must not take part. One comes to understand that the difficulties confronting the appeal to middle level principles can be resolved only by situating the principles within the context of a moral account by which the principles are defined in their own terms and in relationship to one another. To bring these procedures together — specification, weighing, and balancing — these authors use a process of reflective equilibrium.

Still, one may ask: if all of these difficulties beset middle level principles, why should they appear to be so successful? The answer lies in the circumstances that many of those who write books on bioethics in fact share one particular secular moral vision. They then attempt to reconstruct their moral vision, along with their moral sensibilities, in terms of different theoretical approaches. For such theoreticians, the point of departure is a common morality in which they share similar moral sentiments. They simply set about the task of reconstructing those sentiments through different deontological or consequentialist approaches. It should not be startling that the middle level principles they endorse will have similar substance, though different theoretical overtones. It is only when individuals attempt to resolve moral controversies from different ideological understandings (imagine the differences in the understandings of the middle level principles of justice as given by a Rawlsian versus a Nozickian bioethicist) or different religious understandings (imagine the differences in the understandings of the middle level principle of nonmaleficence regarding abortion as given by an observant Roman Catholic versus a secular humanist) that one discovers that middle level principles disclose differences rather than resolve controversies.

A second attempt to avoid the conceptual dilemmas of ethical theory are the recent attempts to appeal to some form of casuistry. Perhaps the best known example is that of Albert Jonsen and Stephen Toulmin.[35] They argue that the failure of moral philosophy to resolve moral controversies is due to the misconception of moral reason. Moral reason needs to be understood as practical, rhetorical reason, not as geometrical or theoretical reason. Jonsen and Toulmin argue that moral controversies are resolved by referring controversies to particular moral paradigm cases. For example, one might resolve the controversy associated with assisted suicide by referring to the paradigm case of murder.

The conceptual problems for a secular casuistry revolve around the need for a content. Jonsen's and Toulmin's appeal to rhetorical, practical reason cannot resolve moral controversies unless there is content for the structure.[36] However, unless the content is commonly shared, there is no way to recognize a moral controversy or its specific character. Furthermore, without a common moral framework, there is no way to know the correct set of paradigm cases that should be applied. In the continuing controversy over abortion, for example, some apply the paradigm of killing while others apply the paradigm of privacy and battery.

In their exposition of casuistry, Jonsen and Toulmin apply an historical example from a very highly defined moral community. The casuistry of Roman Catholicism, which they explore at length, was set within the life of a community with particular moral understandings and a common juridical structure (confessors, bishops, popes) which could resolve ambiguities when it was unclear as to the way a case should be interpreted or which paradigm case should be applied. What Jonsen's and Toulmin's account makes clear is that, if casuistry is to work within a secular, morally pluralistic context, there will have to be some common moral framework. The problem is to find the correct one.

The recognition that a content-full moral framework is necessary has been expressed in various appeals to the existence of consensus. One might think here, for example, of the recent invocation of the notion of overlapping consensus in John Rawls' recent volume, *Political Liberalism*.[37] There is a recognition that, without a common normative framework, one will not possess the thin theory of the good, the canonical moral intuitions, the correct moral sensibilities, needed in order to make moral choices and to endorse particular moral judgments. As a result, much is done in order to manufacture the seeming presence of a consensus. When one impanels national commissions or other bioethics committees to frame public policy or to make bioethical recommendations, one is careful both to choose individuals with much in common and to focus the agenda on issues where common agreement is likely to be attainable. One can only imagine the kinds of prin-ciples that would have been endorsed were the National Commission for the Protection of Human Subject in Biomedical and Behavioral Research to have had as its members Robert Nozick, John Rawls, Jesse Ventura, Ron Paul, Jesse Jackson, Pat Buchanan, and William Buckley. When people talk about a consensus shared in bioethics, they often fail to recall the great range of moral opinions about health care expressed in political campaigns.

Of course, like Richard Rorty, one can accept a particular deliverance of a particular history as normative and speak as "we 20th century liberals."[38] When one speaks of oneself and like minded individuals as inheriting a particular understanding of cosmopolitan and democratic institutions, one accepts a particular contingent history as normative and justified. But, that is to return to something like the secular equivalent of a religious faith. For the Christian notion of a *consensus fidelium*, one substitutes a particular orthodoxy or ideological viewpoint in order to gain content, but with the Holy Spirit. Though it is not a true consensus of all the persons involved, it is considered normative as the consensus of those whose conscience is evoked as if it would have a religious, but still secular, significance.

In examining the history of secular bioethics, one finds that, after trying to come to terms with the difficulties and pluralisms of religious bioethics, secular bioethics has in great measure reiterated the character of religious bioethics. It has substituted particular philosophical and ideological communities for what had been found in religious faith. The result has been a recapitulation of the disagreements that shaped religious bioethical disputes, but now couched in secular terms. This outcome is fully understandable. If one wishes to resolve moral controversies other than by the mere application of force, that is, only with morally authoritative force, one must derive that authority from God, reason, or common agreement. The development of secular bioethics as a response to the diverse ways in which individuals have chosen to hear God led to the attempt to ground bioethics in sound rational argument. But, since this cannot succeed without presupposing particular content-full moral premises, that is, without a prior act of faith or common agreement, a common agreement was silently assumed.

The failure of this project is manifest both sociologically and theoretically. On the one hand, one finds a continuing multiplicity of bioethics, not simply numerous religious bioethics, but secular bioethics as well. The controversies go on and on; they do not appear open to definitive resolution through sound rational argument. As a sociological fact, pluralism has persisted, if it has not been intensified. On the other hand, one can recognize the theoretical basis for the failure. The closure of content-full moral controversies by sound rational argument requires that one employ content-full moral premises. The character of these is exactly what is at issue.

Looking toward the Future: Proceduralism and Institutional Ethics

At the moment, there is no reason to think that the moral controversies in health care will subside in secular nations like the United States. The field has been fueled by scientific and medical advances, moral pluralism, and the questions of the best way to allocate our resources. These are three trends that, in the foreseeable future, will continue to be sources of deep moral controversy.

First, there is the ongoing development of genetic medicine. As our knowledge of the genetic basis of different diseases increases, we will be better equipped to change the genetic structures and develop therapies. While this development offers great hope for many, it will also raise important moral questions about the way we define diseases. It will also raise questions about redesigning the human species and increasing our control over human life. These developments in medicine will lead to a greater need to examine basic philosophical questions about the nature of medicine and health care.

Second, there will be ongoing controversies over health care finance and resources. The technological and scientific advances will open up more and more possibilities for human life. These developments will contribute to an expanding appetite for what is possible. While there will be seemingly limitless possibilities, there will always be limited resources. We live in a finite world and will have to make choices about the way to allocate our resources. We will need to live with a tension that, while there are seemingly limitless possibilities for our interventions, there are not limitless resources to support these interventions.

Third, there is the continuing fragmentation and diversity of moral views in bioethics and in many fields. There is no reason to think that this fragmentation will end. As there is greater freedom of expression and communication in our world, there is every reason to think that moral pluralism will continue to develop.

Is there a future for the field of bioethics? If medicine continues to develop as it has and to produce the kinds of new moral controversies that we have seen, what is the future of this field? There may be another way to identify common moral ground and possible ways to resolve differences in issues in bioethics in a way that will allow us to work together. It is an appeal to "proceduralism."

Proceduralism is a term that focuses on the ways in which common moral authority can be justified. In democratic societies, for example, moral justification rests in some way on the consent of the governed. The moral authority of the procedural approach comes from the consent of the persons involved. In this way, moral "practices" are established. Procedures like informed consent have played critical roles in the development of bioethics. Consent to treatment, advance directives, consent for research are all everyday elements in the practice of medicine. Some thinkers may lament that bioethics has been reduced to empty procedures and mere formalisms. But, are these procedures so empty? It can be argued that procedures are not. Practices like informed consent make sense only if there are underlying moral assumptions about respect for persons.

Embedded in procedures like free and informed consent are not only assumptions about respect for persons, but also moral assumptions about honesty, truth telling, and fraud. These are rich moral concepts. The procedures then are far from "empty."

One can argue that the turn toward procedures is a way to capture moral ties that cut across different moral traditions and communities. The appeal to procedures is a way to identify common moral ground. Procedures have been crucial to the development of bioethics, and it would seem safe to guess that they will develop and grow with the field as medical options multiply, as our moral fragmentation continues, and as our resources are still limited.

Proceduralism, however, points to only one possible direction for the field. It can also be argued that the field will have to develop more in the area of institutional and organizational dimensions of ethics. Earlier in this essay, I argued that one reason for the rise and development of bioethics was the cooperative nature of modern medicine and health care. These goods are neither developed nor delivered without complex social and political structures. The encounter of the patient and the physician is not a one on one encounter. When they meet, there are many others who are present (other health professionals, insurers, hospital administrators, et cetera). One ought not bemoan the "presence" of these others as their presence helps make the encounter possible. It is important that the field bioethics move to take a wider account of the importance of institutional and organizational ethics.[39] Often the questions facing individual actors and decision makers are shaped by the institutional context. (Such influences are manifest in the practice of medicine in a managed care environment.) While institutions and organizations are more difficult to figure out than are individual moral choices, there are important questions to ask. What is the identity of the institution? Does it fulfill its mission and responsibility to the community? Institutions are not just aggregates. They are actors that, like health professionals, have an obligation to enable patients to make as free and rational a choice as possible.

Further, I would argue that the developing institutional complexities of health care and the continuing moral pluralism in secular societies will accentuate the importance of procedural morality and practices in shaping and guiding health care. We can look on these procedures, and their development, as signs of our common moral ground. The proceduralism that has been appealed to begins with an assumption about respect for persons. The appeal to procedures enables us to identify who has moral authority and the extent of that authority. A person, for example, has authority over her/his own self and her/his property. Proceduralism provides a way to outline the lines of authority and helps to produce a maze of moral authority with which we can act.

Just as bioethics has developed a concern for the procedures that govern the relationship of health care professionals and patients and providers, it needs to look beyond these relationships to include the organizations and institutions that provide the context of health care delivery. As we struggle with the impact of managed care, it becomes clear that the questions of bioethics transcend the relationship of physicians and patients. Those relationships are contextualized and embedded within institutions that provide the framework for the delivery of care. So, the future of bioethics must turn more and more to the questions of ethics and organization.

The need for a secular bioethics is real. It will not go away. While there has been a great deal of discussion recently about the role of religion, the number of religious voices keeps increasing. At the same time, there is a continuing movement toward patients' rights as well as the continued fracturing of professional ethics for physicians. To bind together a large scale society with general moral authority and to give moral legitimacy to its health care policy when citizens are members of diverse religious, ideological, and other moral communities, one must be able to justify an account of bioethics that transcends confessional and ideological differences. This is the concern that gave rise to the modern philosophical project and the Enlightenment hope of a general rational justification of a secular morality and of secular governmental authority. The project has failed to date. It has gone aground on its attempt to recapitulate the character of the communities it was designed to transcend. A successful secular bioethics must not simply announce yet one more moral community or one more content-full moral vision. It must draw authority from those who participate in it without requiring them to accept the particularity of yet one other moral vision. It must allow diverse confessional and ideological visions to have their place, as long as they do not involve nonconsenting others. This aspiration may not be oxymoronic. There is an underlying legitimacy to informed consent, the free market, and limited democracy that presupposes only the permission of those collaborating with concurring others. There is *de facto* a web of moral authority that can bind individuals of diverse moral understandings as it does in any market, in any war torn area of the world where members of hostile communities can still trade commodities without sharing a moral vision. There is theoretically the possibility of attending to the ways in which permission suffices to ground general moral authority without concurrence in any particular, content-full moral vision or the presupposition of a commonality of content-full moral premises. This theoretical possibility offers a basis for the general moral justification of a range of limited collaborations that can legitimate a *res publica* and health care policy with robust rights to privacy and space for deviant, but peaceable, consensual undertakings. Something of a secular bioethics can indeed be sustained.

NOTES

[1]This essay is built on earlier work that I did with H. T. Engelhardt, Jr., in an essay, entitled "The Emergence of Secular Bioethics," in *Bioethics*, ed. E. Edward Bittar and Neville Bittar (Greenwich, CT: JAI Press, 1994), 1-15.

[2]Mark A. Rodwin, *Medicine, Money & Morals: Physicians' Conflicts of Interest* (New York: Oxford University Press, 1993).

[3]Albert R. Jonsen, "The Birth of Bioethics," *The Hastings Center Report* 23: 6 (1993): S1-S4, and *The Birth of Bioethics* (New York: Oxford University Press, 1998).

[4]David J. Rothman, *Strangers at the Bedside: A History of How Law and Bioethics Transformed Medical Decision Making* (New York: Basic Books, 1991).

[5]In this essay, I use the term "content-full" to describe any model of moral reasoning which has a set of values and a ranking of them.

⁶A special qualification must be made with regard to the way religious communities understood the particularity of their bioethical commitments. Roman Catholicism is something of a special case. Roman Catholics have traditionally assumed that almost all of the particular content of their bioethics can in fact be established by reason alone. For example, this was the view that the good willed, open minded person, no matter what faith, should understand the Roman Catholic proscriptions about contraception. Edwin Healy wrote: "It matters not whether one be a Roman Catholic, a Protestant, a Jew, a pagan, or a person who has no religious affiliations whatever; he is nevertheless obliged to become acquainted with and to observe the teachings of the law of nature. In the present volume all the obligations which are mentioned flow from the Natural Law, unless the contrary is evident from the context" [Edwin Healy, *Medical Ethics* (Chicago: Loyola University Press, 1965)].

⁷See Gilbert Meilaender, *Body, Soul, and Bioethics* (Notre Dame, IN: University of Notre Dame Press, 1995).

⁸In this essay, the term *secular* is used to mean a morally neutral framework within which individuals of various moral communities can collaborate.

⁹See Daniel Callahan, "Why America Accepted Bioethics," *Hastings Center Report* (November, 1993), Special Supplement, S8-S9.

¹⁰See H. T. Engelhardt, Jr., *Bioethics and Secular Humanism: The Search for a Common Morality* (London: SCM Press, 1991), 20-42.

¹¹See Robert Baker, "A Theory of International Bioethics: Multiculturalism, Postmodernism, and the Bankruptcy of Fundamentalism," *Kennedy Institute of Ethics Journal* 8:201-31; Robert Baker, "A Theory of International Bioethics: The Negotiable and the Non-Negotiable," *Kennedy Institute of Ethics Journal* 8:233-74; Tom L. Beauchamp, "The Mettle of Moral Fundamentalism," *Kennedy Institute of Ethics Journal* 8:389-401; Ruth Macklin, "A Defense of Fundamental Principles and Human Rights: A Reply to Robert Baker," *Kennedy Institute of Ethics Journal* 8:403-22.

¹²Hippocrates, "The Oath," in *Hippocrates*, trans. W.H.S. Jones, The Loeb Classical Library (Cambridge: Harvard University Press, 1962).

¹³Robert M. Veatch, *A Theory of Medical Ethics* (New York: Basic Books, 1981), 22.

¹⁴Robert M. Veatch, "Medical Ethics: Professional or Universal?," *Harvard Theological Review* 65: 559.

¹⁵Alasdair MacIntyre, *After Virtue* (Notre Dame: University of Notre Dame Press, 1981).

¹⁶Tom L. Beauchamp, "Ethical theory and the problem of closure," in *Scientific Controversies: Case studies in the resolution and closure of disputes in science and technology*, H.T. Engelhardt, Jr., and A. L. Caplan, eds. (New York: Cambridge University Press, 1987), 27-30.

¹⁷Beauchamp, 30.

¹⁸See Kurt Bayertz, ed., *The Concept of Moral Consensus* (Dordrecht: Kluwer Academic Publishers, 1994).

¹⁹Beauchamp, "Ethical theory," 31-33.

²⁰See Leslie P. Francis, "Advance Directives for Voluntary Euthanasia: A Volatile Combination?," *Journal of Medicine and Philosophy* 18: 297-322.

[21]Baruch A. Brody, *The Ethics of Biomedical Research: An International Perspective* (New York: Oxford University Press, 1998).

[22]See Beauchamp, "Ethical theory," 30-31, 33-35.

[23]William Blackstone, *Blackstone's Commentaries*, ed. St. George Tucker (New York: August M. Kelly, 1969), vol. V, 42-55.

[24]Patrick Devlin, *The Enforcement of Morals* (London: Oxford University Press, 1965), 136.

[25]H. T. Engelhardt, Jr., *The Foundations of Bioethics*, 2nd edition (New York: Oxford University Press, 1996).

[26]A. MacIntyre, chapters 4 and 5.

[27]Romano Guardini, *The End of the Modern World* (New York: Sheed and Ward, 1956).

[28]John Rawls, *A Theory of Justice* (Cambridge: Harvard University Press, 1971).

[29]Ibid., 396.

[30]Ibid., 152-58.

[31]Ibid., 143, 546.

[32]Ibid., 128.

[33]See Peter Singer, *Practical Ethics* (Cambridge: Cambridge University Press, 1979); Veatch; Edmund Pellegrino and David Thomasma, *A Philosophical Basis for Medical Ethics* (New York: Oxford University Press, 1981); Norman Daniels, *Just Health Care* (Cambridge: Cambridge University Press, 1985).

[34]Tom L. Beauchamp and James Childress, *The Principles of Biomedical Ethics*, 4th edition (New York: Oxford University Press, 1994).

[35]A. Jonsen and S. Toulmin, *The Abuse of Casuistry* (Berkeley: University of California Press, 1988).

[36]Kevin Wm. Wildes, "The Priesthood of Bioethics and the Return of Casuistry," *Journal of Medicine and Philosophy* 18: 33-49; "Respondeo: Method and Content in Casuistry," *Journal of Medicine and Philosophy* 19: 115-19.

[37]John Rawls, *Political Liberalism* (New York: Columbia University Press, 1993).

[38]Richard Rorty, *Contingency, Irony, and Solidarity* (Cambridge: Cambridge University Press, 1989).

[39]Kevin Wm. Wildes, S.J., "Institutional Identity, Integrity, and Conscience," *Kennedy Institute of Ethics Journal* 4:413-19; "Institutional Integrity: Approval, Toleration and Holy Way or 'Always True to You in My Fashion,'" *Journal of Medicine and Philosophy* 16:211-20; Ezekiel Emmanuel, "Medical Ethics in the Era of Managed Care: The Need for Institutional Structures Instead of Principles for Individual Cases," *Journal of Clinical Ethics* 6:335-38; Edmund Pellegrino, "Hospitals as Moral Agents," in *Humanism and the Physician* (Knoxville: University of Tennessee Press, 1979).

Social Ethics in the New Millennium

Judith A. Merkle, S.N.D. de N.

When I began my doctoral studies, I asked a respected professor what he would do if he were beginning a program in social ethics. He looked at me thoughtfully and said, "My dear, I would jump off the bridge!" He may have sensed at that time that not only were the questions changing in social ethics, but also our understanding of the concepts used to answer the questions.

Today we ask: what is the ethic of those who live as one age dies and another is born? Individuals inventory their lives, asking themselves whether they are who they could be. However, the question of social ethics goes beyond personal scrutiny and asks: who are we together? What will become of us? How should we conduct our affairs? What consequences await if we ignore our problems?

At the turn of a millennium, humankind seeks a new place in the scheme of things. We search to exercise our powers in harmony with our place; yet, we establish this place with each new decision. We set about this task in a world where a sense of the whole is absent, a sense that understands the interrelationship of the varied elements of our lives and knows what to do with them. To seek an ethic for a new age uncovers this state of affairs. It stretches us to ask: what habits of heart and mind and what policies and institutions are required in the face of the complexity of the earth, its peoples, economics, religion, and politics?

We are the first generation capable of destroying the earth as we know it. We can no longer say that the environment is a question of concern as if the environment were a world apart from ourselves. The true state of affairs is we are part of the earth. We live

and die as human beings, as nature lives and dies in our transformations of it. The future of humankind stands, not apart from the
earth subduing it, but inextricably dependent on its future for survival.[1] Therefore, in the twenty-first century, we do more than pass
through another era in human history. We face crises which are
civilizational, religious, and geobiological.

In this essay, we will explore this changed context in social
ethics in three ways. In the first part, we will investigate forces that
are changing the face of social ethics today. These forces, like
geological plates, are remaking the economic, political, and religio-
cultural face of the earth. In the second part, we will examine the
role of religion and theology in forming a social ethic to meet the
challenges of this age. In the last section, we will reflect on practice
of ethics by focusing on community and its role in social ethics in
the new millennium.

I. Major Shifts in Social Reality

The images of the earth as a womb and the world as global are
two guiding metaphors for the state of the world today. Lester
Milbrath compares the womb of the earth, which supports all life,
to the slow running of a feature film. The movie takes a full year to
run, from the origin of the earth to the present. Each day of the
movie represents more than twelve million years. On this scale, the
time since the Industrial Revolution has been two seconds so far.[2]

This image certainly conveys the small place modernity holds in
the passing of the millennia. A glance at the energy meter running
on the present globe reveals that everyday the worldwide global
economy burns the amount of energy the planet required ten
thousand years to produce.[3] If we refer to development to mean
movement from a preindustrial society to an industrial one, we
must catch the irony of the phrase as we assess these costs. A truer
picture is that development and progress are demands of civilization which those of us who have lived only in the last two seconds
of the earth's story have put on the human community. Only
twenty percent of the world's population actually profit from the
development and progress we affirm.

In the twenty-first century, we must ask what development really
means if the earth is global and so are its peoples. To seek a sustainable world is to work toward one where nature and our social
systems survive and thrive together. Social ethics in the new millennium is challenged to maintain this inseparable union between
nature and social systems for all of humankind.

Today, scientists claim we live in a period of punctuated equilibrium. In a period of punctuated equilibrium, the environment

suddenly changes, and what has been the dominant species rapidly dies out to be replaced by some other species. Evolution, in other words, takes a quantum leap.

As an image of the world, a period of "punctuated equilibrium" refers to a time of unprecedented change. Massive shifts are caused by the simultaneous movement of factors which can be compared to the geological plates which form the surface of the earth.[4] In geology, movements in the continental plates are driven by currents in the earth's molten inner core, its magna. Today, social, economic, and political "plates" ride on a fluid mixture of changed technology, ideology, and cultural redefinition to provide a new state of the world.

In a period of punctuated equilibrium, these elements do not match. Social and ethical systems no longer control our technology; identities as peoples are no longer defined by the same boundaries, and time held ideas no longer carry meaning or provide insight into solutions to problems. People and nations scramble for identity and position in a world of shifting ground, often by means which tear apart the fabric of our families, communities, and globe. Let us turn to examine these shifts in our world today.

Global Character of Life

The first is the global character of life. Globalization is understood as the increasingly interconnected character of the political, economic, and social life of the peoples on this planet. Robert Schreiter defines globalization in the twentieth century by three important shifts.[5] The first is the collapse of Communism and the bipolar world of the United States and the Soviet Union in 1989. Today, power is distributed in a multipolar world. Territory and contiguity are less important as ways to map reality.

The end of Socialism in all but a few countries has allowed for a worldwide expansion of market Capitalism. This brings about our second shift, the move to a single world economy. This economy ignores national boundaries, moves capital quickly, and engages in short term projects that maximize profits. The end of Communism does more than clear the playing board for all capitalist markers. The end of Communism means that one third of humanity and one fourth of the world's landmass move from a Communist to a Capitalistic economic, political, and social identity. The digestion of this world will change Capitalism and democracy as we know them.[6]

The third characteristic of globalization is the advancement of communications. We now have instant communications across the globe. The networking made possible through communication eludes traditional forms of hierarchical control. Air travel makes the movement of peoples and goods relatively inexpensive.

Changed communication and patterns of travel cause shifts in cultural and political identity. Political borders traditionally mark boundaries of sovereignty, identity, and responsibility. They indicate where social investments are made and administrative guidelines are enforced, where tariffs are collected and legal systems applied. However, shifts in technology, transportation, and communication dictate that things can be made and sold anywhere today. Governments are involved with affairs far beyond their borders. The notion of national economy and identity fades as the tension between global business, which focuses on markets and national governments which are to focus on the welfare of the voters, grows. Will children in the new millennium pledge allegiance to a regional trading block? How do we blend these new realities with the cultural needs of political association?

The relationships of a new world economy are mimicked in our daily lives. Positively, new relationships are produced. Negatively, as loyalties and boundaries of relationships are evaded and broken more easily in the modern society, the result is a sense of fragmentation of family and community.[7] We enjoy maintaining contacts and relationships through the telephone and email that could have been sustained previously only by occasional correspondence. Yet, the rapidity of movement in our world today weakens the significance of the past and makes the future seem short term. The movement of peoples makes the meaning of home as ancestral place less significant. A third of all the people living in Frankfurt, Germany, today do not hold German passports. [8] The role of boundaries in forming identity loses its power as we crisscross the globe.

Even Capitalism is affected by shifts in technology, ideology, and cultural change. Capitalism needs some very long run communal investments in research and development, education and infrastructures, for it to prosper in the new millennium. Yet, Capitalism's normal decision making processes look only eight to ten years into the future. Economists charge that Capitalism has little in its rationale to build the local communities needed to sustain these investments.[9]

Shifts to a multipolar world, the single economic system of international Capitalism, and advancements in communications technology converge to produce a new face on globalization today. The mix of technology and ideology which propel globalization changes culture and redesigns the major institutions of our society.

Effects of Globalization

Globalization extends the effects of modernity to the entire world and compresses time and space. Through the spread of Western culture through globalization, powerful homogenizing systems have been established which function in similar ways from country to country and shape institutions. While there are local and national variations, international science, medicine, education move in a fashion in which standards are maintained across cultures and countries. The global system of capital formation and transfer symbolized by an international stock market that operates twenty-four hours a day is an icon of this homogenization. Homogenized patterns, driven by values of innovation, efficiency, and technical rationality, grow stronger in the world each day.

Benefits and loss come to the world community through this homogenization. While the human community holds onto the positive advances of this century in medicine, education, and nutrition, it is staggered by the fact that eighty percent of the world's population still experience globalization as materially negative. These peoples are in economic decline rather than in economic development, with many facing the loss of their cultures through the economic and cultural force of a global market.

The experience of homogenization in global cultures is further heightened by a hyperculture or an overarching cultural ideal which is not in itself a full culture.[10] The hyperculture of our global world today is one based on consumption and marked by icons of consumption derived from the United States; T-shirts, McDonald's, Coke, American films, videos, and music circle the world.[11] Benjamin Barber refers to this new world of universalizing markets as McWorld. The window of McWorld is the American television industry, exported globally. However, the typical TV family of American television is four times wealthier than the average American family.[12] What McWorld does not tell the globe is that a significant number of the citizens of the United States simply flip hamburgers.

The link between a single economic system and the exportation of a hyperculture is striking. In this decade, the one hundred largest corporations in the world had more economic power than eighty percent of the world's population had. In 1991, the aggregate sales of the world's ten largest industrial enterprises, employing only five hundreths of a percent of the planet's population, controlled twenty-five percent of the planet's economic output. The l992 sales revenue of General Motors alone ($133 billion) was about the same as the combined GNP of eight countries whose combined population is one tenth of the world's: Tanzania, Ethiopia, Bangladesh, Zaïre, Nigeria, Kenya, Nepal, and Pakistan.[13]

Governments, caught in the hyperculture of globalization, lower investments in the future to raise consumption in the present. Governments that should be representing the future to the present generation act in the opposite direction. The growing bipolar world today is not between the old enemies of the Cold War, but between those who enjoy the fruits of global Capitalism and those who do not. In this Invisible War, the well off world and their governments increasingly ignore the poor. In such a single system world, it becomes increasingly difficult to imagine alternatives. Even religion struggles against being coopted by the culture of media and consumerism.[14]

Changing Demographics

A fourth shift in world reality is a massive change in demographics, represented by new migration and changing age distribution. Former colonial people are flooding into Britain, France, Portugal, producing multicultural societies in previously monocultural situations. The expectation is that, sometime approaching the year 2030, the population will stabilize at about ten billion people, five times the number in 1950. The World Bank projects an increase in the world's population by 2050 to be a fifty percent increase of what it is today. What is striking is that two billion of these new 2.8 billion people will be born in countries where daily earnings are less than two dollars.[15]

Population growth in poor countries is a serious challenge facing us. Population growth is approximately three percent in the Middle East and Africa and two percent in south Asia and Africa. With such large populations, these countries can have real growth, yet make no progress in raising per capita incomes.[16]

However, a more grim forecast comes from the World Health Organization which estimates that one quarter of the adult populations of Zimbabwe and Botswana are infected with the virus that causes AIDS, a situation unparalleled since the bubonic plague swept through Europe in the fourteenth century. United Nations projections show India may add six hundred million more people by 2050, overtaking China as the world's most populous country. However, India faces serious water shortages. Social unrest, as in the longstanding conflict between the Tutsis and the Hutus in Rwanda, are fed by population pressures which reduced cropland to a point where it could no longer feed those who lived on it.[17] Similar conflicts can be sparked by demands on the world's fisheries and shared water resources.

The world is on the move; however, this is not the first vast migration of people. Between 1750 and 1930, fifty million Europeans migrated, one fifth of the entire European population. Recorded emigration had never happened on that scale, as the population increased more than fourteen times over.[18] Today, more than one hundred million people live outside the country in which they were born; twenty-three million of these people are refugees.

What causes migration at this rate today? Miserable conditions in the Third World and hope of better incomes in the First World propel population movements that the world has never seen. While the United States and Canada struggle with their immigration policies, we recognize that the Republic of Congo, during the African conflict at its border, proportionately took in more refugees per year than did the United States, with a national economy far less able to care for new peoples.[19]

People migrating today, however, differ from their predecessors of the last two centuries. They are moving into countries that do not need people or unskilled labor. Cheap transportation costs and images of a better life from the electronic media push skilled people into the United States as well as into France, Spain, and Italy. Movements of a century ago were from reasonably well off countries to empty lands. Today, migration is from poor to rich, from war torn to places of asylum. To be fully integrated into new societies, new peoples will require massive investments in their skills.

A recent study by the Rand Corporation of legal and illegal immigration in the state of California found for low skill workers: 1) a steady drop in earnings and employment prospects; 2) minimal job skills and little or no progress after they arrive; 3) the cost of providing services to immigrants, mainly education, adding considerably to the state's fiscal burden. Immigrants are paid less than native workers at all skill levels, but are equally productive employees. Business does profit from immigration. Yet, new patterns of immigration set up a new competition for low skilled native citizens.[20]

If First World countries refuse to educate their immigrants, they are implicitly deciding to produce a Third World within the First World. People are not going to go home, because they will not get educated at home either. At the same time, low skilled First World workers will not be paid First World wages for doing work that can be supplied by the Third World . The unskilled labor force in the First World will not have First World cushions to its lifestyle. Unless better programs of skill training and wage calculations occur, low skilled workers in the First World will experience a Third World lifestyle in a First World environment.

Governments in the past could curtail in-country exploitation of the worker with minimum wage laws, unemployment insurance, and safety regulations. All were advocated by the social teaching tradition of this century. But, we are now challenged to set and enforce such standards where unrooted countries, capital, and communications chase low wage labor from country to country as they please.

Aging Population

Changing demographics are also reflected in an explosive aging population in the world. For the first time in human history, our societies will have a very large group of economically inactive elderly people who have money, who vote, who require expensive social services such as health care, and who depend on the government for much of their income. In the United States, those more than sixty-five receive about forty percent of their incomes from the government. Approximately forty percent of these elderly receive eighty percent or more of their income from the government.[21] Excluding interest on the national debt, half of the federal budget goes to the elderly. By the year 2030, two thirds of the budget will go to older Americans.[22] Today's baby boomers are saving only one third of what they need in order to have the standard of living in retirement that their parents currently enjoy.[23] Some estimate that government expenditures for the elderly are currently nine times those spent on the young.[24]

Some project the federal government will stagger under the weight of the baby boom generation as they retire. Others hold that disability and morbidity will continue to become more compressed, leading to healthier years later in life. In other words, the average retirement age will rise.[25] Whatever the projections, the challenge remains that other investments have to be made that will not, or can not, be made unless benefits to the elderly are under control.

The challenge here is not just financial; it is political. Democracy might be tested to its core as the voting power of human history's largest group of elderly voters assess needed investments in education, infrastructure, skills, and knowledge which will not bring them tangible benefits in their lifetimes.

Changing Nature of Wealth and Power

Our fifth shift in the world reality is the changing nature of wealth. Brainpower is becoming the main source of strategic competitive advantage in our global economy. This poses new problems. How is the economic system to function in a brainpower era when brainpower cannot be owned? How do governments measure capital formation when so much new capital is intellectual?[26] How does one regulate or control such capital? For example, a computer wizard with a new program can cross an international boundary, paying no tariffs and asked no questions. Yet, the assets represented by the program in her head might be more than those contained in a thousand cargo ships. Balancing the ownership and reproduction of intellectual capital with the needs and contributions of the society at large will require new agreements on what is yours, mine, and ours.

A sixth shift is a multipolar world where there is no dominant economic, political, or military power. The earth serves as an icon of the variability of power across the globe today. Political power and ecological integrity can not be separate categories of global analysis in the future. Those who hold one will hold the other. In the new millennium, the human community will ignore, only at its peril, the connections between the sustainability of the earth and the distribution of power among the peoples of the earth.[27]

We cannot detach the multipolar nature of political power in the world today from the ecological realities in which it is inserted for three reasons. First, the technoeconomic power has been fashioned which is sufficient to destroy the material conditions of human and other life. This power can be exercised by rich or poor nations. Second, the human population has exploded. The economically dominant peoples of the earth are barely replacing themselves. Growth in nondominant populations will account for immigration driven growth in First World countries, while a youthful medium age in poorer countries will increase the world's population in 2050 to double the population in 1967.[28] These new peoples will need access to the world's resources and will move toward powerful cultural and ethnic identities, land, and political alliances to get it. Third, human consumption, at least in some sectors of the planet, has reached unparalleled heights. Twenty to twenty-five percent of the world's population, the advanced industrial countries, produce and consume four fifths of all goods and services.[29] This continuing pattern is not the recipe for a secure global community or for a sustainable earth.

Changes in access to the earth and its species will cause shifts in human power. Powerful interventions into nature affect everything that has life and is necessary for life, even across political boundaries. Will an army, a strategic arm, water, or a germ be the basis of power in the new millennium?

Power and ecology cannot be divorced in the new millennium. Nature is not just a human resource; rather, real nature lives and dies in our transformations of it for good or for evil. What we call human power over nature can be actually the power exercised by some people over others, using nature as a tool.[30] Sustainability, in this sense, is a planetary requirement in a multipolar world, since the biosphere itself is under siege and uses of power over nature, a global public worry.

These slow, almost imperceptible, changes in our global reality affect social ethics. To adapt, Christian ethics will change the way it responds to traditional problems and to the methods and ideas used to answer new questions. As Christianity engages with global-ization, it will question the adequacy of the vision of life, success, and happiness that drives modern culture. Yet, it will also use the new resources and opportunities of our global world to make a positive contribution to humankind. Christianity, too, will be changed in the process. While Christianity will not be the only ac-tor in social ethics in the future, it must gain insight into its own identity and role in order to be effective in wider civic and global circles. In the next section, we will inquire into the transformation in thinking and acting that this new age will require for Christian social ethics.

Challenges to Christian Social Ethics

Changes in the world reality influence the way we approach social ethics in the Christian community. Changes in global reality raise special issues for Christian ethicists since they stand within a communal religious tradition as they carry out their task. Moral methodology in Christian ethics is not just an academic system, but it involves a way of life and requires a community. Changes in the way we approach social ethics change the way we live in the Chris-tian community, and the way we live or do not live in Christian community radically affects our approach or method of Christian social ethics.

According to Brian Johnstone, moral methods are processes "by which a community of persons adopts, founds, validates and com-municates a moral way of life."[31] These processes must be clear enough so that they can be followed intelligently in a way of life. They also must be coherent in that the starting points, sequences, and conclusion are in a practical harmony with one another.

In Christian morality, the internal order of a method is not just academic, but it is related to its capacity to coherently direct a way of life. Coherence requires that a change in one pole in a rela-tionship brings changes in the others. Shifts in our world stimulate change in our self understanding as Christians and influence the way we understand the relevance of Christian revelation for the world. The search for a more adequate moral method in Christian social ethics will question the role of religion and theology in social ethics in the new millennium.

II. Religion and Theology in Social Ethics

Modern society does not lack the systems to meet its needs. It often lacks the focused leadership and vital moral vocabulary to change itself. Religion enters into the condition of modern society with the choice to collude or not with this situation. The sociologist, Max Weber, has stated that a main indicator of the way religion functions in a society is its capacity to lead that community to transform itself. Weber likened the role of religion to that of a magician or a priest. A magician does not lead a community to transform itself or reach out to the new challenges called forth by changes in the environment. Rather, the magician manipulates the gods to conform to the expectations of the people as they are now. When religion functions as a magician, it comforts, but offers no challenge.

A priest, on the other hand, leads a community to transformation: to face, and then to adapt to, the perplexities of a new environment. The priest calls the community to change. He or she challenges the community to leave behind its self centered desires to resist the calls of reality in its life. The priest uses the sacred rituals of religion to remind the group of their need to move outward and links them with the transcendent vision necessary to do so.[32] When religion functions as a priest, it challenges as well as comforts.

Religion today has a role which only the conditions of our secular society draws out of it: to speak to the end and purpose of existence without abstracting them from experience.[33] Religion must be able to talk about what is ultimate in life in a way that the sciences cannot: ultimate destiny, meaning, origins, and values. Yet, religion must speak of transcendence in terms which have historical ramifications.

Religion's role in social ethics is to insist that the larger meanings of life are present in ethical deliberation and that their implications for behavior find public and institutional forms. James Cone captures the priestly role of religion well. Religion must be able to point to something in its living that is not simply a religious legitimation of the values of the society in which it lives.[34] Religion's search is dialectical. It moves between a description of the world as it is and the articulation of an integral sense of the whole that carries us beyond present division and destruction.[35]

The Church today struggles to hold onto a sense of transcendence which religion protects and an account of history which ethics requires. When the tension between transcendence and history collapses, religion and the ethics it inspires dance between a fundamentalism, on one hand, and a relativism, on the other. The connection, which religion is charged to maintain, between transcendence and history becomes either too tight or too loose.

The efforts of religion to link transcendence and history can also be blocked. The incorporation of history into Christian ethical deliberation requires some shifts in the Church community as to the way we think about social problems. The equation of transcendence and irrelevance in the public mind often excludes religion from discussions of a public nature. In the next section, we will address some challenges both of these questions pose for a Christian social ethic.

The Question of History in Social Ethics

A shift in an understanding of the world, of God, or of human beings brings a subsequent shift in an understanding of social ethics in the Christian life. We can observe such a methodological shift as we examine the way a turn to history poses problems for a religious approach to social ethics. By a turn to history I mean the way the contextual nature and variability of human experience impacts an ethical problem. I will address the question in Roman Catholicism since it is the tradition with which I am most familiar.

Roman Catholicism, in the last century, has made a shift within its own ethical tradition from a Scholastic to a Personalist approach to ethics. This shift makes history, rather than timeless nature, a key referent in ethical reflection.[36] In a prior neoScholasticism, there was no room for the experience based thinking of history. Farley comments that, while Aquinas himself exhibited a certain amount of caution about the absoluteness of specific conclusions from general principles, his followers in neoScholasticism did not. Influenced by the Cartesian and Kantian drive toward clear concepts and absolute norms, morality tended toward an ahistorical system which controlled experience rather than explored it.[37]

Attention to history has called for a movement away from Integralism in social ethics, the presupposition that human persons simply put theory into practice in the social realm. Integralism approached the world and its history as simply the material field in which human action is carried out. Integralism assumes that this world is sufficiently predictable, malleable, and submissive to human will to make such a procedure possible.[38]

The challenge of a turn to history and experience in social ethics is the question of how one justifies and validates a moral decision which does not deny the relativities of history, yet does provide an objectivity short of absolute claims.[39] John Paul II cautions that detaching human freedom from its essential and constitutive relationship to truth leads to contemporary relativist currents of thought.[40] Also, failure to search for the truth of human dignity in its transcendent and permanent nature undermines the vision needed for essential political conditions in our world. Only a belief in the transcendent nature of human life, for instance, grounds openness in public administration, the rejection of illicit means in order to gain or increase power, respect for the rights of political adversaries, and others.[41] A turn to history and human experience without attention to the ethical relevance of transcendence is done at the peril of society. Yet, in practice, the human community often absolutizes a cultural sense of truth, freedom, or nature as it does social ethics, which ultimately obscures the sense of transcendence these terms are meant to uphold.

Truth and History

The turn to history affects core visions of truth, freedom, and nature which are used in social ethics. Church teaching has affirmed that freedom must be related to truth and that human autonomy has to be related to community. Yet, when the human community engages in social ethics, it searches for guiding principles in key relationships of social, political, and economic life that convert these philosophical relationships into policies for action. At the point of ethics, the tension between history and transcendence can be collapsed, and the transcendence of truth, freedom, or nature can be so identified with their cultural forms that they are idealized to protect the status quo or left as irrelevant.

For example, Vaclav Havel reminds us of a wary alliance between truth and a historical human system as he reflects on the "correct system" of the Communist régime. The *Power of the Powerless* is a reflection on the experience of the totalitarian Communist system. Communism offered ready answers to any questions whatsoever. It was a totalitarian system which could not be accepted in part. To accept it had profound implications for human life. In an era when metaphysical and existential certainties were in a state of crisis, Communism provided a home for the mind. All one had to do was accept it, and, suddenly, what was dark and anxious became clear. Havel remarks, "One pays dearly for this low-rent home: the price is abdication of one's own reason, conscience, and responsibility, for an essential aspect of this ideology is the consignment of reason and conscience to a higher authority."[42]

The center of power in the Communist system is the center of truth. For those in the Communist block, the loss of the transcendence of truth also meant a subsequent loss of freedom. Havel cautions that the freedom that people under Communism lost through accommodation to the system can also be lost in the West. The numbing force to freedom and truth in the West is not the State, but the soul owning market. While the West enjoys a type of political freedom not afforded in the Communist block, it, too, can live only the illusion of freedom, for it can make the market its center of truth.

The only corrective for freedom in either system, according to Havel, is living in truth. For the West, moral purpose and commitment to the truth are necessary to sustain its own freedom. The question is: does the West have this ethical commitment and does its religion foster it? John Paul II echoes Havel's concerns as he reminds us that the free market economy can actually resemble Marxism in the sense it totally reduces humanity to the sphere of economics and the satisfaction of material needs.[43] This operative "truth" of the Modern Age must be challenged.

Like Pilate, the human community asks today, what is the truth? The truth in social ethics is not just speculative, but it is linked to life itself. Liberation theologians remind us that truth makes a difference to some one, some place, and at some time. The truth of ethics does not keep humankind trapped in their failures and their living conditions; instead, it assures them of the meaningfulness of their life project, even when it does not fit into the parameters of First World consumer success.[44] The truth of Christian vision is always linked to hope for every man and woman. Each culture in our world today has visions of reason and "truth" which enable some and damn others. Religion must examine the adequacy of these ideas as they are enculturated into the systems and institutions of each nation and question the way each contributes to, and detracts from, the formation of a social ethic.

In First World culture, for example, rationality is often limited to technical rationality. This translates in ethical decision making into a simple utilitarianism: what works is what is right. Reason, in this sense, is not called upon to deliberate ends and norms that ought to govern our lives. Means and ends get confused. Theologian Juan Luis Segundo claims the greatest dilemma of modern times is not ordering means to ends, but deciding on what scale of means is appropriately human.[45]

The scale and complexity of the means utilized in our world today often make it impossible to decide exactly what ends these mechanisms are serving. For example, at what point do nuclear stockpiles cease serving needs of security? In this context, religion is called upon to work with the social sciences to construct tools by which communities can determine whether both ends and means are in harmony with values to be served. Technical rationality alone can not achieve this goal.

Cultural forms of rationality can also dim the capacity to think about issues of a public nature. Theologian Shawn Copeland charges that accepted standards of racism, sexism, and classism undermine people's ability to think and feel and thus dim the public vision of a wider public good.[46] The cultural individualism of our age, or the sense that only the individual is real, is a social blindness which obscures the full truth of the social situation. Sociologist Robert Bellah claims it is hard for the average American to even think at the communal level.[47] Individualism so captures our minds that such communal issues as how shall we live and for what shall we live can not be considered beyond choices made in private. Pursuit of personal goods is affirmed in the mentality of the market. However, this climate leaves social goods to be imposed and enacted by force.

Religion and theology help in the pursuit of a public rationality by retrieving from the Christian life values which are accessible to all and by speaking them in the public domain.[48] Here, religion is not seeking to establish a civil religion, but to look at the nation's public life for signs and calls of transcendent meaning and to point to them. Religion can aid in the understanding of the American experience in the light of ultimate universal reality and, thus, can better link history and transcendence in the public domain.

Freedom and History

Truth is not the only category of a social ethic transformed by history, but freedom also is challenged. While the Christian tradition has an operative definition of human freedom, religion today must call the human community to consider freedom also in the context in which it is lived. Roger Haight claims that, while human freedom has always been a tenet of Christian theology, the unanswered question of our global reality remains: is freedom meant only for some? If freedom implies being directed or attracted by some goal, something ahead that one can choose and strive for, and if it is this that gives meaning to human life, can life which has no options share in this meaning of freedom?[49] We meet this situation on massive scales in the world today.

What does it mean to say that human existence is free if so many human beings are in fact not free? Is there any meaning in my ex-

istence if half of the human race seems to be trapped in an existence that seems meaningless, pointless, leading nowhere? In
other words, if one participates in a common humanity, then the
value, worth, importance, and meaningfulness of each of us and
our freedom are called into question by the massiveness of the
seeming senseless existence of so many of us.

To do social ethics, we must consider freedom in the social
ethic, not only in its essential meaning, but also in its context. The
contextualization of freedom does not limit freedom, nor explain
it away, nor remove it from its roots in Christian doctrine, but gives
it direction. It directs discussion of freedom toward consideration
of the real people involved, and it directs the energies of freedom
toward the other. Freedom in action is characterized precisely by
what we strive for. Every ethic presupposes an eschatology, a goal
for which we strive, a hoped for future entailed in every decision.
The essence of freedom is lost, then, when we work with views of a
world and human freedom which fail to take into consideration
the human hopes, fears, goals, values, and culture of the real people involved in our global policies.[50]

Christian theology affirms that freedom from sin empowers the
Christian to work, not just for personal salvation, but also toward
liberation from concrete social evil for the neighbor. Freedom
"from" in Christian theology is always meant to be a freedom "for."
Christian freedom today enables us to redefine the priorities and
hierarchies of values that form the basis of economic and political
choices across the globe, not simply to accept things as they are.[51]
The human community owns and appropriates its freedom in its
praxis. Human freedom, in this sense, is the link between the transcendent and historical dimensions of human experience. It always
gives rise to hope through enabling of actions of hope.

We will not arrive at a more historically grounded sense of freedom without cultural criticism. Stephen Carter, in his recent book
Civility, claims Americans have a problem understanding what it
means to be free. The freedom that humans possess is not the freedom to do what we like, but the freedom to do what is right.
Freedom requires the truth of transcendence which draws us
toward the needs of the other. By forgetting what it means to be
free, we allow our "collective amnesia" to put at risk our claim of
civilization.[52] John Paul II states that a notion of freedom which
detaches itself from obedience to the truth absolves itself from the
duty to respect the rights of others. The wars of the last century
testify to this.[53]

We recognize that Catholic Social Teaching consistently contributes to a sense of freedom linked to history and one adequate
for a social ethic. In Church teaching, freedom is directed toward

a responsible societal life. State and society are distinguished by the imperative that the latter is never absorbed into the former, thus better enabling communities of free association.[54] Subsidiarity affirms the importance of social pluralism and intermediate groups, recommending as much centralization as is necessary for human flourishing, but as little as possible while pursuing legitimate goals.[55] All these insights are to protect the meaning of human freedom within society. They root freedom in history and protect a societal understanding of freedom by linking it to the truth of transcendence.

Lastly, to do social ethics in the new millennium, we must think of nature with an eye on history. As we seek to justify the moral rightness of human conduct in a world with only relative values, we cannot simply affirm nature as it is to the neglect of what it ought to be or ignore the consequences of our use of nature for the future.[56] Rather, a sense of nature linked to history reminds us that nature is not yet what it could be, nor fully revelatory of God. An ahistorical view of nature alone or a vision that a harmony of social and natural interests exists somewhere just below the surface of life can easily mask the struggle and conflict that are the status quo.[57] The status quo that is racist, élitist, militaristic, sexist, and destructive of peoples and cultures in turn undermines the future of the earth. We maintain that facts of nature are relevant in material norms of behavior for a Christian social ethic; however, the facts of nature rarely specify material norms of behavior entirely.[58]

How, then, do we honor the moral tradition of dwelling in the Wisdom of God and of maintaining God's covenant with us in the social conditions of our times? We do this by understanding, pondering, evaluating, and judging the human goods and values involved in our social conduct in relation to human persons, located in concrete social situations, yet conditioned by, and influencing, problems of humanity interpersonally, societally, and globally.[59] We ask, given these conditions, what is the modicum of freedom of which humans are capable necessary to promote the greatest good and eliminate the greatest evils in this situation and, in fact, to promote human dignity? John Paul II gives us an image of an ethic that links history and transcendence when he proposes the "humanistic criterion." This is a standard for evaluating and choosing among various social systems, institutional reforms, or legal reforms: The "humanistic criterion" is "...the measure in which each system is really capable of reducing, restraining and eliminating as far as possible the various forms of exploitation of man and of ensuring for him, through work, not only the just distribution of the indispensable material goods, but also a participation, in keeping with his dignity, in the whole process of production and in the social life that grows up around that process."[60] While we can see that truth, freedom, and nature divorced from history are a poor substitute for a needed sense of the absolute or transcendence, we must ask: can there be an ethical absolute in the new millennium?

An Ethical Absolute in the New Millennium?

We know today that, in the midst of history without a sense of an ethical absolute, there is no social ethic, and actions are abandoned to total arbitrariness or modern utilitarianism. In a world that recognizes the problem of history, however, the absolute can not be equated simply with cultural standards. It cannot even equal universally valid, or broadly and generally acknowledged, norms. History teaches us that consensus itself often fails the moral good. No one cultural vision exhausts the meaning of the social good, for there are a plurality of cultures.

A notion of the absolute, which also takes history seriously, envisions the absolute as that which is objectively and unconditionally valid within each relevant ethical system, taking into consideration all the ethically relevant circumstances.[61] The absolute must be interpreted. It is not self evident. Persons who are dependent upon previous intellectual systems and attitudes and yet seek a truth to be realized, not only now, but also in the future, do this interpretation. The absolute in this sense is always situated.

The absolute is not an unambiguous, unconditioned higher order that compels persons in ethical dialogue and leads them into one insight, no matter where they stand on the globe. Josef Fuchs reminds us that an ethical consciousness can not possibly exist that is at once concrete in its presentation and identical in its universality.[62] Rather, the ethical imperative, the call of transcendence, or the absolute, is experienced only by people who through reason arrive at an ethical judgment in often complex situations and seek to solve problems through limited means at their disposal.[63]

From Paul VI onward, Catholic social teaching has recognized that social ethics can not be pursued on a global level, apart from regional communal discernment.[64] Catholic Social Teaching alone does not attempt to offer a sense of the "absolute" which can simply be applied in a local situation. Community and solidarity with those not profiting from a particular social configuration are essential ingredients of Christian ethical social reflection. Commitment to others in community through faith and solidarity influences insight into the social good and sustains the will to pursue it. This matrix of contemporary social discernment includes sensitivity to the infinite varieties of culture in the world today and the capacity to evaluate the worth of the various ideologies. The challenge of a turn to history and experience in social ethics is the search to validate our moral decisions in a manner which does not deny the relativities of history, yet has an objectivity short of absolute claims. This search requires the formation of communities of discernment.

Modern anthropocentrism is a block to this necessary communal vision today. It is based on an Enlightenment vision of the human subject in history as one with nature at its feet, living out the command to subdue the earth. It is a vision of humanity as the dominator. The Church affirms the essential dignity of the human person, but there is no sense of personhood in the Church which is detached from community.[65]

In contrast, modern anthropocentrism can attempt to ground a social ethic on a vision of the human person who is detached from the dependencies of everyday life or the consequences of his or her actions on the future of the humanity of others or the earth. Rasmussen claims we must face the "lost integrity" of modernity whose sense of the human person is often divorced from primal connections to the earth, to the future of humankind, and to each other. We cannot ground social ethics in the "inalienable rights" which only some people on the earth actually enjoy or in the notion of *homo sapiens* as being capable of knowing nature and the world and regarding itself the pinnacle of creation and Lord of the world. According to Havel, this world of "modern anthropocentrism" is deeply, even fatally, flawed, for it is divorced from the truth of human existence as connected to the earth, the global community, and the truth of freedom.[66]

In light of the changing character of the mental tools within religion for social ethics, we see that the significance of Catholic Social Teaching goes beyond the principles it offers for the solution of social problems in the world. More basic to the future of social ethics, social teaching "coheres around a theologically inspired communitarian social ethic which has yielded a cluster of shared, integrated insights concerning religious, political, familial, economic and cultural relations in society."[67] By requiring a sense of community and solidarity, social teaching corrects an anthropology that is detached from others, the earth, and global humanity. The latter easily become mere statistics in a First World mind, ceasing to obligate or merit concern.

Religion and theology contribute to a social ethic by holding out to the human community a sense of the transcendence it requires and to humankind a vision of community needed for survival. The communitarian aspect of social teaching may be its greatest contribution to social ethics in the new millennium.

However, claims to the importance of community cannot be innocent. Without a sense of transcendence, a vision of community
turns demonic. While we recognize religion's role to uphold and
contribute a sense of transcendence in the public realm, we must
face our second question: whether religion is up to the job.

Religion and the Public Realm

Is religion really doomed to be a magician rather than a priest
in face of the complexities of the third millennium? Certainly, the
experience of Auschwitz challenged the Churches to ask whether
their failures before Nazism were ones of finitude before evil or
sins of omission prompted by patterns of thought and behavior
which crippled their Christian witness. Had modern religion so
identified with modern culture that it, too, accepted that religion
is a private matter? Did the moral belief that Christians were to
avoid the world and evil lead to a secularization of politics and a
quietist interpretation of Christian authenticity?

Had the two kingdom theory of the Protestants and the two
spheres vision of Catholics confined religion and conscience to
personal life, turning society over to simply a politics of power?[68]
Could a vision of religious practice characterized solely by ritual
fidelity and a moral life preoccupied with the efficacy of licit or
illicit acts stand before a scientific explanation of the world?[69]

No greater question has been asked religion in the last two hundred years than the Marxian challenge to its adequacy in the
public realm. A positive answer to Marx's question is essential, not
only for the future of the world, but for the future of religion.
Religion stands on trial in the new millennium regarding its capacity to point to transcendence in a worldly way and to draw out
its significance for human affairs. Humankind experiences transcendence through a plurality of forms and religions. However,
ethically it translates into an experienced need to be in harmony
even with what we ourselves are not and to continue to seek the
unifying force to which all are mysteriously linked. John Paul II
reminds us that human beings are always called to direct their
steps toward a truth which transcends them.[70] It is this sense of
transcendence that links humankind together and reminds us that
we live with global problems in a single world. Humankind's awareness of transcendence is the only real alternative to extinction.[71]

Religion's role in social ethics is not just cosmetic. Solving serious social ethical problems is not just a matter of increasing the
GNP or better juridical or social organization. Rather, it will call
for a renewed sense of ethical values and a new commitment to
religion itself. While the Church recognizes that those without

religion will have a significant role in providing the social question with its necessary ethical foundation, religion itself holds a preeminent role.[72] Together with others of good will, it must translate the harmony of transcendence into practical terms. Religion will be refined in the new millennium as it takes on its public responsibility. It, too, will be changed in the crucible of the mounting social inequalities in our world. Asian theologian Aloysius Pieris comments that the future religion of Asia will be that religion which adequately addresses Asian poverty.[73] North American theologian Frederick Herzog asserts that public concerns will define religion in the new millennium. According to Herzog, the primary questions of the early Church were devoted to the closeness of God to Jesus. In the Reformation era, it was God's closeness to the human being. Today, the concern is God's closeness to history in the struggle for justice.[74]

Religion witnesses to the transcendent by saying "no" to the world as it is and "yes" to something better.[75] Human societies need a vision of something better. They need utopias. Utopias are always simply those things that cannot be built. However, utopias provide elements that can be integrated into the present order so that societies can adapt to new circumstances. Christianity's sense of hope is rooted in its faith in Jesus Christ and the meaning of his redemption for all humankind and all of history. However, this hope grounded in faith also must take concrete forms. Religion today must face the fact that our present crisis involves a lack of vision of alternatives to a single market economy and the style of global human community which results. This political and cultural crisis precipitates a theological crisis within Christian faith itself.[76]

Theology and the Task of Religion in Society

Religion assumes its proper role in the transformation of society with the help of theology. The theological task is a vocation that is initiated and lived in the center of the believing community. Theology serves the evangelizing mission of the Church.[77] In the history of the believing community, we have had many forms of theology, with none totally identified with faith. While the Church, according to tradition, holds the deposit of faith, theologies live as long as the conditions that gave them origins exist.[78] The questions of our globe challenge Christian theology to provide a light to their solutions in the human community. In carrying out this gospel task, theology itself is changed.

Throughout this century, Christian theology has circled themes of finitude, creativity, and limits and critiqued, invoked, retrieved, and transformed the tradition to link a vision of the Christian life to the transformation of the society. Theology today continues this task. It discovers and communicates socially significant meanings of Christian symbols and traditions.[79] It takes up its hermeneutical task of interpreting basic Christian symbols in a way that believers can discover the full meaning of those symbols for their social life. Since theological symbols carry public meanings, theology is charged with uncovering those meanings. However, theology and religion today stand on the same shifting fault lines that challenge social ethics. They, too, must cope with uncertainty in face of change and pluralism before the need for unity and relevance in a world that explains them away.

In the last decades, liberation and political theologies have pointed to the political dimension of the whole theological enterprise.[80] Yet, when theology stands before the phenomenon of globalization, the role of theology can be expanded to another level. Robert Schreiter argues that forces of globalization today summon theology to go beyond the traditional articulation of the social significance of Christian symbols. In addition, Christian theology has the opportunity to participate in global theological flows that offer in the world today an alternative voice to the forces of globalization as we experience it. What gives identity to these flows is not a single theological meaning system, but their common resistance to poverty and political oppression in the world.[81]

New Tasks for Theology

A theological flow differs from a theology. While flows do not exhaust theology's role and function in the Church or the world, they are significant for social ethics. "Flow" is a term which arises out of the information age. It is used in anthropology, sociology, and communications to denote cultural and ritual movements, a circulation of information that is visible, yet hard to define. Just like a river, a flow can cross geographic and other cultural boundaries, change the landscape, and leave behind a sediment and silt that change the local ecology.[82] The image of a flow is used for ideas which circulate the world for the good, have diverse cultural and religious context, yet a universality which invites and unites members of the world community into movements for change. While Christian theology can not be reduced to its role in these theological flows, participation in these flows represents one way it can contribute to social ethics in the coming years.

As the trajectory of globalization crisscrosses the world, it carries with it notions of progress, equality, and inclusion. While it is debatable whether religion itself is a global system on a par with the forces of globalization, its global presence can be felt as a language of contrast. Religion can be a major force which unmasks the lies of progress, equality, and inclusion for many that live today in the economic global system. Theology can ask: whose progress is involved with our changing markets? What equality is accomplished as new nations form? What does inclusion mean in a world of ethnic cleansing? One way which religion combines its own language of belief and tradition with the concerns that threaten our civilization is through global theological flows.

Global theological flows are theological discourses. They are not uniform or systemic, yet represent a series of linked, mutually intelligible discourses that address the contradictions or failures of the global systems. They are theological in that they speak out of the realm of religious beliefs and practices. They are not uniform because they arise from, and are committed to, specific cultural and social settings. They are intelligible to others in diverse settings because others experience the same failure of global systems and raise the same kind of protest. Schreiter suggests there are four such global theological flows in the world today: they are voices of liberation, feminism, ecology, and human rights.

These flows arise out of the religious practices of solidarity and commitment to justice issues on a local level, yet in their specificity rest in their ability to address the failure of the global system as they are experienced in a specific context. As flows, they function as an expression of religion before the challenge of social ethics. They speak to the end and purpose of human existence without abstracting them from experience by speaking in a language of contrast. They uncover a sense of the ultimate through the lens of human dignity and insist that the larger meaning of life has implications for behavior and the shape of public and institutional forms. As language about the end and purpose of life, they evoke in others solidarity, even across geographic, ethnic, and gender lines. Certainly, the social teaching of the Church finds a new context within these global theological flows as it offers a theologically inspired communitarian social ethic.

Christian theology can link a vision of the Christian life to the transformation of the society. Yet, we can not adequately envision a role for Christian theology in public religion's call to foster a social ethic without recognizing the shadow side of theology in the public realm. The issue of global fundamentalism is, and will be, a caveat in public religion of the twenty-first century.

Fundamentalism and the Public Role of Religion

As the economic, social, and political plates of our world shift, the gap between the rich and poor widens. A comparable split in religious practice appears across the globe as both ethnic and religious division grows. Old calls for pluralism in American religion, calling for Catholics, Protestants, and Jews to unite around shared beliefs, no longer define the real battles in religion and in the name of religion in society today.[83] Today, the culture wars of our nations and globe stem from differences in faith and ideology which intersect denomination, ethnic, and cultural lines.

Uncertainty in the world breeds concern for moral order.[84] As religion seeks to bring a sense of transcendence to public order today, it must recognize the tension between a fundamentalist and wider religious vision of this order and its impact on a social ethic. Fundamentalism perceives the nature and meaning of this order and the nature of justice and freedom in a manner that builds a sense of identity within at the expense of its capacity to relate to others who are different in the society. In contrast to a religious liberalism that collapses the tension between Christianity and culture, fundamentalism claims the normative story of a nation's founding and its meaning gives it ownership of the ideals of the social good in a manner which is mutually exclusive with other groups in a society. In this way, religious fundamentalism produces a world of certainty in place of a world of uncertainty.[85]

The phenomenon of fundamentalism is a response to modernity. Martin Marty views religious fundamentalism at the turn of the millennium as a tendency, a habit of mind, found within religious communities which manifests itself as a strategy by which beleaguered believers attempt to preserve their distinctive identity as a people or group.[86] Religious identity, renewed through a selective retrieval of doctrines, beliefs, and practices from a sacred past, becomes the exclusive and absolute basis for a recreated search for political and social order of the future.

Fundamentalist tendencies provide the basis of major political and military forces in our world today. At first glance, fundamentalists seem to offer the globe a concern for transcendent values. They seek to remake the world of the future by resubmitting all things to the divine. Through this strategy, they face the future and engage in self preservation.

However, fundamentalists characteristically preserve themselves and their social order by neutralizing a threatening Other. Integral to a fundamentalist stance is the identification of an enemy and the formation of community bonds and identity in response to the threats of this enemy to their survival and future.

Fundamentalist perspectives influence religious, political, social, and economic analyses.[87] They differ from other attempts by religion to bring its values to all aspects of society by their nonresponsiveness to information inconsistent with adopted positions. Even when empirical evidence is inhospitable to shared beliefs, fundamentalists do not shift their perspectives, nor do they give up their insistence that their beliefs are equally binding on everyone. Fundamentalism is a complex global reality in its basis, identity, and future as an actor in the global reality. At its core, fundamentalism is more than a religion; it is a view of reality which seeks stability before rapid change through rigid boundaries of religious, ethnic, and social identity. It is a major threat to world peace. Yet, it does not stand alone in this capacity.

Benjamin Barber argues that fundamentalism partners with the forces of globalization in undermining the conditions for the pursuit of social ethics in the new millennium. The forces of globalization, expressed in global Capitalism or McWorld, and fundamentalist movements, or Jihad, are radically different, yet live in a condition of powerful and paradoxical interdependence in our world today. Whether driven by parochial hatred or a universalizing market both overlook the disciplines and institutions required for civil society. In Barber's words, "Neither Jihad nor McWorld aspires to secure the civic virtues undermined by its denationalizing practices; neither global markets nor blood communities service public goods or pursue equality and justice."[88]

Fundamentalism does not always forge communities based on blood exclusion, but it characteristically produces a type of consensual tribalism. For those who are wealthy, fundamentalism can provide a buttress against changes that threaten their way of life, privilege, and status. For the poor, with no prospects for the future, for those out of work whose savings are eroding before their eyes, for the immigrant whose cultural heritage and home have to be left behind, fundamentalism offers an escape from anxiety and even a reprieve from having to think. In Christian circles, fundamentalism appears as an interpretation of Christianity in which a charismatic leader locates, with easy certitude in chosen words, doctrines, and practices, the miraculous actions of a strict God saving an élite from an evil world.[89] It is easy to see in this definition a tendency to excess in religion itself as it searches for identity in a changing world.

The rapid spread of fundamentalism across the globe challenges all religion to adopt its priestly, rather than magical, role in the new millennium. At its core, fundamentalism raises the question: how will religion contribute to a search for identity before the convulsion of global forces that reshape the cultural, economic, and political face of the world and the future of the earth?

Fundamentalism, Faith, and Ideology

Fundamentalism collapses the balance necessary between faith and ideology inherent in healthy religion. Theologian Juan Luis Segundo defines faith as the capacity to confide one's life to the unverifiable and thus to relate to life through a center of meaning in the creation of values. In order to find meaning in life, human beings have to choose a goal which is above all others and order other satisfactions by it. This goal or value serves as an absolute against which they can form judgments.[90] Faith in this sense is always exercised in the concrete world of objective reality. For Christians, religious faith is locating ultimate value and meaning in life in Jesus Christ.

Ideology, in contrast, is a way of knowing related to efficacy. Ideology is the systematization of one's perception of reality.[91] Ideology involves the way one sees the world, its tools, its mechanisms, and one's understanding of these elements.

Faith and ideology operate in the concrete world of objective reality. Between these two zones, that of ultimate data and concrete reality, there exists an area where the two are mixed. As we draw on our faith and ideology, life is viewed in such a way that the ultimate data over reality illumine what reality can offer us. Faith and a sense of transcendence are merged with data and one's perception of the significance of those data and brought into ethical reflection.

How does religion fit into this schema of faith and ideology? It is human nature to identify the absolute value in one's life with religion. However, a person's ultimate value and a person's religion are not always the same.[92] Religion alone can simply be an ideology or set of ideas given an authority apart from their relevance to human need or to God. One's functional religion can be materialism or group identity. "True religion" is an attitude of the heart that searches for the will of God. It is attuned to transcendence. True religion causes one to expand one's faith and correct one's ideology or perceptions of the world. True religion establishes a dynamic cycle of conversion between the two.

Religion and Public Criteria

Segundo's notion of faith and ideology offers some criteria to judge whether the transcendence of God is upheld by religion in the public realm. The transcendence of God is preserved in human judgment only by linking religion to what is effectively good for human beings.[93] It is here that fundamentalist trends, which can claim to speak for God, as well as liberal trends, which can claim that God is silent before culture, fail the test of true religion.[94] Religion, as it pursues the social good, is ambiguous. What is good or valuable is not something defined by a reference first to the divine. Rather, it is defined first by reference to what is actually and effectively good for human beings.[95] Human good and evil can and should be determined before resorting to the religious realm. It is the human criteria, those things which arise from a sense of responsibility in the face of the visible needs of one's fellow human beings, which really measure whether the integrity of the transcendence of God is being respected in human judgment. John Paul II echoes this judgment when he affirms that all routes for the Church are directed toward the human person.[96]

The truth of the God-human relationship does not mean human beings have to transfer God's absolute quality to some construct of an absolute value in life in order to render it valuable.[97] The ethical truth which religion seeks to uphold in society is marked by criteria which are valid in themselves. Because of God's respect for human freedom, it is not necessary that we establish that our values in a concrete situation are ones directly established by God. It is necessary only that these values are consistent with the knowledge of life that we gain in this covenant relationship.

Religion and theology can contribute to ethics an unquestioned deepening and continual recognition of a more extensive absolute. The absolute held in religious ethics is the assertion that there are but one single ethical order and one single ethical consciousness for and in humanity. This order corresponds to the fact that humanity is one, and this ethical order is concrete, going beyond the formal principle to do good and avoid evil. The concreteness of the moral imperative, however, has to be read by consciences living in many cultures and situations. Religion helps to focus these consciences in hope, to sustain their faith, and to foster their compassion for human fraility through its spiritual life.

Religion cannot simply generate ethical decisions, though religions can, in practice, solve the ethical problematic for many persons through their directives. But, religious directives are not sufficient to solve the problem of ethical responsibility in society today.[98] Theology alone can not solve the problem of social ethics either. The only metaethical principle known to theological ethics is a twin assertion of the moral capacity of the human person and the primary law that good is to be done and evil left undone. Everything further requires empirical data, research, conversation, and political process. Religion, therefore, discerns the human values in the social sciences, without negating their own independence.

Public religion can interact with the social sciences without denying the legitimate autonomy of social institutions from it. It enters the forum where policy and principles are mixed and related and searches for new ways for its own institutions to influence the public realm. It can offer clear critiques of existing societal practices. Finally, religion joins in movements, programs, and alternative institutions which better witness to the spiritual values it upholds.[99]

Religion's contribution to the public realm should lead to a variety of ethical systems in the world community today, arising from the unique ways human communities respond to the problems which confront their lives.[100] No locality receives global influence in a totalizing way. Rather, local community reshapes and reexpresses the forces that impinge upon it, according to its culture and capacities. Social ethics is done between the local and the global, needing structures to act communally on both the local and global levels.

The social problems of the new millennium need religion because they require more than technological solutions alone. The ethicist Larry Rasmussen reminds us that the unsustainability of our present world order is a cosmological and moral disorder tied into a cultural, social, and environmental one. Global communities of the future will require different orientations and habits, not only different technologies. Religion in this sense continues in its traditional role of helping people to seek moral goodness before the transcendent reality of a God who loves them. It fosters and directs energies toward influencing public policy, personal character, family values, and religious formation. These, in turn, influence characters and communities who form public policy.

Religion reaffirms the primal confidence of transcendental faith, life has meaning, and, because of that, each person and community must assert the courage to be. Religion's role as a priest rather than as a magician to challenge a community to seek the truth, however, rests on the future of community itself. It is to this last topic I now turn.

III. Community and the Global Future

Is community the most endangered species on the moral terrain of social ethics in the new millennium? We cannot recreate the communities of the nineteenth century. Stephen Carter argues that whatever community we had at the end of the twentieth century came from the World War II generation.[101] Their shared experience of sacrifice established the moral consensus of the WWII era. However, this consensus is collapsing and dying with this generation. The absence of a shared moral understanding, developed through a shared experience of sacrifice in the post WWII generation, has led to the kind of radical individualism that causes ordinary social interaction to become both stressful and dispensable. The current lack of civility in our society indicates that we assume we are not fellow travelers in life; rather, we go through life alone. The world today is a society of strangers, and one knows well that it does not count if you hurt a stranger.

While social analysts claim that community ties are weak today, community has a role as a corrective in a vision of social ethics in the new millennium. Sustainable development and sustainable community are contrasting paths to the future, carrying with them different notions of the structure of human society and responsibility. The World Council of Churches points out that, under reigning approaches to sustainable development, formation of community is often ignored. Domestic and global wealth is generated without eradicating poverty or making local communities more viable and sustainable.[102] In reigning development approaches, the image of a good society is equated with a growing gross domestic product, period.

Economic growth alone does not make a good society. We can observe this on two fronts. For those above the poverty line, human happiness does not necessarily correlate with increased consumption and incomes. Growth in the gross domestic product does not necessarily bring a better quality of family life and friendship, satisfaction with work, more leisure, and a sense of spiritual richness. Rather, pursuit of money alone is more easily correlated with the greed, weakening of family relationships, and psychological and spiritual emptiness which characterize current First World culture.

As to those below the poverty line, reigning views of development do not provide a viable vision of their future. Even at a three percent growth rate, a growth impossible for many poor countries, yet an optimal development index, only seven poor countries could close the gap with the First World in one hundred years and only nine countries in one thousand years. A truer picture of the world's development has one billion like ourselves, living a good quality of life, 3.6 billion as the managing poor, and one billion at the bottom living on less than one dollar a day. The World Bank predicts that the real future will mark a growth in the bottom two divisions.[103]

A major challenge to religion in the new millennium is to ransom a vision of a sustainable world from the assumption that a globalizing economy will save us. The global economy is here to stay. However, a more adequate view of global development must concern, not just economies, but the distribution of power among peoples of the world.[104] As power shifts from local communities to transnational capital and institutions that wield and regulate it, the Churches seek today visions of development which foster community responsibility, ecological sensitivity, as well as economic productivity.

Views of development must involve the way to live in a sustainable relationship with the rest of the earth. Sustainability in this sense is the capacity of natural and social systems to survive and thrive together. If human life is not just economic, then community plus economics have to be maintained. Without this sense, North and South in the new millennium will describe totally different ways of life based on class and culture rather than indicating geography.[105]

Alternative views of development increase local economic self reliance within a framework of community responsibility and ecological balance, along with developing webs of social relationship that define human community. In such a view, regeneration occurs, not only of the earth, but also of human communities who depend upon it. An alternative view of development gives to community a major role in social ethics in the new millennium.

Community and the Carrying Capacity of Social Ethics

Some ecologists say it is not the general conditions of an ecosystem that ultimately determine its capacity to sustain itself, but that single factor that is in short supply in a given system which determines its carrying capacity.[106] One wonders whether community is that single factor which marks our capacity to carrying on a tradition of social ethical reflection and action in the new millennium.

Martin Luther King once asked: where do we go from here, chaos or community? King questioned the possibility of community in society. But, he more seriously pondered the chance for a society without community. In order to respond to the pressing problems of globalization, Christian ethicists today must inquire about the state of the moral ecology of community. Is it an endangered species across the globe?

The search for community is not a call to recreate the community of the past. The changed social conditions of today will not recreate it. We have learned in our own century that a rational quest for self interest alone will not establish community, since community requires sacrifice. Coercive external authority cannot form community. Rather, the human community itself must build a new type of community in the new millennium, freer from the limitations of the past, yet able to form the humanity of the future.

What is community? Community is a center of multilayered interactions among people. There, traditions and rituals are
preserved and developed. Life skills are learned and called forth.
Discipline is nurtured and expected. Fidelity and accountability to
the community are practiced. At its best, community is a way of life
that shapes and defines a member's identity. True community
shows itself in an alliance for a common cause, a life beyond itself.

Community is required for the social conscience which, in turn,
builds constructive social relationships in the new millennium.
The human spirit must have experiences that hold, as it were, the
historical forms of the criteria which will provide ethical guidance
in the new millennium. It is only by participating in the truth of
such values as equality, respect, and dignity that one understands
them. It is the bonds created with significant others which form
the data about life and its transcendent values which ultimately
bring value to the world.[107] We learn values in relationship.

Americans tend to place the burden of ethics on the development and sanctity of individual conscience. Yet, Robert Bellah
reminds us that even our respect for conscience in American society is vulnerable without a sense of community. In an address to
the American Academy of Religion, "Is There A Common American Culture?," he reminds us that culture does not float free from
institutions.[108] As we seek to validate the sacredness of the individual conscience in society, we must face the fact that our capacity to
imagine a social fabric that would hold individuals together is
vanishing.

Bellah charges that our sense of conscience as Americans is
highly esteemed in our culture, yet stands on shaky ground. It is
not based in a proper relationship between the individual and the
group. We ground conscience in a religious individualism that
does not need Church. Our religious individualism, in turn, is fed
by a climate of economic individualism that, ironically, knows
nothing of the sacredness of the individual. Its only standard is
money, and the only thing more sacred than money is more
money. What economic individualism destroys and what our kind
of religious individualism cannot restore is solidarity, a sense of
members being in the same body. This is essential for establishing
a sense of obligation to another. As religious people seek to re-
trieve a necessary respect for the individual in their Churches,
families, and societies, they engage in a futile effort if they simply
mimic a cultural individualism that cannot save.

Even though normal community life is filled with argument,
controversy, conflict, and pluralism, without a minimal degree of
solidarity the project of greater recognition of individual dignity
within the group collapses in on itself. Community dysfunction is

no bearer or protector of individuality. Without community and the solidarity with others it implies, real individuality is lost. Such conditions turn individual dignity into a façade which belongs to a very small minority, those with access to money and decision making power.

The Church today should not assume it can easily foster community. The Church, too, lives in a wider culture which is highly influenced by the State and the market with their agencies of socialization: the media and education. Neither is hospitable to the notion of community. In simpler societies, kinship and religious communities could withstand cultural pressure and provide models of difference. But, in our society, families and Churches are often too colonized by the market and the State to provide much of a buffer. Bellah charges that Churches share with families today a fragility in providing a radical alternative to our culture or even a perspective to criticize it and alter it. Since, in order to uphold a sense of transcendence in society, religion is responsible for engaging in cultural criticism, religion must be lived in a community capable of the task. In this light, the establishment of a better sense of community becomes essential for social ethics in the new millennium.

Toward a Community and a Social Ethic of the Future

If we desire a community that is different from that of the past and able to be sustained in the conditions of the future, what would be its characteristics? Theorists claim that a shared history, identity, mutuality, plurality, autonomy, participation, and integration mark modern community.[109] We recognize in these values a changed type of community elicited from and for a new set of circumstances. If our capacity to shape a social ethic for the new millennium is as strong as the quality and direction of our communities, might these qualities have expressions in a viable social ethic for the new millennium? In conclusion, let us engage in a thought experiment and explore the relationship between a healthy community and the characteristics of the ethic that flows from it.

A *shared history* assumes that customs, language, geography, shared events, and crises bond a community more than do abstract ideals. A community shares a Story through which each member's story is interpreted. Ethical vision is latent in a community's shared culture. However, in the new millennium, a community's history has to be multicultural, first, to bond the real people on the move in the world and, second, to produce a social vision that respects diversity: racial, ethnic, economic, age, and religion. Yet, *shared history* alone is not sufficient to bond a community.

Aspects of a *shared history* can be pathological, as we see in various ethnic divisions in the world, rising fundamentalism, and wars of ethnic cleansing. *Shared history* and a sense of belonging are important for community, but the content of that belonging has to be open to moral criticism and ongoing reflection by all the members. The community of the future has to be built differently, if it is to be more than a tool for hatred or an enclave for group preservation.

The social ethic that arises from a community is a social construct. It involves a balance in the play of human power: whose history counts, who speaks, who sits at the table, whose issues are addressed, who votes, whose values and character mark the decision and whose generation is represented, and who speaks for the future. The history of this community must also include awareness of the history of the earth upon which it depends for sustainability. Hence, the ethic which comes from a community with a *shared history* is one marked by *participation*. *Participation* is the optimal inclusion of all involved voices in society's decision and in the sharing of the burden as well as of the benefits of society and of nature together in a given locality.[110] If *participation* were not just a quality of the ethical community, but a goal of its ethical pursuit, the resolution of international issues like debt crisis, for example, would be a *sine qua non* of this *participation*.[111]

Identity refers to the kind of persons being formed by a community. The formation of *identity* in community involves a sense of "we" which does not destroy individuality and is not based on a hostile moral tribalism where "we" is seen always opposed to a "they." *Identity* in the modern era, however, has to embrace a pluralism. A climate of civility must exist where individuality and *identity* are centered in a respect and loyalty that establish healthy boundaries.

Unlike the nineteenth century where geography, ethnic ties, and common values bonded community, modern community will be more diverse and pluralist. People will disagree, and there will be *pluralism* of thought. *Pluralism*, however, can be a hiding place for incivility, and under its guise people can generate new fiefdoms of "truth." Here, reality is formed rather than reflected. We see this false *pluralism* in the shadow side of modern communications. For instance, the web opens us to the world, yet it also generates focus groups for hate. The web cannot substitute for the healthy *pluralism* of *community* because it cannot supply the ingredients for *identity*.

Identity requires that *community* be a place of manifold engagement.[112] *Community* is an inclusive whole where people live interdependently with one another, sharing both a private and a public life. In *community*, one generation initiates the next into a way of life. As center of manifold engagement, *community* gives each member a significant place in day-by-day *participation*. Manifold engagement forms important bonds which tie the members together and give them a sense of *identity* in the group,

The social ethic which flows from a *community* of *identity* is marked by *responsibility*. Consequences are not lost in scales of action whose range of impact makes no one responsible. A workable *community* establishes *responsibility* on a scale that people can handle and makes plans which are subject to alteration and correction by the members.[113] A *community* with a sense of *identity* thus overcomes the modern pathology of authority perceived as uninhibited power and nonapproachable disinterestedness. This climate feeds the violence which cripples our schools, families, and society as models of "power over" others are acted out in relationships.

Experiences of *responsibility* in *community* where members make, break, and remake meanings which guide their lives and live in groups which are clear about what can and can not be done will demand structures of *responsibility* at both local and higher levels of society and globe. Without *identity* and the *responsibility* which flows from it, the human *community* will not produce the global systems of checks and balances required for the survival of the global *community*. Since World War II, social teaching has called for these structures of international agencies and world government.[114]

Mutuality is the atmosphere of interdependence and reciprocity in a group. People sense they need one another in some way and gain from cooperating with each other. A *community* of *mutuality* provides a vision for a world order where race, class, and gender relationships will be restructured. The international concerns of women raised by the Beijing conference, tribal equity in the Congo, and affirmative action policies in the United States all require this sense of *mutuality*.

Mutuality builds on a sense of *responsibility* and promotes a climate of *accountability*. As the structuring of *responsibility*, both to others and to the earth, *accountability* marks a social ethic with structures and procedures for holding decision makers accountable. It checks a growing world reality where the weak have no influence on those in charge. In this climate, the "weaker" can resist only by negation of whatever the powerful want them to be, whether this negation is expressed through terrorism, germ warfare, or paralyzing cynicism.[115] A *community* grounded in *mutuality* builds accountable structures which can deal with such new problems of the millennium as climates of total war. Here, goals are not just to win conflicts, but absolute domination of the other side by destroying the other's capacity to resist through propaganda, lies, and terror tactics.[116] This ultimately undermines the social ecology of a people and destroys any possibility for a climate of *mutuality* in the *community*.

Plurality is perhaps the most "modern" of the characteristics of *community*. It connotes that people will belong to more than one community at the same time. Modern *community* is not a totalizing one. Membership in a variety of groups does not threaten a group, but enhances it. It extends the *community* into wider spheres of influence and brings to the *community* the well being of family, occupation, recreational, ethnic, and religious groups other than its own. *Plurality* is held in relationship to the other values of *community*, *identity*, and *mutuality*. In this sense, plural membership has to be balanced with sufficient presence to make *community* life a reality.

Equity marks the social ethic of a pluralistic *community*. Like basic fairness in distributive and procedural justice, *equity* is required to bridge the *pluralism* of rich and poor nations, the growing divisions between generations and their needs, and respect for species and their biotic integrity. This requires renewed investment in corporate *responsibility* across the global economy and new visions of national *identity* as we integrate new peoples.[117]

Autonomy is the ability of a *community* to develop responsible individuals while it incorporates them into a complex of relationships which gives them a social self or "we." Genuine *autonomy* is the capacity to foster self direction that avoids both the illusion of unlimited choices within the group and a brutal crushing effect of the group on the individual.

Autonomy fosters in the individual a sense of self which includes the group in its well being and a sense of group that includes the flourishing of its members. Loyalty helps the group take the individuals seriously and supports the individuals to make the emotional investment necessary to incorporate the group into their self identity.

Sufficiency flows from and fosters the *autonomy* of a *community*. As the commitment to meet the basic material needs of all life, it requires careful organization of exchange and visions of economic life that involves both ceilings and floors for consumption. It takes into consideration the ecoefficiency of its life and sees sustainability as involving both material simplicity and the maintenance of communal spirituality. Major disparities of wealth and poverty generate the instability of the human *community*, but so do cultures with no soul or a life vision that addresses the spiritual needs of their peoples. An ethic of *sufficiency* grounded in the *autonomy* of local communities will no longer tolerate the international problem of child labor, but will require communities to give their children back their childhood.[118]

Integration is a quality of *community* that balances and mixes the other qualities. No one value alone is a mark of a healthy *community*. A healthy *community* will involve a mix and match of the above qualities. It is the relationship of the qualities to one another that makes a sustainable *community*. There is no one magic combination that must be present at all times. There are many possibilities that work.

A *shared history* has to be balanced by a sense of pluralism, or there will be a closed group. *Autonomy* needs a good sense of *mutuality* and *participation*. *Identity* alone is insufficient because growing *identity* must be open to change in the world of the new millennium.

Integration is the capacity to keep a healthy tension among qualities of *community* in a manner that is unique to the group, the culture, and the context. Differences in *community* will be marked by the way groups stress one over the other. Essentially, *integration* will bring about *intimacy*, instead of fragmentation, in a *community*.

A *community* requires *intimacy* to ground its members. Lack of *intimacy* will be experienced as no *community*, the state of affairs in many of our neighborhoods and cities today. As Martin Luther King noted, without *community* we have only chaos to look forward to. The chaos of drive by shootings, brutal racist murders, militant religious suicides, our elderly living in fear in the high rises of our towns, our children fearful to go to school, or our families racked by divorce will continue unless we rebuild our communities.

Community today is not based just on technical or organizational skill, but on a sense of *responsibility*, care, and commitment that both resides in characters already formed and forms characters entrusted to it. Tolerance, respect, and loyalty are insufficient to hold a *community* together unless these qualities are evident in a group which has sufficient face-to-face relationships so that people can experience trust and *mutuality*. While social ethics in the new millennium will require technical and political and economic analyses of the multiple factors influencing our globe, without the availability, investment, witness, and credibility of *community* formation there will be no global society. For, *community* is a place where the experimentation with *community* needed in society always occurs. The person of the new millennium who will do social ethics is not just the economic person, but the communal one. To go beyond the utilitarian ethic of our culture will require a type of capacity for solidarity that is learned only in *community*.

Social ethics in the new millennium will not arise out of the universalizing forces of globalism; it will emerge only from a sense of *community* grounded in the local which can hold the global and local in tension and respond. Religion in this matrix continues to have the role of priest rather than that of magician in fostering both a sense of transcendence that has markers in history and a community life which grounds people in a conscience capable of social ethics.

In summary, amid the shifting ground of conditions across the globe, three ethical issues stand out as core tasks before us in the new millennium. First, the development of an effective social policy to counteract growing disparity between rich and poor; second, the production of a vision of development more in coherence with the earth; third, the peaceful formation of sustainable *community* across the globe before the universalizing force of globalism. As religion addresses these tasks in the new conditions of our times, it has before it the tools of life and death generated by our age. May those of us who have the privilege to be alive as we begin the new millennium set the course of our new age to a fuller humanity and fulfillment for all peoples.

NOTES

[1]Larry Rasmussen, *Earth Community, Earth Ethics* (New York: Orbis Books, 1997), 48.

[2]Lester W. Milbrath, *Envisioning a Sustainable Society: Learning our Way Out* (Albany, N.Y.: State University of New York Press, 1989), 1-2.

[3]Rasmussen, 59.

[4]We find this image in Lester C. Thurow, *The Future of Capitalism* (New York: William Morrow and Company, 1996), chapter one.

[5]Robert Schreiter, *The New Catholicity* (New York: Orbis Books, 1997), chapter 1. I am indebted in part to Schreiter's analysis of globalization in this section of the essay.

[6]Thurow, 8; see also chapter 3.

[7]Larry Rasmussen, *Moral Fragments and Moral Community* (Minneapolis: Fortress Press,1993).

[8]Schreiter, 11.

[9]Thurow, 16, 257.

[10]Schreiter, 10.

[11]Benjamin R. Barber, *Jihad vs. McWorld:How Globalism and Tribalism Are Reshaping the World* (New York: Ballantine Books, 1996).

[12]Thurow, 86.

[13]Rasmussen, *Earth Community, Earth Ethics*, 64.

[14]Robert Wuthnow, *Christianity in the 21st Century: Reflections on the Challenge Ahead* (New York: Oxford Press, 1993), chapter two.

[15]William G. Hollingsworth, "Population Explosion: Still Expanding," *USA Today,* July, 1998, 127/ 263, 28.

122   SOCIAL ETHICS IN THE NEW MILLENNIUM

16"Growing Population," *The Economist*, 20 May 1995, 116.

17Mary Hager, "How Demographic Fatigue Will Defuse the Population Bomb," *Newsweek*, 2 November 1998, 12.

18Rasmussen, *Earth Community, Earth Ethics*, 45.

19National Issues Forum, *Admissions Decisions: Should Immigration Be Restricted?* (Dubuque, Iowa: Kendall/Hunt, 1994).

20William O'Neill, S.J., "Rights of Passage: The Ethics of Immigration and Refugee Policy," *Theological Studies* 59/1 (March, 1998): 85.

21Thurow, 96-97.

22Robert J. Samuelson, "Off Golden Pond," *The New Republic*, 12 April 1999, 36ff.

23"The Economics of Aging," *Business Week*, 12 September 1994, 60.

24National Issues Forum, *The National Piggybank System: Does Our Retirement System Need Fixing?* (Dubuque, Iowa: Kendall/Hunt, 1996).

25Ronald Lee and Jonathan Skiner, "Will Aging Baby Boomers Bust the Federal Budget?," *Journal of Economic Perspectives* 13/1 (Winter, 1999): 115ff.

26Barber, 241.

27Rasmussen, *Earth Community, Earth Ethics*, 15.

28Hollingsworth, 28.

29Rasmussen, *Earth Community, Earth Ethics*, 151.

30Ibid., 48.

31Brian Johnstone, "Moral Methodology," in *The New Dictionary of Catholic Social Thought*, ed. Judith Dwyer (Collegeville, Minnesota: The Liturgical Press, 1994), 597.

32For a commentary on Weber's thought on this point, see Gregory Baum, *Religion and Alienation* (New York: Paulist Press, 1975), 86ff.

33Rasmussen, *Earth Community, Earth Ethics*, 185.

34James E. Cone, *Speaking the Truth:Ecumenism, Liberation and Black Theology* (Grand Rapids, Michigan: William B. Eerdmans, 1986), 118.

35Rasmussen, *Earth Community, Earth Ethics*,19.

36Johnstone, 602.

37Margaret Farley, " Feminism and Christian Ethics," in *Freeing Theology*, ed. Catherine Mowry LaCugna (San Francisco: Harper, 1993), 215.

38Karl Rahner, "Theological Reflections on the Problem of Secularization," in *Theological Investigations*, X (New York: The Seabury Press, 1977), 322. See also Avery Dulles, "The Problem of Method: From Scholasticism to Models," in *The Craft of Theology: From Symbol to System* (New York: Crossroad, 1992), 41-52.

39David Hollenbach quotes James Gustafson on the relevance of historical understanding in ethics. See "Tradition, Historicity, and Truth in Theological Ethics," in *Christian Ethics: Problems and Prospects*, ed. Lisa Sowle Cahill and James F. Childress (Cleveland: The Pilgrim Press, 1996), 61.

40John Paul II, *Veritatis Splendor* (Vatican City: Libreria Editrice Vaticana, 1993), no. 4:8.

41Ibid., no. 101:151.

42Vaclav Havel, *The Power of the Powerless* (New York: M.E. Sharpe, Inc., 1985), 25.

43John Paul II, *Centesimus Annus*, 19.5-20, in *Proclaiming Justice and Peace: Papal Documents from Rerum Novarum to Centesimus Annus*, ed.

Michael Walsh and Brian Davies (Mystic, Connecticut: Twenty-Third Publications, 1991), 447.

[44]James F. Keenan and Thomas R. Kopfensteiner, "Moral Theology out of Western Europe," *Theological Studies* 59/1 (March, 1998): 117. See John Paul II, "Faith and Reason," *Origins*, 22 October 1998, #11, 321. Here, John Paul II links the truth Jesus spoke about God to his manifestations of this truth in words and deeds.

[45]J. L. Segundo, *Faith and Ideologies*, trans. John Drury (New York: Orbis, 1984), 260.

[46]Anne E. Patrick, *Liberating Conscience* (New York: Continuum, 1997), 222.

[47]Robert Bellah et al., *Habits of the Heart: Individualism and Commitment in American Life* (Berkeley: University of California Press, 1985).

[48]Michael J. Himes and Kenneth R. Himes, O.F.M., *The Fullness of Faith: The Public Significance of Theology* (New York: Paulist Press, 1993), 21-2.

[49]Roger Haight, S.J., *An Alternative Vision* (New York: Paulist Press, 1985), 35.

[50]Keenan and Kopfensteiner, 115.

[51]John Paul II, *Centesimus Annus*, 28.2, *op. cit.*, 453.

[52]Stephen Carter, *Civility: Manners, Morals and the Etiquette of Democracy* (New York: Basic Books, 1998), 78.

[53]John Paul II, *Centesimus Annus*, 17, *op. cit.*, 445.

[54]Thomas Massaro, *Catholic Social Teaching and United States Welfare Reform* (Collegeville, Minnesota: The Liturgical Press, 1998), 28.

[55]John Coleman, S.J., "Development of Church Social Teaching," in Charles E. Curran and Richard A. McCormick, S.J., eds., *Readings in Moral Theology No.5: Official Catholic Social Teaching* (New York: Paulist Press, 1986), 183.

[56]John Haught, *The Promise of Nature* (New York: Paulist Press, 1993), 110-12, 113-14, as referenced in Rasmussen, *Earth Community, Earth Ethics*, 240.

[57]Rasmussen, *Earth Community, Earth Ethics*, 240.

[58]Josef Fuchs, *Moral Demands and Personal Obligations* (Washington, D.C.: Georgetown University Press, 1993), 41.

[59]Ibid., 35.

[60]John Paul II, "Address to the United Nations on the Declaration of Human Rights," *AAS* 1156, para. 17, as quoted in Donal Dorr, *Option for the Poor, 100 Years of Catholic Social Teaching* (New York: Orbis, 1992), 275.

[61]Fuchs, 16, 22.

[62]Ibid., 22-23, 40ff.

[63]Liberation authors remind us of the "praxis" required for ethical insight that flows from commitment to justice in a local situation. See Jon Sobrino, *Christology at the Crossroads*, trans. John Drury (New York: Orbis Books, 1978).

[64]Paul VI, *Octogesimo Adveniens*, 4: "In the face of such widely varying situations it is difficult for us to utter a unified message and to put forward a solution which has universal validity. Such is not our ambition, nor is it our mission. It is up to the Christian communities to analyse with objectivity the situation which is proper to their own country, to shed on it the

light of the gospel's unalterable words and to draw principles of action from the social teaching of the Church."

[65]John Paul II, *Centesimus Annus*, 11.2, *op. cit.*, 441.

[66]Rasmussen, *Earth Community, Earth Ethics*, 17.

[67]Michael J. Schuck, *That They Be One: The Social Teaching of the Papal Encyclicals, 1740-1989* (Washington, D. C.: Georgetown University, 1991), 180. We say this noting also this body of teaching has weaknesses in its treatment of women. See Christine E. Gudorf, *Catholic Social Teaching on Liberation Themes* (Washington, D.C.: University Press of America, 1981), 249-328.

[68]Gustavo Gutierrez, "Liberation Theology and the Future of the Poor," in *Liberating the Future: God, Mammon and Theology*, ed. Joerg Rieger (Minneapolis: Fortress Press, 1998), 96-123.

[69]Juan Luis Segundo, *Evolution and Guilt*, trans. John Drury (New York: Orbis Books, 1974), 62.

[70]John Paul II, *Faith and Reason, op. cit.*, #5.

[71]Rasmussen, *Earth Community, Earth Ethics*, 19.

[72]John Paul II, *Centesimus Annus*, 60.1,2, *op. cit.*, 477.

[73]Aloysius Pieris, S.J., *An Asian Theology of Liberation* (New York: Maryknoll, 1988).

[74]Frederick Herzog, *God-Walk: Liberation Shaping Dogmatics* (New York: Orbis Books, 1988) 46.

[75]On the experience of moral contrast, see Edward Schillebeeckx, *Church: The Human Story of God* (New York: Crossroad, 1990), chapter one.

[76]Jürgen Moltmann, "Political Theology and Theology of Liberation," in *Liberating the Future*, 63.

[77]Gutierrez, 98.

[78]Stephen B. Bevans, *Models of Contextual Theology* (New York: Orbis Books, 1992), chapter 1. On the strong contextual nature of early Christian theology, see David Bosch, *Transforming Mission: Paradigm Shifts in Theology of Mission* (New York: Orbis Books, 1991), 190-213.

[79]Himes and Himes, 4.

[80]Ibid., 13.

[81]Schreiter, 99.

[82]Ibid.,15-16.

[83]James W. Fowler, *Faithful Change: The Personal and Public Challenges of Postmodern Life* (Nashville: Abingdon Press, 1996), 162.

[84]Wuthnow, 117.

[85]Thurow, 17.

[86]Martin E. Marty and R. Scott Appleby, eds., *Fundamentalisms and the State: Remaking Politics, Economies and Militance* (Chicago: The University of Chicago Press, 1993), 3.

[87]Timur Kuran, "Fundamentalisms and the Economy," in *Fundamentalisms and the State*, 289-301.

[88]Barber, 6, 9.

[89]Thomas P. O'Meara, O.P., *Fundamentalism: A Catholic Perspective* (New York: Paulist Press, 1990), 18.

[90]Segundo, *Faith and Ideologies*, 25.

⁹¹Ibid., 109.

⁹²Ibid., 17.

⁹³Ibid., 47. See also Gregory Baum, *op. cit.* Baum discusses the ambiguity of the function of religion in a society.

⁹⁴Jim Wallis, *Who Speaks for God?* (New York: Doubleday, 1996).

⁹⁵Segundo, *Faith and Ideologies*, 47.

⁹⁶John Paul II, *Redemptor Hominis*, 14.

⁹⁷Segundo, *Faith and Ideologies*, 79.

⁹⁸Fuchs, 60.

⁹⁹J. Brian Hehir, "The Right and Competence of the Church in the American Case," in John A. Coleman, S.J., ed., *One Hundred Years of Catholic Social Thought* (New York: Orbis Books, 1991), 66-9.

¹⁰⁰Fuchs, 15.

¹⁰¹Carter, 91.

¹⁰²Rasmussen, *Earth Community, Earth Ethics*,149.

¹⁰³Ibid., 150.

¹⁰⁴John Paul II, *Centesimus Annus*, 58.

¹⁰⁵Rasmussen, *Earth Community, Earth Ethics*, 132.

¹⁰⁶Ibid., 39.

¹⁰⁷Juan Luis Segundo, *The Liberation of Theology*, trans. John Drury (New York: Orbis Books, 1976), 150.

¹⁰⁸Robert Bellah, "Is There a Common American Culture?," *Journal of the American Academy of Religion* 66/3 (Fall, 1998): 613-25.

¹⁰⁹The following analysis is based on, and adapted from, the work of Larry Rasmussen, *Moral Fragments, Moral Community, op. cit.*, 110ff., and his use of the work of Philip Selznik, *The Moral Commonwealth:Social Theory and the Promise of Community* (Berkeley: University of California Press, 1992), 183-90, 357-65.

¹¹⁰Rasmussen, *Earth Community, Earth Ethics*, 172. I draw on Rasmussen's reflections on a vision of sustainability in this section of the essay.

¹¹¹United States Catholic Conference of Bishops, *Relieving the Third World Debt* (Washington, D.C.: USCC, 1989).

¹¹²Rasmussen, *Moral Fragments, Moral Community*, 139.

¹¹³Richard Sennett, *Authority* (New York: Knopf, 1980), 168.

¹¹⁴John Paul II, *Centesimus Annus*, 58.

¹¹⁵Michael Lerner, *The Politics of Meaning: Restoring Hope and Possibility in an Age of Cynicism* (New York: Addison-Wesley, 1996).

¹¹⁶John Paul II, *Centesimus Annus*, 15.

¹¹⁷Dennis P. McCann, "On Moral Business: A Theological Perspective," *Review of Business* 19/1 (1997): 9ff.

¹¹⁸S. L. Bachman, "Young Workers in Mexico's Economy," *US News and World Report* 123/8 (1997), 40.

Feminist Ethics in the New Millennium: The Dream of a Common Moral Language

Anne E. Patrick, S.N.J.M.

When the bishops of the Second Vatican Council spoke of "signs of the times" and "questions of special urgency," few of them were thinking of the women's movement for justice, and probably none anticipated that something called feminist ethics would soon appear on the Catholic theological scene. But, arguably the Council itself catalyzed this development in ways that are worth recalling today, in this context of millennial musings on what ethics should be like in the new century. The document, *Gaudium et Spes* ("Pastoral Constitution on the Church in the Modern World"), stated that God intends a society in which the essential equality of women and men is recognized, and declared that, where the "fundamental rights of the person" are concerned, discrimination based on sex "is to be overcome and eradicated as contrary to God's intent" (#29).[1] The same document also affirmed that history is the locus of the activity of God's Spirit and God's people are led by this Spirit in their efforts to "build up a better world in truth and justice":

> In each nation and social group there is a growing number of men and women who are conscious that they themselves are the craftsmen and molders of their community's culture. All over the world the sense of autonomy and responsibility increases with effects of the greatest importance for the spiritual and moral maturity of mankind (#11, 55).

127

In addition to affirming women's dignity and equality and commending historical efforts on behalf of justice, *Gaudium et Spes* contributed directly to the development of feminist ethics, at least of the Catholic sort, by voicing the hope that "more of the laity will receive adequate theological formation and that some among them will dedicate themselves professionally to these studies and contribute to their advancement" (#62). By thus welcoming formerly excluded Catholics to the guild of theology, the Council opened itself to ideas that would soon transform the enterprise in ways that no one could anticipate in 1965. Furthermore, by articulating the value of freedom of intellectual inquiry, *Gaudium et Spes* implicitly deepened its endorsement of the possibility of significant change:

> In order that such persons [those trained in the sacred sciences] may fulfill their proper function, let it be recognized that all the faithful, clerical and lay, possess a lawful freedom of inquiry and thought, and the freedom to express their minds humbly and courageously about those matters in which they enjoy competence (#62).

Finally, in another document promulgated on that busy December 7, 1965, the Council singled out moral theology as especially in need of development. In their "Decree on Priestly Formation," *Optatem Totius*, the bishops declared: "Special attention needs to be given to the development of moral theology. Its scientific exposition should be more thoroughly nourished by scriptural teaching. It should show the nobility of the Christian vocation of the faithful, and their obligation to bring forth fruit in charity for the life of the world" (#16). The effect of this statement is to establish norms for the practice of moral theology. It should be accountable to science, nourished by Scripture, inspiring in its articulation of the ideals of Christian living, and of practical benefit to the world. We may discern a fifth norm in the passage from *Gaudium et Spes* about freedom of inquiry and expression, for with such freedom comes the responsibility to pursue truth rigorously and to express one's findings appropriately, in the words of the Council, with humility and courage.

The fact that these bishops called for the *development* of moral theology indicates their recognition that our ethical tradition had not been living up to its potential and that the world has been the poorer as a result. The Council's insistence that moral theology "bring forth fruit in charity for the life of the world" suggests that past emphasis had been too individualistic and too otherworldly, too preoccupied with the future state of believers' souls, to take sufficient notice of its effects on the worldly welfare of persons within and beyond the Catholic community. Today, decades after the Council, this call for the development of moral theology still stands in need of fulfillment. Progress has been made, but the discipline is not yet sufficiently integrated with biblical spirituality nor is it fully adequate to meet the needs of our world.[2]

I believe the challenges to moral theology are deeply religious and moral ones. We are being called, on the one hand, to foster a more radical trust in God and, on the other, to develop a more thoroughgoing ethic of justice. To me the situation calls for change greater than anything we have yet seen; we need no less than a revolution of Catholic consciousness. A profound conversion is called for, a shift of attention, a turning from certain preoccupations to new topics and new ways of seeing old ones.[3]

My thesis here is that Catholic feminist ethics is contributing to this process of conversion and is fostering the development of moral theology called for by the Council. I also think that we may hope for the "planned obsolescence" of feminist ethics to be underway at some point in the new millennium, ideally within the next century. Although I do not expect this to happen in my lifetime, I believe feminist ethics should have a limited life span and should make a graceful exit once its goals have been achieved. We will be ready for its departure when women are recognized as fully human and fully capable of moral decisionmaking, sacramental leadership, and Church governance; we will be ready when women's moral experience is routinely incorporated into moral reflection at every level of the Church and the academy. We are far from ready now, but we came some distance in the twentieth century, and there is reason to hope for a future that is better than the past we have known. This future is the dream of my title, adapted from the poet Adrienne Rich, "The Dream of a Common Moral Language."[4] Rich gave her original title, *The Dream of a Common Language*, to a volume of love poetry, something not at all removed from theology, if one shares Gustavo Gutierrez's notion that theology can be "a love letter" to God and the Church.[5] In any case, the "dream of a common moral language" is certainly one that fits well with the Natural Law tradition of Catholic moral theology, which aspires to communicate and collaborate with all persons who strive to know and do what is right and good.

For the present essay, I have narrowed the topic of feminist ethics to that practiced in the Catholic context, not only because this is my own tradition, but also because Catholics have been leading contributors to feminist religious thought. If the hopes of the Second Vatican Council are to be realized, it will be up to Catholics to bring this about, and the more of us who see feminism as central to the reform of our tradition, the sooner this reform will be likely to happen. Of course, Catholics who do feminist ethics are

often in conversation with Jewish, Protestant, and secular feminist
thinkers, and sometimes with those from other traditions as well.
My focus here, however, will be on the way feminist ethics contributes to the Conciliar mandate to make moral theology, and
by extension the ethical lives of Catholics, more fruitful for the
common good of all the earth's inhabitants, both now and in the
future. I have reviewed Conciliar influences on the development
of feminist approaches to Catholic moral theology because it is
crucial to situate this enterprise solidly in the tradition that gave it
impetus. Certainly, there remain tensions between Catholicism as
we have known it and feminism, but we have found considerable
common ground already. My discussion that follows is divided into
three sections:

1. Feminist Ethics: Vision and Voices;
2. Harbingers of Hope: Feminist Ethicists as Theorists and Practitioners of Solidarity;
3. Living in the Meantime.

Finally, I conclude by returning to the ideal of my subtitle, "the
dream of a common moral language." This is the situation toward
which feminist ethics is working, when sufficient attention to par-
ticularities of difference will have transformed ethical discourse
to a point of full inclusivity. At this point, feminist ethics itself can
leave the platform because its goals will have been reached.
Women will no longer be perceived or treated as a lesser form of
humanity, but will view ourselves and be recognized by men as fully
human and fully capable of moral decisionmaking, sacramental
leadership, and Church governance; our moral experience will
routinely be incorporated into moral reflection at every level of
the Church and the academy. In view of this long term goal, then,
I begin by offering some definitions of terms and historical background, preliminary information that provides a basis for thinking
about the future. Here, I address the questions: "What is feminism?" and "What led to the emergence of feminist ethics in
Catholicism?"

I. Feminist Ethics: Vision and Voices

Just as maps are not actual territory, but representations that
orient and guide us, so verbal definitions are not full depictions of
"reality," but resources that aid our understanding of such complex movements and enterprises as "feminist ethics."

Feminism: There are many definitions and types of feminism,
with considerable controversy about the meanings and implications of the various types. All feminists agree that there has been a

historic bias against women, and they seek to overcome the problems known as sexism, androcentrism, and patriarchy. Where definitions of feminism are concerned, one crucial distinction should be noted. Some definitions emphasize the participation of women as *subjects* of their own liberative process against sexism, stressing the fact that women, not men, must liberate themselves from injustice. Other definitions emphasize the fact that human beings of both sexes are capable of recognizing and seeking to remedy sexism. These two types, designated respectively as "woman-centered feminism" and "inclusive feminism," are different, but each captures true aspects of the movement and has useful applications.

Historian Gerda Lerner provides an example of a **woman-centered** approach when she describes feminist consciousness as

> [. . .] the awareness of women that they belong to a subordinate group; that they have suffered wrongs as a group; that their condition of subordination is not natural, but is societally determined; that they must join with other women to remedy these wrongs; and finally, that they must and can provide an alternate vision of social organization in which women as well as men will enjoy autonomy and self-determination.[6]

I do not believe Lerner means by this definition to exclude men from sharing in the alternate vision or working toward its social realization, but her definition recognizes that there is indeed a difference between being the subject of a liberative process and participating empathetically in such a movement when one does not suffer the precise injustice oneself.

While accepting the value of Lerner's approach, I have also found it useful to employ an **inclusive** definition of feminism and have suggested that feminism is a position that involves two elements: (1) a solid conviction of the equality of women and men, and (2) a commitment to reform society so that the full equality of women is respected, which requires also reforming the thought systems that legitimate the present unjust social order.[7] This implies that men and boys can be feminists and, indeed, do well to assume this moral stance. Finally, however one defines the term, it needs to be said that feminists differ widely in their analyses of injustice, levels of commitment to liberating action, degrees of explicitness of commitment, and opinions regarding specific problems and their solutions.

Sexism, patriarchy, androcentrism: Various thinkers distinguish "patriarchy" and other key terms of feminist thought in slightly different ways, but there is basic agreement that bias against females has both social-systemic and intellectual-attitudinal components.

Theologian Elizabeth A. Johnson provides a helpful analysis in her groundbreaking volume, *She Who Is*. Johnson regards sexism as a "social sin that has debilitating effects on women both socially and psychologically, and interlocks with other forms of oppression to shape a violent and dehumanized world." She names the "twin faces" of sexism as "patriarchy" and "androcentrism."[8] In a later volume, Johnson stresses that sexism is "a pattern of thinking and acting that subordinates women on the basis of their sex." Sexism expresses itself *structurally* as *patriarchy*, "the social arrangement where power is exercised of necessity by the dominant males, with others ranked in descending orders of dominance," and *intellectually* as *androcentrism*, "the thought pattern that takes the human characteristics of the adult male as normative for the whole of humanity, consigning whatever deviates from this to the outer realms of otherness or deficiency." Whether social or ideological in expression, Johnson argues, sexism has the effect of "making women mostly invisible, inaudible, and marginal, except for the supportive services they provide."[9]

Patricia Beattie Jung has developed a cogent ethical analysis of the relationship between sexism and feminism in a 1984 *America* article, entitled "Give Her Justice." Jung's argument is elegant in its simplicity: sexism involves an unjust distribution of the benefits and burdens society has to offer, and feminism is the commitment to right that imbalance. Not to be committed to feminism, in other words, is to be complicit in sexism.[10]

I find Jung persuasive on this point — that feminism is a moral position highly to be commended, since it is the name for the willingness to overcome the injustice of sexism — and I have long been comfortable describing my own work as theologian and ethicist in these terms. I am aware, however, that ambiguities of definition, and especially of connotation, have colored the meaning of feminism for many persons, and there are some good reasons that others are less comfortable accepting or proclaiming that their efforts are "feminist." In the first place, there is the basic concern of men not to claim themselves as subjects of a liberative process that is not actually their own. Secondly, there is the strategic choice of women and men not to complicate what may already be difficult rhetorical challenges when they are seeking to influence an audience that cannot hear them further if the term "feminism" is dropped within fifty feet of their paragraphs. Finally, and most importantly, from the vantage of women of color there has been the need to dissent from the racism and false generalizations long associated with white feminism in this country, which has too often spoken about women as if the experiences of European American females were the only ones that mattered.

Thus, a number of African American and Latina scholars have claimed more precise designations for their own efforts, employing the novelist Alice Walker's term "womanist" in the former case and theologian Ada María Isasi-Díaz's parallel term *mujerista* in the latter. At the same time, these scholars usually acknowledge, explicitly or implicitly, that their work on behalf of justice for women is a dimension of feminism when it is properly understood and functioning in a genuinely pluralistic way.[11] Two representative contributors to Catholic feminist ethics from these groups are discussed in more detail later on — M. Shawn Copeland and Ada María Isasi-Díaz — but, for now I want to address the nervousness about claiming feminism that affects European Americans who believe in women's equal dignity, but are reluctant to use the designation "feminist."

Ironically, "feminism" is the moral position that dare not speak its name in certain circles. Catharine R. Stimson notes that feminism has become an "F-word" of sorts, and ethicists may sometimes prefer not to employ it in a climate in which the concept has been trivialized, demonized, or otherwise burdened beyond recognition. Nevertheless, I believe Stimson is right to assert that feminism brings several gifts to society: "a moral vision of women in all their diversity, and of social justice; political and cultural organizations (like battered women's shelters); and psychological processes that enable men and women to re-experience and re-form themselves."[12] Stimson acknowledges, however, that "[e]ven feminists fear feminism." They may feel conflicted about gender and social change and may be inclined to whisper that they are feminists while adding under their breaths that they regret having to be. Nevertheless, the moral vision and programs of feminism are "too compelling to ignore," and I agree with Stimson's conclusion that only the appropriate and frequent use of the term is likely to restore its ethical meaning and reasonableness to the public at large.[13]

For this reason, I believe theologians and ethicists do well to claim their commitment to feminism explicitly whenever it is relevant to their efforts, for, by doing so, they keep the essential meaning of feminism as a commitment to justice before the Church, which is historically so implicated in sexism. To women, who have inherited the opportunities to teach and publish as the result of long struggles by foresisters who entered these professions in times much less favorable to females than are our own, I say it is important to claim the moral vision of feminism explicitly. This forthrightness will keep us from being what Stimson has called "languid heiresses," who are "living on a trust fund from history," spending the money, but failing to add the principal. It will also bring more positive connotations to the minds of others who will grow to understand the value and complexity of feminism more readily as more of us claim and clarify the designation.

To men, whose feminism is different from women's, I say that their commitment will be most edifying when they speak well of the moral vision of feminism and act in ways that clearly manifest their desire to remedy past injustices. I commend the example of such theologians as Walter Burghardt, Charles Curran, and Richard McCormick, who have served Catholic feminism in ways that make their opposition to sexism quite clear. As editor of *Theological Studies*, during the 1975 International Women's Year, Burghardt devoted an entire issue to the subject of "Woman: New Dimensions," providing a forum for the thought of scholars like Rosemary Radford Ruether, Elisabeth Schüssler Fiorenza, Mary Aquin O'Neill, and Margaret A. Farley to reach a wide and influential audience of Catholic theologians. The fact that Raymond Brown and George Tavard also contributed to that December, 1975, issue of *Theological Studies* was important, too, for their presence in the volume on women encouraged the collaboration necessary for significant change to occur.

A few years earlier, a regular contributor to *Theological Studies*, Richard A. McCormick, had advanced the cause of feminism by including a discussion of the women's liberation movement in his "Notes on Moral Theology" for March, 1972. McCormick's notes, which appeared annually in *Theological Studies* for two critical decades following the Second Vatican Council, from 1965-84, have been influential for the Church internationally. Moreover, by the time McCormick wrote about women's liberation in late 1971, he had received the highest honor from the Catholic Theological Society of America (then known as the Cardinal Spellman Award, 1969) and had just completed his year as president of the CTSA (1970-71). He thus brought considerable stature to the discussion of women's liberation and would have been more likely heard by theological colleagues than would have been a less powerful figure. It is worth quoting McCormick here and recalling or imagining a situation quite different from our own, a time when very few women were teaching in graduate programs in moral theology or Christian ethics. Margaret Farley may have been the only Catholic woman doing so; in March, 1972, she was in her first year as professor at Yale Divinity School, with her dissertation not quite complete. McCormick begins his 1972 reflections on women's liberation by citing a thinker associated with the Grail Movement:

> As Janet Kalven points out, women's liberation has come into existence against the background of the black movement, student movements, and the third-world emergence and has adopted very often their heady rhetoric, guerilla tactics, and shrill anticapitalist

ideology. But surely it would be a pity if these sometimes bizarre tactics and the violent rhetoric blinded us to the genuine moral dimension cast up by the new feminism.[14]

He concludes by declaring that theology's task concerning women's liberation is threefold. It must critique unjust models of women's humanity and replace them with just ones, shaped from the "richness of the Christian tradition." Secondly, theology must "put its own house in order by encouraging the emergence of women theologians of competence and influence in far greater numbers." And, finally, theology must

> insist that the Church . . . must teach what it is to be human by her own inner life. If her own structures and ministry continue to speak of humanity in terms of but one sex, must we not think that the Church is seriously compromising her mission in the contemporary world? I believe so. Granted, there are hosts of practical pastoral problems to work out; but here is a chance for genuine leadership. Too often in the past the Catholic community has almost reluctantly accommodated after everybody else has shown the way.[15]

Perhaps McCormick had in mind here the hierarchy's opposition to women's suffrage, which had been voiced by many American bishops in the first two decades of the last century, perhaps most eloquently by Cardinal James Gibbons in a 1911 interview with the *N.Y. Globe*:

> Women's suffrage? . . . I am surprised that one should ask the question. I have but one answer to such a question, and that is that I am unalterably opposed to woman's suffrage, always have been and always will be. . . . Why should a woman lower herself to sordid politics? Why should a woman leave her home and go into the streets to play the game of politics? . . . When a woman enters the political arena, she goes outside the sphere for which she was intended . . . [and] loses the exclusiveness, respect and dignity to which she is entitled in her home.[16]

Cardinal Gibbons, who is rightly remembered as a progressive leader where the rights of working men were concerned, certainly spoke for the old order when it came to women's suffrage. His confidence that the nature, scope, and purpose of women's lives should be determined by men is something he shares with certain Church officials alive today, who have progressive views on many other questions, but are unwilling even to allow discussion of change on such matters as tubal ligation or women's ordination. In 1972, when McCormick published his appreciative discussion of the women's movement in *Theological Studies*, it is likely that the hierarchy's belated endorsement of women's political rights was among the items he had in mind in lamenting that "[t]oo often in

the past the Catholic community has almost reluctantly accommodated after everybody else has shown the way." He voiced the hope
that this pattern would change, that there might be some "fresh . . .
bold move," but recognized that there was not much precedent for
the kind of boldness he envisioned. Nevertheless, McCormick concludes his groundbreaking discussion by insisting that women's
liberation confronts the Church with a "serious moral problem
and, it would seem, an idea whose time has come."[17]

McCormick's leadership on this matter did not end in 1972. A
decade later he discussed "the most important areas within the
field of moral theology in need of exploration and research over
the next five to ten years" at the moral theology seminar of the
CTSA. The list he presented to a roomful of generally male colleagues at this June, 1982, gathering in New York began with
"moral issues related to feminism."[18] He urged attention to the
question of women's ministry and declared that, although "no
individual can claim an unqualified right to ordination as a priest,"
still "a class of persons could argue that, if there is no solid theological justification, this exclusion is a denial of a right: a right not
to be *unfairly* interfered with in the *pursuit* of a possession or a
goal." He also pointed out that one might claim that the faithful in
general "have a right to the *fullness* of priestly ministry as they
work out their salvation," and, because theological justifications
for the current exclusion of women have not been convincing,
"the matter must be viewed as unfinished and open to further
development."[19]

On this subject, it is worth adding that Bishop Raymond Lucker
of New Ulm, Minnesota, is also among clerics long on record as
pointing to the need for the Church to overcome sexism. Indeed,
in 1991, Lucker observed that the fact that women's ordination
cannot be discussed is "a sign of injustice."[20] He published this
opinion in 1991, three years prior to Pope John Paul II's apostolic
letter, *Ordinatio Sacerdotalis*, which sought to close the question by
declaring "that the church has no authority whatsoever to confer
priestly ordination on women, and that this judgment is to be defini-
tively held by all the church's faithful."[21] The Catholic Church is,
for the time being, in a period of official silence on the question
of women's ordination, but works published earlier can hardly
be taken off the shelves, and new reflections will find their way
into print, albeit through independent publishing houses. For
example, when the Benedictine monks, who sponsor the Liturgical
Press, obeyed an injunction not to distribute Lavinia Byrne's study,
although it had already been advertised in their 1996-97 catalog,
the independent publishing house, Continuum, brought it out
promptly in New York.[22]

Returning to Richard McCormick, a recent and important instance of his support of feminism involves the publication, in collaboration with Charles Curran and Margaret Farley, of the ninth volume in a series of *Readings in Moral Theology* he had previously coedited with Curran. The publication of this work in 1997 keeps the importance of feminist ethics before the guild of Catholic moral theology and also makes it easier for students to have access to otherwise fugitive contributions by leading contributors to feminist ethics. Among the twenty-five essays in this anthology, several are by scholars in such related disciplines as historical theology or biblical studies, but most are by women (and one man) who are well established in the field of Christian ethics.

This background information from the last three decades amounts to a story with a moral. Christian ethics, including the feminist variety, is at its best when it is judiciously proactive about where it puts its efforts and when it tackles difficult topics in a way gauged to help change the world for the better. Richard McCormick is an outstanding example of such proactivity, demonstrating an effective solidarity with a marginalized group. Whether or not he is appropriately called a feminist can be argued either way, but this is not quite so important as what he has done with his power as a leading practitioner in the guild of Christian ethics. His decision to write appreciatively on women's liberation in 1972 helped promote a climate in which Rosemary Radford Ruether's volume of *Liberation Theology*, also published in 1972, could be received more favorably and by a wider Catholic audience than might otherwise have been the case.[23] It also seems likely that many of the women whose feminist essays were published in the anthology, *Readings in Moral Theology No. 9*, benefited from the climate to which Burghardt and McCormick contributed in the seventies, especially those who were in graduate school or seeking employment at that time, when very few women were tenured as theologians.[24]

Consider the mandate McCormick set in 1972, that male theology must "put its own house in order by encouraging the emergence of women theologians of competence and influence in far greater numbers." This has happened, and it has not happened by accident. The participation of women in the CTSA is a case in point. The first women to be admitted as active members of this formerly male and clerical organization were Elizabeth Jane Farians and Cathleen M. Going, who joined in 1965. By 1977, female membership had reached five percent, and, by 1992, it stood at seventeen percent; presently, I would estimate that it is approximately twenty percent.[25] But, today women are perceived as much more numerous than we actually are because we have been elected to leadership in this society disproportionately to our numbers, and I have to infer that other male theologians have been sharing the moral vision articulated by McCormick a quarter century ago, for we women would not have had the votes to bring this off by ourselves. Agnes Cunningham was the first woman elected to presidential office, in 1977, and, since then, two women were elected in the 1980s and four in the 1990s. The current president is Margaret Farley who designed a convention that took place in Miami in June, 1999, on the theme of "Development of Doctrine." The papers and conversations that resulted from her efforts are helping to nudge the tradition into the new millennium with appropriate verve, faith, and commitment.[26] The emergence of women in the field of theology is change that can be measured, and the case suggests to me that ethicists will also do well to think even more practically about the way feminist values can become realized in the new century.

Of course, women's own efforts and commitments were the primary factor in our entering the guild and developing a new approach to ethics, and that is a story too complex to tell in any detail here. Suffice it to say that the first generation of women scholars in this field set an impressive example by their commitment to a methodology that gave priority attention to women's experience in its diversity and complexity as they reflected on various theoretical and practical questions in ethics. Margaret Farley notes in her entry on "Ethics and Moral Theologies" for the *Dictionary of Feminist Theologies* that there are two factors that make Christian feminist ethics "feminist": In the first place, "it is opposed to the subordination of women to men on the basis of gender," and, in the second, "it incorporates a central methodological focus on the experience of women."[27] The reasons for this methodological commitment are well stated in the Introduction to the first volume of religious feminist ethics published in this country: "The patriarchal legacy of the West has hidden women's experience from ethical view. . . . Too often, society creates a vision of 'feminine' experience which keeps women subservient to men, alienated from our own human wholeness, and isolated from other women."[28] These pioneering editors sound a theme that will be plumbed often by subsequent authors, namely, the diversity of female experience:

> There is no homogeneous woman's experience. Women's lives are very different. Among the differences which seem the most significant are the following: Some women are mothers; others are not. Some women come from upper class backgrounds; others, from the middle class; still others, from the working class or from poverty. Some are lesbian; some heterosexual. Women are black, native

American, Asian American, or Latina. . . . Women have very different work experiences as homemakers, clerical workers, service
workers, factory operatives, managers, or professionals. If feminist
ethics is to be based upon the experience of *all* women, then such
differences in experience must be acknowledged and incorporated
into feminist theory.[29]

Although this diversity entails that one cannot generalize
uncritically about something called "women's experience," and
especially that women from more powerful groups cannot presume to speak for all women, feminist ethics should not for this
reason drift into a skeptical relativism. Indeed, it has not usually
done so, certainly not in the case of the Catholic authors included
in the volume mentioned above. Along with recognizing diversity
among women, these thinkers are also conscious that all women
share female embodiment and suffer some injustice on account of
gender. Therefore, many claims about what is harmful and beneficial to women do have validity: for instance, claims about the evils
of malnutrition, rape, and battering.

Lisa Sowle Cahill used the occasion of her 1993 presidential address to the CTSA to argue this point cogently in a lecture, entitled
"Feminist Ethics and the Challenge of Cultures." The insights of
such postmodern philosophers as Foucault and Habermas about
the limits of reason notwithstanding, our common humanity inspires
Cahill to affirm the basic insight of the Aristotelian-Thomistic
Natural Law tradition: "a commitment to an objective moral order,
knowable by reasonable reflection on human experience itself,
especially on the purposes and values all societies share."[30] There
can, in other words, be "intercultural ethics," and, given the "cry-
ing injustices worldwide of poverty, war, hunger, and oppression
of whole peoples, and of women among all peoples," there must
be sustained efforts to reach agreement on matters of justice and
human well being.[31] This position is widely shared by other
Catholics who do feminist ethics.

Besides its commitment to justice for women and its methodological focus on women's experience, Catholic feminist ethics is a
highly theological enterprise. It shares the liberationist perspective
of feminist theology in general, whose aim has been well described
by systematic theologian Elizabeth Johnson: "By Christian feminist
theology I mean a reflection on God and all things in the light of
God that stands consciously in the company of all the world's
women, explicitly prizing their genuine humanity while uncovering and criticizing its persistent violation in sexism, itself an
omnipresent paradigm of unjust relationships."[32] The principle of
the "preferential option for the poor," so central to liberation theology and important also to recent Vatican teaching, leads Johnson

to state as the aim of feminist religious discourse a goal that is widely shared by Catholic feminist ethicists: "the flourishing of poor women of color in violent situations."[33] When women from the most oppressed situations flourish, it seems clear that we can safely assume that life is better for everyone.

The vision of feminist ethics, in sum, is one of justice, mutuality, and inclusivity. The last three decades of the twentieth century have seen the emergence of women into the field of moral theology, thanks to their own efforts and to the proactive welcome extended by men who shared this vision. Now that women's voices have come into the discussion, what new things are stirring? What harbingers of a hopeful future are with us as we enter the new millennium?

II. Harbingers of Hope: Feminist Ethicists as Theorists and Practitioners of Solidarity

The most crucial thing that needs to happen as we enter the new century involves a refocusing of moral energy, which I have called the "turn to the oppressed." If moral theology is to fulfill the mandate of Vatican II and inspire the faithful to "bring forth fruit in charity for the life of the world," somehow Catholics' moral energy must burst through the casing of legalism and of dutiful individualism that were stressed in their moral formation. Only then can it blossom into an effective responsibility that will bear fruit for the life of the world. When I survey the many contributions of Catholic feminist ethicists since the 1970s, one especially encouraging theme is solidarity, a newly emphasized virtue and practice, which is necessary for realizing the ideals of justice central to feminism and Christianity alike. Without solidarity, moral theology is at risk of lapsing into "gourmet ethics," a preoccupation with individual moral righteousness, especially among those whose affluence allows them to worry about choices that are beyond the realm of possibility for most human beings, particularly the poor.

Solidarity can also help feminist ethics avoid the theoretical paralysis that may otherwise happen as a result of the rapid proliferation of subfields in ethics, whether those of such "identity groups" as Latinas and African Americans or those of such topical fields as bioethics, ecology, sexual ethics, and so on. Obviously, these subdivisions have purpose and value, but the insights from each need to be brought together for everyone's practical benefit. A spirit of solidarity can inspire those with particular interests to gather the gleanings from specialized work and make these available for wider discussions of the common good. It is surely a sign of hope that reflections on solidarity and an ethical methodology that expresses solidarity are prominent in the writings of many Catholic feminists who do ethics.

According to Matthew Lamb's discussion of "solidarity" in the *New Dictionary of Catholic Social Thought*, the term was first employed in papal teachings in the early twentieth century in an effort to shape a social theory that avoided both the individualism of liberal Capitalism and the various problems of authoritarian Commu-nism. "Solidarity" is the English translation of a modern German word, *Solidarismus*, originally linked with the labor movement, and its first Magisterial use seems to have been in Pope Pius XI's encyclical of 1931, *Quadragesimo Anno*, which had been written by the social theorist, Otto von Nell-Breuning. As Lamb indicates, "Catholic solidarism aimed at transposing pre-modern understandings of natural law, of human being as essentially social, and of society itself as organic and cooperative, into the modern contexts of industrialized societies with complex exchange commodities."[34] The term "solidarity" was later used in the encyclicals of Pope John XXIII, *Mater et Magistra* and *Pacem in Terris*, as well as in the Conciliar document, *Gaudium et Spes*, and Pope Paul VI's encyclical, *Populorum Progressio*. It has been especially prominent in the writings of Pope John Paul II, and its association with the Polish labor movement that played such a key role in dismantling the Communist bloc in Eastern Europe is well known.

Lamb notes that Pope John Paul II was the first to employ the term solidarity to denote a virtue which he characterizes in his 1987 encyclical, *Sollicitudo Rei Socialis* ("On Social Concern"), as more than mere feelings of compassion, but, rather, "'a firm and persevering determination to commit oneself to the common good,'" which is to be practiced, not only between individuals and sociopolitical entities, but between human beings and the natural environment.[35] Solidarity, moreover, goes beyond simple "interdependence" and is very close to classical understandings of charity. According to Pope John Paul II, solidarity

> helps us to see the "other" — whether a person, people or nation — not just as some kind of instrument, with a work capacity and physical strength to be exploited at low cost and then discarded when no longer useful, but as our "neighbor," a "helper," to be made a sharer on a par with ourselves, in the banquet of life to which all are equally invited by God.[36]

Liberation theologians, such as Jon Sobrino, have also emphasized solidarity, but it is especially prominent in the writings of Catholic feminist theologians, perhaps because they have reason to think that the Magisterium itself needs to be more consistent in practicing solidarity with regard to women.

The virtue and practice of solidarity begins with the commitment to the oppressed which, in liberation theology, has been called the "option for the poor." Solidarity, above all, requires a disposition to give priority to those who are voiceless, marginalized, or oppressed in any situation about which we do moral reflection. Its first moment must be one of attention and, especially, of listening. Such listening requires more than mere politeness; rather, it presumes a real openness and a willingness to be affected and to change as a result of what has been heard.

The importance of such listening is illustrated in the examples I discussed earlier, the decisions of Walter Burghardt and Richard McCormick to use the power of their social location in a field that had traditionally marginalized women, namely, Catholic theology, to provide a space where women's voices could be heard and eventually transform the field. Now that women are established in the theological community, they have not only enriched the theoretical meaning of solidarity, but have also exemplified the virtue in much of their own practice. These Catholic women ethicists are harbingers of hope for a better future, helping to span the gap between a century that has known too much violence and injustice and a new millennium that can be considerably more peaceful, compassionate, and just, if we, with God's help, make it so.

There are many Catholic feminist thinkers whose work is relevant here, although for reasons of space I have selected six for discussion below: Ada María Isasi-Díaz, Margaret A. Farley, Patricia Beattie Jung, Barbara Hilkert Andolsen, M. Shawn Copeland, and Rosemary Radford Ruether. All these scholars have set new directions, and their very practice of ethics exemplifies what solidarity entails and thereby deepens our understanding of its meaning and requirements. These thinkers have been building a bridge to the new millennium, and we will do well to cross it in their company. If we do, we shall also encounter many others who have valuable things to teach us along the way.

Ada María Isasi-Díaz is a Latina born in Cuba who has lived in the United States for almost forty years. A leader of the Women's Ordination Conference in the late 1970s, she later studied theology and ethics at Union Theological Seminary. She now teaches in the Theological School at Drew University and publishes works that demonstrate a distinct emphasis on solidarity. In 1988, she coauthored a volume with a Mexican American colleague, Yolanda Tarango, which was largely built from interviews with women from diverse Latina backgrounds, including Mexican, Puerto Rican, and Cuban. This work emphasizes the actual words of the women interviewed, thereby affirming with unprecedented immediacy the experiences of those previously marginalized from theological scholarship.[37] This book also provides summaries of each chapter in Spanish, a practical way of broadening the circle of those who have access to the work and a subtle reminder to Anglo readers of the importance of the language spoken by the fastest growing segment of the Catholic population of the United States. In 1993, Isasi-Díaz published a work elaborating her *mujerista* theology. This book is more theoretical than the one she wrote with Tarango, but it still draws from an organic process of listening to women from a broad range of Latina cultural and economic backgrounds.[38] In her most recent book, *Mujerista Theology* (1996), Isasi-Díaz devotes an entire chapter to "Solidarity: Love of Neighbor in the Twenty-first Century." There, she describes solidarity as "the appropriate present-day expression of the gospel demand that we love our neighbor."[39] She indicates that solidarity is a matter of effective, cohesive struggle governed by an understanding of interconnected issues; it goes well beyond mere agreement with, and support of, a people's cause. Solidarity requires mutuality as well as praxis, she insists, and its "goal is not the participation of the oppressed in present social structures but rather the replacement of those structures by ones in which full participation of the oppressed is possible."[40]

Although she has an academic position, Isasi-Díaz continues to work with grassroots Latinas and endeavors to bring their experiences into her reflections on theological and ethical topics. I have never forgotten the powerful words she quoted in her first book from a Puerto Rican woman in her early sixties. This mother of twelve said about her decision to have a tubal ligation despite the objections of doctors, husband, and priest: "I would have had twenty-four children if I had listened to them."[41] I hope that Magisterial authorities will listen more attentively to such women, something that Isasi-Díaz's books certainly facilitate. If they listen, they will have to discover a way of allowing for reasonable exceptions to current policies that absolutely prohibit sterilization, even under conditions where pregnancy poses a serious threat to a woman's health.

Margaret A. Farley: A similar methodological interest in the diverse experiences of those who have not made the ethical rules is evident in Margaret Farley's important study from 1986, *Personal Commitments.* Her opening chapter describes instances where a commitment vowed in marriage or religious life has meant joy, growth, and fulfillment — not without struggle, to be sure, but, on the whole, a positive experience. But, she also describes instances where such commitments have brought largely negative results, including pain, tragedy, and despair. Keeping this mix of experience in mind, Farley reflects on the meaning and obligatory force of

personal commitments in a context where people "find [them]-
selves faced with an ever widening range of options . . . and a
confusing rate of change that never lets [them] rest from making
decisions."[42] Her conclusion is balanced and well grounded theologically. Because only God is to be loved absolutely, our human
commitments to love within such finite frameworks as marriage or
a religious community will appropriately be assessed in light of
whether they actually allow for the focused love that was promised
to endure and flourish or whether, for some reason, they have become inimical to this flourishing of love and perhaps even harmful
to the well being of persons. Human loves and the frameworks
designed to serve them must be assessed in light of the norm of
justice, Farley believes. In some cases, this norm will require that
the framework should be maintained until death, whereas in others
justice may oblige a person to change the framework of a commitment, for example, by obtaining a divorce or a dispensation from
religious vows. Nevertheless, she concludes that the original commitment to love does continue to bind the one who made it:

> Should we be justified in changing the framework of a commitment,
> the special claim we have given to our love still obligates in some
> way. Even when we must end a marriage or leave a community or
> withdraw from a project, the special right of the other at least ob-
> ligates us, to the extent we are able, to change the commitment with
> care, without violence on our part, with some form of fidelity to the
> love we originally promised. . . . [T]he commitment-obligation to
> a fundamental love does hold even through the changing of the
> instrumental commitment that was meant to serve it.[43]

In subsequent writing, Farley lives up to her own commitment
to attend to the experiences of those who have been on the margins when the tradition was shaped. Her work in progress on
sexual ethics has been informed by the voices of persons whose
experiences have much to teach the tradition, especially women
and sexual minorities.[44] At the same time, her knowledge of, and
esteem for, the classical tradition is evident in her writings and is
praised by her scholarly colleagues. In 1992, Farley became the second woman in the history of the CTSA to receive its John Courtney
Murray Award for achievement in theology. (Systematic theologian
Monika Hellwig had been so honored in 1984.) The following
excerpt from the citation, read on that occasion by CTSA
President Michael J. Buckley, conveys the balance and solidarity
that characterize Farley's work:

> With the 1992 John Courtney Murray Award, the Society honors a
> scholar who bears out Murray's own commitment to public respon-
> sibility and social justice. Like Murray, our recipient draws on St.

Thomas' concern for reasonable moral discourse and the integration of love and justice. Reinterpreting Aquinas and Murray for the post-Vatican II world, this theologian makes a special commitment to justice and equality for those excluded from power — especially for women — in family, society, and Church.[45]

With Lisa Sowle Cahill, Farley is one of only two Catholic women who have been elected president of both the Society of Christian Ethics, where she served in 1993, and the CTSA, where she assumed the presidency in 1999. In stating her goals for the latter office, Farley stressed her intent to make the organization an even more welcoming forum for the full range of theological voices, so that minorities — whether of gender, racial/ethnic background, or place along the conservative/progressive spectrum — can enjoy full access to the give and take of theological conversations.[46]

Patricia Beattie Jung, who teaches at Loyola University in Chicago, is a third feminist ethicist whose writings exemplify the sort of proactive solidarity that is requisite for the development of moral theology. Two books of hers are especially notable. In preparing them, she worked collaboratively with male scholars, one Catholic, the other Protestant. It took courage and generosity for her and Thomas A. Shannon to publish in 1988 an anthology of essays, entitled *The Catholic Abortion Debate*, in order to make widely available a range of arguments about the moral, political, and ecclesial dimensions of this topic. Jung and Shannon sought "to present the middle ground of the abortion debates," because they believed that "on both sides of the debate it is possible to develop reasonable arguments based on commonly held principles." These editors deliberately omitted perspectives from the "radical right and left," but included contributions by cardinals of the Church and by a diverse group of Catholic feminists, among various others chosen because their arguments seemed "responsible," "complex," and "often not that far apart."[47] In the heated, and often disrespectful, context of late twentieth century abortion politics, Jung and Shannon knew they risked trouble by undertaking this publishing project, and they might well have gathered essays on a controversy with a lower decibel rating. But, they resisted the temptation to self censorship and undertook a task they anticipated might be thankless, in a spirit of solidarity with many Catholics of conscience who have been endeavoring to discern a reasonable and responsible position on a public policy question that is more complex than it has been portrayed.

More recently, Jung has published a work on another topic that will be engaging reflection in the Churches well into the new century. This is a study from 1993 which she authored jointly with the late Ralph F. Smith, then a professor of liturgy and colleague of Jung at Wartburg Theological Seminary, a Lutheran institution in Dubuque, Iowa. In this book, Jung and Smith conduct an ethical analysis of their topic that involves careful attention to the biblical and Natural Law traditions as well as to the human costs of maintaining the "reasoned system of prejudice" they designate as "heterosexism."[48] Their study serves an ecumenical community that is currently struggling with many questions on this issue and predictably will continue to do so well into the twenty-first century. It exemplifies one of the aspects of solidarity that I have mentioned above: the willingness to listen to marginalized others to the point of being affected by what they say and possibly changing as a result. Jung and Smith, who characterize themselves as "heterosexual persons of different genders, each married [to other partners] with children," were transformed by sustained listening to their students from the gay community. In the "Introduction," they voice their realization that publishing this work on behalf of justice for sexual minorities would entail some risks:

> Speaking publicly on homosexuality in the present climate means facing on occasion the kind of condemnation and ostracism that gay men and lesbian women face daily. The personal and professional risks borne by others who have taken this path before us are plain to see. . . . With this book we acknowledge that the life stories of gays and lesbians, like the life stories of women and people of color, have helped to persuade our hearts and minds that we cannot stand by while injustice reigns.[49]

Barbara Hilkert Andolsen: A fourth Catholic feminist whose ethical writings are notable for their solidarity with persons who live at some remove from the centers of power is Barbara Hilkert Andolsen who teaches social ethics at Monmouth University in New Jersey. Her doctoral dissertation, published in 1986, was a study of racism in the nineteenth century white women's movement and is entitled *Daughters of Jefferson, Daughters of Bootblacks*. In subsequent books, she has continued to focus on issues of gender, race, and class.[50] In 1989, she wrote *Good Work at the Video Display Terminal: An Ethical Analysis of the Effects of Office Automation on Clerical Workers*. There, she called attention to the various health and economic justice concerns that computers and other technologies have raised for the largely female clerical work force.[51] In her most recent book this feminist reaches an interesting insight about solidarity with respect to the employment patterns now practiced in the United States. She notes that there has been a transition from a traditional employment paradigm in which a diligent and skilled worker could often expect long term employment with the same company to what is now a much less secure labor sit-

uation, even for middle class, white collar workers. This new paradigm, known as the "employability" model, "does offer workers a
chance to develop skills that will make them 'employable' in the
external labor market," but does not provide the security typical
before corporations adopted the tactic of "downsizing" to remain
competitive in a rapidly changing global economy.[52] Corporations
today are also turning more and more to "contingent workers,"
that is, "part-timers, temporary workers, and contract workers,"
who typically lack health and retirement benefits and who face
considerable economic insecurity. Women comprise the majority
of these contingent workers, and Andolsen is "disturbed that contingent work continues a pattern of insecure work for many persons
of color and for some white women." But, her research shows that
the new "employability" paradigm also means that "many men, including many white men, are losing ground in this economy, while
some economically privileged (primarily white) women are doing
much better."[53] Her nuanced conclusion voices an important challenge where solidarity is concerned:

> Women as a group have not achieved economic parity with their
> male peers. Nevertheless the substantial economic progress
> made by some women raises . . . sharp questions about the moral
> responsibility of economically "successful" women. What are the
> possibilities of a solidarity that will bind those privileged women to
> the women and men who are excluded or marginalized in the labor
> markets of the information age?[54]

Andolsen believes there are important resources for answering this
question within Catholicism, both in its tradition of social thought
that calls for "a conversion to solidarity with the socially disadvan-
taged" and especially in the "eucharist as a source of motivation to
act in solidarity with the many workers and their dependents
whose employment security has been seriously diminished as a
result of the shift to the new employability contract."[55] Sadly, however, Andolsen acknowledges that the Eucharist itself is burdened
by sexism and sometimes by racism as well and is presently an ambiguous sacrament for feminists of both sexes. Nevertheless, she
values the Eucharist as a celebration between our present "broken-
ness" and our hoped for "wholeness," which is eminently capable
of nourishing "solidarity with economic 'outcasts' in the global
labor market." Thus Andolsen commends Eucharistic spirituality
as a way of growing in awareness of the problematic aspects of the
seemingly thriving economy of the United States: "Regular participation in the eucharist — with an openness to the values that it
embodies — should create and strengthen in worshipers a sense of
the connectedness among human beings, with the whole created
world, and with the Creator/Redeemer."[56]

The last two thinkers I shall discuss, **M. Shawn Copeland** and **Rosemary Radford Ruether**, are not active in the specialized guild of ethics or moral theology, but rather are identified with liberationist and political approaches to historical and systematic theology. Each is centrally concerned with matters of justice, however, and has published works that are appropriately called "feminist ethics."

M. Shawn Copeland, whose contributions to Black theology and liberationist political theology more generally date from the 1970s, even prior to her doctoral studies, now teaches at Marquette University. Like Andolsen, she has a particular interest in the situation of workers, especially factory and domestic workers, and the links between solidarity and Eucharistic practice. In an important essay published in 1995, she argues that "the Eucharist with its precise denotation of the meaning of the Incarnation of the Second Person of the Trinity as Jesus of Nazareth and his sacrifice for us illustrates in a most striking and accessible way the meaning of solidarity for Christians."[57] But, the Eucharist will be an "empty gesture," she maintains, "if we have not confessed our sins; repented of our participation and/or collusion in the marginalization of others. . . .if we have not moved to healing and creative Christian praxis." Copeland continues:

> The Eucharist is at the heart of the Christian community. . . . Eating the bread and drinking the cup involve something much deeper and more extensive than consuming the elements of this ritual meal. . . . there are social as well as sacramental consequences to the Eucharist. For to be one in Christ Jesus is to reject those systems of living that deprive women and men of human and political rights, that oppress the poor, that suppress women, that authorize racism, that promote discrimination against men and women because of fear of their sexual orientation, that obstruct the self-determination of the peoples of the world.[58]

In a 1987 essay, Copeland called for a "critical feminist theology" of global dimensions, "which refuses to rank or order oppression; which takes up the standpoint of the masses, the marginated and those beyond the margins; and which is committed to justice in the concrete." Overcoming the collusion of Christianity in the oppression of women and of people of color, Copeland points out, requires the collaboration of theologians with other analysts within and beyond the tradition, especially those trained in critical understandings of economics, sociology, and politics.[59]

In recent years, Copeland has bridged the discussion between womanists and other feminists, most explicitly in a groundbreaking 1994 address to the College Theology Society, which was quoted above for its insights on the Eucharist and solidarity. This lecture challenges Christian feminist theologians of all back-grounds to go beyond the *rhetoric* of solidarity and commit themselves to the *critical practice* of solidarity. Speaking at St. Mary's College, Notre Dame, on the occasion of the fiftieth anniversary of the first Catholic graduate program in theology open to women in this country, Copeland argues that

> focus on solidarity not only problematizes the practice of theology for Celtic, Anglo, European-American feminist theologians, but also for indigenous North American and Asian American women theologians, for *mujerista* and womanist theologians. Focus on solidarity calls for an end to facile adoption of the rhetoric of solidarity by Celtic-, Anglo-, European-American feminists, while they ignore and, sometimes, consume the experiences and voices of the marginalized and oppressed, while, ever adroitly, dodging the penitential call to conversion — to authenticity in word and deed.[60]

Authentic solidarity, she observes, means recognizing that common problems do not automatically lead to sisterhood and that differences must be respected, but not absolutized. Her suggestions for getting beyond "naïve, 'politically correct,' clichéd rhetoric of solidarity" to authentic Christian praxis are twofold. In the first place, she calls for "active and attentive listening" to differentiated voices within and beyond one's own community. Such listening demands different virtues of those who are relatively more implicated in systems of oppression than of those who are less so. Thus, she enjoins white women to practice humility, resolve, and relinquishment in an ongoing effort to balance attentive listening with appropriate speaking. She urges red, brown, yellow, and black women to forgo manipulative stances in favor of honesty, courage, and appropriate self criticism. And, she invites everyone to practice patience and restraint, "an ethics of respectful listening and an ethics of thinking before speaking," which is grounded theologically in the experience of God's liberating Word.[61]

In addition to this disciplined process of hearing and speaking, Copeland insists that a complex form of social analysis is also needed for the praxis of solidarity. This analysis involves critiquing one's own horizons, developing general descriptions of the factors at play in oppressive situations, probing the patterns that emerge from such descriptions, judging the incongruities thus uncovered in the light of the Gospel, and coming to specific decisions and commitments for action. The process is a continual one, and it is possible only in community and through the gift of God's Spirit.[62]

The implications of Copeland's critical perspective may be seen in a volume she coedited in 1994 with New Testament scholar, Elisabeth Schüssler Fiorenza, *Violence Against Women*. This book is a Christian theological and ethical analogue to such secular feminist works as the volume, *Transforming a Rape Culture*, published in 1993.[63] It gathers essays by women from Europe, Asia, and the Americas that explore the sociocultural factors, particularly gender construction and religious ideology, associated with violence against women in systems of patriarchal power. In a concluding essay, Copeland makes several proactive suggestions for change on the basis of her critical analysis of the material in this anthology. First, the Church must repent its historic misogyny as well as its ambivalence, complicity, and direct engagement in violence against women: ". . . the blood of raped, battered, abused and murdered women summons the church to its own *kenosis*," or self emptying in effective acts of penance that contribute to real change. Second, the Church must develop a new model of pastoral care that values women's experience and replaces the "aesthetic of submission" associated with so much religious imagery and ritual in favor of an "aesthetic of liberation" that will inspire a "non-oppressive, non-sexist truly human and Christian future." Third, the Church must adopt a renewed theological anthropology and challenge media and religious influences that reinforce unjust patterns in domestic relations, distort understandings of sexual desire and pleasure, and promote dualist or reductively "essentialist" views of women. Finally, the Church must develop a pastoral ministry that heals the effects of clergy sexual misconduct against women and children, thereby restoring their bodies to "erotic and spiritual integrity" and the Body of Christ to "ontological and sacramental integrity."[64]

Rosemary Radford Ruether: The sixth feminist ethicist is the most prolific, and I emphasize here only one dimension of her many contributions, namely, her recent work on ecofeminism, a topic that undoubtedly will increase in importance in the new century. What is now called ecofeminism is not a new interest for Ruether, however, for one of her earliest books deals with the connections between gender injustice and mistreatment of the earth.[65] Her analysis has deepened in subsequent years, and, in 1992, she published a wide ranging and scientifically informed work, *Gaia and God: An Ecofeminist Theology of Earth Healing*. There, Ruether argues that we must respect the interdependence of human and nonhuman living creatures and take action "in defense of the global commons of forests, oceans, and atmosphere." Major changes are needed, including the willingness to acknowledge that "life is not made whole 'once and for all,' in some static millennium of the future. It is made whole again and again, in the renewed day born from night and in the new spring that rises from each winter."[66] Her 1998 book, *Women and Redemption: A Theological History*, takes the argument from there and probes the way different interpretations of this central religious mystery have developed in Christian history, culminating in the new possibilities emerging from contemporary feminist theologies. Drawing on her training in classics and historical theology, Ruether traces the connections between ideas of gender and redemption in the New Testament and in the patristic, medieval, and reformation periods of Church history. The theme is then pursued in several chapters dealing with particular regions: one discussing North American Shakers and feminist abolitionists of the nineteenth century, and three that survey recent feminist theologies in Europe, North America, and the vast territories of Latin America, Africa, and Asia. She looks especially to these last approaches for insight toward building "a more authentic basis for solidarity among women, and between men and women, to rebuild more life-sustaining societies in their own lands and between nations on a threatened Earth."[67]

Ruether's commitment to solidarity with marginalized groups is longstanding. She took part as a Delta ministries volunteer in Mississippi in 1965 and spent her first years of seminary teaching (1965-1976) at the Divinity School of Howard University, an historically Black institution in Washington, D.C.[68] In a groundbreaking 1974 study, she challenged Christians to rethink their attitudes towards Jews, and, more recently, she has also lifted up the concerns of the Palestinians and drawn attention to the sufferings brought upon the people of Iraq by the airstrikes and economic sanctions of the United States.[69] Her interests in ecology and in justice for women everywhere led her to edit an anthology in which she brings voices from Africa, Asia, and Latin America to a wide readership in North America and Europe.[70]

There is a prophetic urgency to Ruether's Introduction to this collection in which she surveys North American feminisms and finds some lacking, especially when they fail to make the connections between "their actual social context as heirs and beneficiaries of [patriarchal] conquest as First World affluent people." Merely to deal with the psychospiritual level by reconnecting with nature and celebrating embodiment, she maintains,

> can become a recreational self-indulgence for a privileged countercultural Northern elite if these are the *only* ideas and practices of ecofeminism; if the healing of our bodies and our imaginations as Euro-Americans is not connected concretely with the following realities of over-consumerism and waste: the top 20 percent of the world's human population enjoys 82 percent of the wealth while the . . . poorest 20 percent of the world's people, over a *billion* people — disproportionately women and children — starve and die early from poisoned waters, soil, and air.[71]

Ruether discerns two notable differences between the Northern ecofeminists and those writing from Asian, African, and Latin American contexts. In the first place, the latter group is much more vividly aware of the human and economic factors involved in ecological devastation, for these women know on a daily basis the way drought and deforestation cause hardship and death. Secondly, they are more likely to be realistic in recognizing the ambiguities both of Christian and tribal traditions, instead of tending, as many Northern women do, rigidly to condemn their own Western Christian heritage while romantically idealizing tribal cultures. Ruether believes that studying the analyses from African, Asian, and Latin American women's perspectives can inspire European and North American feminists to keep more focused on the connections among their own economic privileges, the impoverishment of the world's majority, and the diminishing quality of earth's soil, air, and water. She also hopes that the examples of "third world" women will encourage Northern ecofeminists to be "less dogmatic and more creative about what is good and bad, usable and problematic, in our own cultural legacies," drawing out the good from traditions that range from Hebrew, Greek, and Christian, to Nordic, Celtic, Slavic, and modern.[72]

   Additional examples of solidarity: As I indicated at the outset of this section, the above list is limited to six authors simply for reasons of space. Among many other Catholic feminist ethicists whose work exhibits the quality of solidarity with those who are "other," three deserve special mention because of their stature in the field. **Christine E. Gudorf**, whose writing is included elsewhere in this volume, is the author of important books on victimization and sexual ethics.[73] She has also worked with others to prepare volumes of case studies for discussion by students, most recently a forward looking collection coedited with Regina Wentzel Wolfe.[74] **Lisa Sowle Cahill**, whose books deal with a range of topics including bioethics, sexual ethics, and issues of war and peace, has also written on feminism with particular attention to crosscultural concerns.[75] Cahill used the occasion of her 1993 presidential address to the CTSA to probe "Feminist Ethics and the Challenge of Cultures," concluding with a challenge to her colleagues: "How can the Catholic theological academy both account for theoretically and underwrite practically the struggle of women worldwide to live their lives for themselves and for others with human dignity?"[76] Finally, **Mary E. Hunt**, who, like Ruether, is an activist as well as a theologian, has not only written an important study on friendship, but has also encouraged networking among feminists of various backgrounds and callings, especially through the organization she founded in 1983 with Diann L. Neu, the Women's Alliance for Theology, Ethics, and Ritual (W.A.T.E.R.).[77] Of particular interest here is Hunt's leadership in promoting conversations among ecofeminists in the Americas through a series of gatherings in 1997 and 1998 called "A Shared Garden." Graciela Pujol, a Uruguayan who participated in these meetings — held first in

Santiago, Chile, next in Washington, D.C., and then in Recife, Brazil — observes that they have been "irreplaceably rich experience[s]," especially for "women who had never before left their homeland or their city." She comments thus on what participants concluded after visiting several poor neighborhoods in northeast Brazil: "Change was not viewed among these women as anything in the near future . . . . But they did have a stubborn trust in solidarity, as the one way to survival."[78]

A commitment to solidarity characterizes the work of a number of other Catholic feminists who are working in the field of ethics, in addition to those who have been mentioned above. Their efforts, as well as the efforts of those who labor in other theological disciplines and in various practical ministries, are helping to shape a future that will be more just, less violent, and friendlier to the earth than the past we have known in the twentieth century has been.[79]

III. Living in the Meantime

I find it daunting to imagine what challenges the new millennium will bring to feminist ethics, and I am not enough of a futurist to feel confident in listing priorities even where the twenty-first century is concerned. Certainly, such political and economic developments as new forms of warfare (for instance, air campaigns that minimize risk to the military personnel of the powerful, democratic nations while tolerating "collateral damage" to civilians in the enemy countries) and the globalization of banking, industry, and commerce, will call for creative responses from ethics. Certainly, concerns about the environment, health care, and technologies of all sorts will mount, especially those that affect the genetic makeup and reproduction of our species. Feminist ethics will, I hope, bring to these issues its commitment to the well being of women and its attention to women's experience in all its complexity. I believe it will contribute much to the discussions, since women's well being is constitutive of the wider common good that all ethics must seek.

My emphasis in terms of future recommendations will be more general here, however. Ethics has grown very much specialized in the twentieth century, and, although the complexity of new problems warrants this development, I would like to see Catholic feminist ethics contribute a balancing emphasis on some matters that cut across the various subfields that have developed within ethics, not only those organized around such practical topics as bioethics and sexual ethics, but also those designated as "feminist," "womanist," "*mujerista*," and so on into the increasingly diverse future. Of course, these specialties are important, and it has been

important to name and describe them, but, whatever else femi-
nist/womanist/and *mujerista* ethicists are doing, I hope that we will
feel sufficiently established as we enter the new millennium to give
our energies to matters that transcend these projects. I also hope
that feminist ethics in the future will rise to four challenges that it
faces:

1. *Staying ecclesial,* despite discouraging signals from the hierarchical Magisterium where certain topics of great concern to
women are involved. I agree with Barbara H. Andolsen and M.
Shawn Copeland that the Eucharistic community is important for
fostering the practical solidarity that the feminist ethical agenda
require, and I also think that we need this community to sustain
our faith, hope, and love on a long term basis. Eucharist done in
memory of Jesus and the divine gift of salvation can be an occasion
of grace and solidarity for all. Where else is it likely that the poor,
middle class, and wealthy members of society will encounter one
another as persons? Where else can those blinded by greed and
paralyzed by fear learn to let go of what blocks their human flourishing and set out with new energy to live justly and walk humbly
with their God? Surely, God's grace is not confined to the rituals of
any tradition and, surely, a principled absence from services that
are noninclusive and alienating can be justified as a survival strategy. But, Christian feminists who do observe this contemporary
version of "Eucharistic fast" will need to find satisfying answers to
the "where else" questions I have raised, for a spirituality cut off
from communion with the poor and disenfranchised members of
society, who tend to show up in Church more often than they do
in spas and conference centers, is at risk of becoming one more
consumer item. Moreover, the ongoing reform of the Church requires the presence of members who claim to have the vision of
what God is calling the Church to become.

2. *Gaining a public voice,* now that the academic one seems reasonably secure in view of so many women having gained tenure
and recognition in professional circles. I hope the twenty-first century will see more women trained in moral theology who write
regularly for the Catholic and secular press and who appear as
experts on radio and television. Such thinkers have much to bring
to public debates on such matters as genetic research, the use of
fetal tissue in developing medical treatments, the problem of gun
violence, and other issues that will emerge in the future. Rosemary
Radford Ruether writes often on current issues in the *National
Catholic Reporter,* Lisa Sowle Cahill contributes occasionally to
America, and Carol A. Tauer brings insight to bioethics discussions
on *Almanac,* a local public affairs program produced by the PBS af-
filiate in St. Paul-Minneapolis (KTCA), but, for the most part,
Catholic feminist ethicists have not broken into the national secu-

lar media. We should challenge ourselves and encourage each other to send essays to such journals as *The Atlantic Monthly* and *The New Yorker* and op ed pieces to such newspapers as *The Washington Post, The New York Times,* and *The Los Angeles Times.*

3. *Contributing more directly, not only to virtue theory, but also to the education of persons, especially the young, to virtue as it is coming to be newly understood.* This will mean collaborating with other fields beyond ethics, notably with experts in education and the helping professions.[80] These fields are less prestigious and well heeled than medicine, a prominent conversation partner with ethics in the twentieth century, but they are, nonetheless, crucial for changing a society that now promotes greed and consumerism as if they were social goods. Besides solidarity, my wish list of virtues to be emphasized includes newly interpreted versions of justice, patience, chastity, sobriety, and hope.

4. *Giving thought to the practical details of shaping a new order* that avoids the injustices of patriarchy while carrying on the necessary functions that this problematic form of social organization has, despite its faults, accomplished in the past. In other words, now that the feminist critique of patriarchy has gained a solid footing, we should give more attention to constructing and sustaining alternative social patterns.

IV. Conclusion: The Dream of a Common Moral Language

The present essay has argued that Catholic feminist ethics is contributing to the renewal of moral theology called for by the Council and that it is poised to do much in the new millennium toward realizing the Conciliar goal of "bearing fruit for the life of the world." I have indicated that the practice of solidarity by men of justice was instrumental in women's gaining access to the guild of theological ethics and that, since gaining access, these women have enriched our understanding of what solidarity entails, not only by their theoretical reflections, but also by their own practice. I have articulated several challenges now facing the field, and I conclude by observing that the labors of these feminists are helping the wider human community to implement four principles that were agreed to in 1993 by representatives of various traditions as part of a "Declaration Toward a Global Ethic." These principles are:

1. Commitment to a culture of nonviolence and respect for life.
2. Commitment to a culture of solidarity and a just economic order.
3. Commitment to a culture of tolerance and a life of truthfulness.
4. Commitment to a culture of equal rights and partnership between men and women.[81]

Signatories to this 1993 Declaration included persons from many faith traditions: Bahais, Brahma Kumaris, Buddhists, Christians, Hindus, Jains, Jews, Muslims, Neopagans, Sikhs, Taoists, Theosophists, Zoroastrians, and representatives of several indigenous religions (including Akuapi, Yoruba, and Native American) as well as a few interreligious organizations. Catholics contributed much to this Declaration, and our moral tradition has a great deal of wisdom to bring to the task its signatories identified as incumbent on all religions today, namely, to convert the world's peoples to "a common global ethic, to better mutual understanding, as well as to socially-beneficial, peace-fostering, and Earth-friendly ways of life."[82]

It has been my contention here that Catholic feminist ethics is playing a crucial role in helping to bring about this conversion to a common global ethic. For the first part of the new millennium, it will continue to have a distinct identity and to play this role. But, eventually, its goals will have been reached, and feminist ethics can then make a graceful exit from the scene. Thanks to the divine Spirit, who works mysteriously in our ambiguous lives and history to renew the face of the earth, Catholics will eventually succeed in clearing the impediments of patriarchy from the stream of moral wisdom that is our heritage. We will then begin to realize the dream of a "common moral language" through which insights and questions can be shared among ourselves and with others in ways that are both intelligible and beneficial.

NOTES

[1]Quoted here from Walter M. Abbott, ed., *The Documents of Vatican II* (New York: The America Press, 1966), 227-228. Subsequent references to Conciliar documents are from this widely studied edition. For a new, inclusive language translation, see Austin Flannery, O. P., ed., *Vatican Council II: Basic Edition* (Collegeville: Liturgical Press, 1996). For a fuller discussion of the impact of *Gaudium et Spes*, see Anne E. Patrick, "Toward Renewing 'The Life and Culture of Fallen Man': *Gaudium et Spes* as Catalyst for Catholic Feminist Theology," in Judith A. Dwyer, ed., *Questions of Special Urgency: The Church in the Modern World Two Decades after Vatican II* (Washington, D.C.: Georgetown University Press, 1986), 55-78.
[2]My own volume, *Liberating Conscience: Feminist Explorations in Catholic Moral Theology* (New York: Continuum, 1996), from which I draw occasionally in the present essay, aims to contribute to this task of developing moral theology.
[3]Ibid., 12-13.
[4]Adrienne Rich, *The Dream of a Common Language: Poems 1974-1977* (New York: W. W. Norton & Company, 1978).
[5]See Gustavo Gutierrez, *A Theology of Liberation*, rev. ed. (Maryknoll, NY: Orbis, 1988), xlvi.
[6]Gerda Lerner, *The Creation of Feminist Consciousness* (New York: Oxford University Press, 1993), 14. She believes that patriarchy depends on mis-

taken assumptions about gender, which "constructed the male as the norm and the female as deviant; the male as whole and powerful; the female as unfinished, physically mutilated and emotionally dependent" (p. 3).

[7]This definition is discussed in Patrick, *Liberating Conscience*, 7-8.

[8]Elizabeth A. Johnson, *She Who Is: The Mystery of God in Feminist Theological Discourse* (New York: Crossroad, 1992), 22.

[9]Elizabeth A. Johnson, *Women, Earth, and Creator Spirit* (New York: Paulist, 1993), 24.

[10]Patricia Beattie Jung, "Give Her Justice," *America* 150 (April 14, 1984), 276-78.

[11]For influential examples of these approaches, see Delores S. Williams, *Sisters in the Wilderness: The Challenge of Womanist God-Talk* (Maryknoll, NY: Orbis, 1993), and Ada María Isasi-Díaz, *Mujerista Theology* (Maryknoll, NY: Orbis, 1996). Alice Walker's original description of "womanist" opens her volume, *In Search of Our Mother's Gardens: Womanist Prose* (San Diego: Harcourt Brace Jovanovich, 1983), xi-xii.

[12]Catharine R. Stimson, "The 'F' Word," *Ms.* (July/August,1987), 80.

[13]Ibid., 196.

[14]Richard A. McCormick, *Notes on Moral Theology 1965 Through 1980* (Washington, D.C.: University Press of America, 1981), 385.

[15]Ibid., 392.

[16]*N.Y. Globe*, 22 June 1911 (*Documents of the Catholic Bishops against Women's Suffrage, 1910-1920*; Sophia Smith Collection, Smith College). Quoted here from Rosemary Radford Ruether, "Home and Work: Women's Roles and the Transformation of Values," *Theological Studies* 36 (1975): 653.

[17]McCormick, 392.

[18]David Hollenbach, "Seminar on Moral Theology: The Future Agenda of Catholic Moral Theology in America," *CTSA Proceedings* 37 (1982): 176. Hollenbach summarized several panelists on this topic, including McCormick, whose reflections were revised and published elsewhere; see note no. 19 below.

[19]Richard A. McCormick, "Moral Theological Agenda: An Overview," *New Catholic World* 226 (Jan./Feb., 1983): 4-5.

[20]Raymond A. Lucker, "Justice in the Church: The Church as an Example," in *One Hundred Years of Social Thought*, ed. John A. Coleman (Maryknoll, NY: Orbis, 1991), 100. The late auxiliary bishop of Baltimore, P. Francis Murphy, was also outspoken on this topic. Indeed, in an editorial published shortly after his funeral, the *National Catholic Reporter* noted that "Murphy was unyielding in his support for women's ordination, even in an era when many bishops refrain from making any favorable comment on the issue in public for fear of reaction from the far right and discipline by the Vatican" ("For the Bishop, a Fittingly Provocative Sendoff," 24 September 1999, p. 32).

[21]Pope John Paul II, "Ordinatio Sacerdotalis," #4 ("Apostolic Letter on Ordination and Women"), *Origins* 24 (9 June 1994): 51.

[22]Lavinia Byrne, *Woman at the Altar: The Ordination of Women in the Roman Catholic Church* (New York: Continuum, 1998). The work was originally published by Cassell in Great Britain in 1994.

[23]Rosemary Radford Ruether, *Liberation Theology: Human Hope Confronts Christian History and American Power* (New York: Paulist, 1972).

[24]For example, one of my own early articles, "Women and Religion: A Survey of Significant Literature, 1965-1974," was written at Burghardt's invitation during my second year of studies at the University of Chicago Divinity School and published in *Theological Studies* 36 (December, 1975): 737-66.
    [25]*CTSA Proceedings* 50 (1995): 302. Current statistics are available in the latest directory.
    [26]*Proceedings of the Catholic Theological Society of America* 54 (1999). General information about the CTSA is available at: **http://carver.holy-cross.edu/organizations/ctsa.html.**
    [27]Margaret A. Farley, "Ethics and Moral Theologies," in Letty M. Russell and J. Shannon Clarkson, eds., *Dictionary of Feminist Theologies* (Louisville: Westminster /John Knox Press, 1996): 89.
    [28]Barbara Hilkert Andolsen, Christine E. Gudorf, Mary D. Pellauer, eds., "Introduction," *Women's Consciousness, Women's Conscience* (Minneapolis: Winston Press, 1985), xii-xiii.
    [29]Ibid., xv.
    [30]Lisa Sowle Cahill, "Presidential Address: Feminist Ethics and the Challenge of Cultures," *CTSA Proceedings* 48 (1993): 73.
    [31]Ibid., 77.
    [32]Elizabeth A. Johnson, *She Who Is*, 8.
    [33]Ibid., 11.
    [34]Matthew L. Lamb, "Solidarity," in Judith A. Dwyer, ed., *The New Dictionary of Catholic Social Thought* (Collegeville, MN: Liturgical Press, 1994), 908.
    [35]Pope John Paul II, quoted in Lamb, 909.
    [36]Pope John Paul II, *Sollicitudo Rei Socialis*, #39, quoted here from Jean-Yves Calvez, "Sollicitudo rei socialis," *The New Dictionary of Catholic Social Thought*, 915.
    [37]Ada María Isasi-Díaz and Yolanda Tarango, *Hispanic Women: Prophetic Voice in the Church* (San Francisco: Harper & Row, 1988).
    [38]Ada María Isasi-Díaz, *En La Lucha: A Hispanic Women's Liberation Theology* (Minneapolis: Fortress, 1993).
    [39]Ada María Isasi-Díaz, *Mujerista Theology: A Theology for the Twenty-first Century* (Maryknoll: Orbis, 1996), 32.
    [40]Ibid., 35.
    [41]Isasi-Díaz and Tarango, *Hispanic Women*, 53.
    [42]Margaret A. Farley, *Personal Commitments: Beginning, Keeping, Changing* (San Francisco: Harper & Row, 1986), 7.
    [43]Ibid., 99.
    [44]Margaret A. Farley, *Just Love* (New York: Continuum, 2000). Earlier works include the articles, "Sexual Ethics," in Warren T. Reich, ed., *The Encyclopedia of Bioethics* (New York: Macmillan Library Reference, 1998), and "An Ethic for Same-Sex Relations," in Robert Nugent, ed., *A Challenge to Love* (New York: Crossroad, 1983), 93-106.
    [45]"Secretary's Report: John Courtney Murray Award," *CTSA Proceedings* 47 (1992): 185.
    [46]*CTSA Proceedings* 54 (1999).
    [47]Patricia Beattie Jung and Thomas A. Shannon, eds., *Abortion and Catholicism: The Catholic Debate* (New York: Crossroad, 1988), 4.
    [48]Patricia Beattie Jung and Ralph F. Smith, *Heterosexism: An Ethical Challenge* (Albany: State University of New York Press, 1993), 13.

[49]Ibid., 10.

[50]Barbara Hilkert Andolsen, *Daughters of Jefferson, Daughters of Bootblacks: Racism and American Feminism* (Macon, GA: Mercer University Press, 1986). Recently, Andolsen edited the professional resources section of *The Annual of the Society of Christian Ethics* on "Selected Topics in Feminist and Womanist Ethics" (Washington, D.C.: Georgetown University Press, 1994), 257-305.

[51]Barbara Hilkert Andolsen, *Good Work at the Video Display Terminal: An Ethical Analysis of the Effects of Office Automation on Clerical Workers* (Knoxville: University of Tennessee Press, 1989).

[52]Barbara Hilkert Andolsen, *The New Job Contract: Economic Justice in an Age of Insecurity* (Cleveland: Pilgrim Press, 1998), vii.

[53]Ibid., 4-5.

[54]Ibid., ix.

[55]Ibid., 119.

[56]Ibid., 137.

[57]M. Shawn Copeland, "Toward a Critical Christian Feminist Theology of Solidarity," in Mary Ann Hinsdale and Phyllis H. Kaminski, eds., *Women and Theology* (Maryknoll: Orbis, 1995), 27.

[58]Ibid., 30-31.

[59]M. Shawn Copeland, "The Interaction of Racism, Sexism and Classism in Women's Exploitation," in *Women, Work and Poverty*, ed. Elisabeth Schüssler Fiorenza and Anne E. Carr (Edinburgh: T & T Clark, 1987), 25-26.

[60]Copeland, "Toward a Critical Christian Feminist Theology of Solidarity," 3.

[61]Ibid., 25-26.

[62]Ibid., 28-29.

[63]Emilie Buchwald, Pamela R. Fletcher, and Martha Roth, eds., *Transforming a Rape Culture* (Minneapolis: Milkweed Editions, 1993). The editors define a "rape culture" as "a complex of beliefs that encourages male sexual aggression and supports violence against women" (p. vii).

[64]M. Shawn Copeland, "Editorial Reflections," in Elisabeth Schüssler Fiorenza and Copeland, eds., *Violence Against Women* (Maryknoll, NY: Orbis, 1994), 121-22.

[65]Rosemary Radford Ruether, *Liberation Theology*; the chapter, "Mother Earth and the Megamachine: A Theology of Liberation in a Feminine, Somatic and Ecological Perspective," is especially relevant (pp. 115-26).

[66]Rosemary Radford Ruether, *Gaia and God: An Ecofeminist Theology of Earth Healing* (San Francisco: HarperSanFrancisco, 1992), 272-73.

[67]Rosemary Radford Ruether, *Women and Redemption: A Theological History* (Minneapolis: Fortress Press, 1998).

[68]Rosemary Radford Ruether, "The Development of My Theology," *Religious Studies Review* 15 (January, 1989): 1.

[69]See Rosemary Radford Ruether, *Faith and Fratricide: The Theological Roots of Anti-Semitism* (New York: Seabury, 1974); Rosemary Radford Ruether and Herman J. Ruether, *The Wrath of Jonah: The Crisis of Religious Nationalism in the Israeli-Palestinian Conflict* (New York: Harper & Row, 1989); and, Rosemary Radford Ruether's dedication in *Gaia and God*: " . . . to Adiba Hkader and her four daughters, Ghada (twenty-one), Abir (seven-

teen), Ghalda (fourteen), and Ghana (twelve), and all the other mothers and children who died in the early morning of February 13, 1991, in a bomb shelter in Baghdad that was shattered by two American 'smart bombs.'"

[70]Rosemary Radford Ruether, *Women Healing Earth: Third-World Women on Ecology, Feminism and Religion* (Maryknoll, NY: Orbis, 1996).

[71]Ibid., 5.

[72]Ibid., 7.

[73]Christine E. Gudorf, V*ictimization: Examining Christian Complicity* (Philadelphia: Trinity Press International, 1992), and *Body, Sex, and Pleasure: Reconstructing Christian Sexual Ethics* (Cleveland: The Pilgrim Press, 1994).

[74]Regina Wentzel Wolfe and Christine E. Gudorf, eds., *Ethics and World Religions: Cross-Cultural Case Studies* (Maryknoll, NY: Orbis, 1999); see also Robert L. Stivers, Christine E. Gudorf, et al., eds. *Christian Ethics: A Case Method Approach*, 2nd ed. rev. (Maryknoll, NY: Orbis, 1994).

[75]Lisa Sowle Cahill's recent books include a volume coedited with Margaret A. Farley, *Embodiment, Morality, and Medicine* (Dordrecht: Kluwer Academic Publishers, 1995), as well as two studies she authored, *Sex, Gender, and Christian Ethics* (Cambridge: Cambridge University Press, 1996), and *Love Your Enemies: Discipleship, Pacifism, and Just War Theory* (Minneapolis: Fortress, 1994).

[76]Lisa Sowle Cahill, *op. cit.*, 83. A revised version of this paper is published under the title "Feminist Ethics, Differences, and Common Ground: A Catholic Perspective," in C. Curran, M. Farley, and R. McCormick, eds., *Feminist Ethics and the Catholic Moral Tradition* (Mahwah, NJ: Paulist Press, 1992), 184-99. See also Cahill, "Moral Theology and the World Church," *CTSA Proceedings* 39 (1984): 35-51, and "Feminist Ethics," *Theological Studies* 51(March, 1990): 49-64.

[77]Mary E. Hunt, *Fierce Tenderness: A Feminist Theology of Friendship* (New York: Crossroad, 1991). Besides publishing *WATERwheel*, a newsletter containing brief essays and lists of resources, Hunt and Neu maintain a website of information on feminist issues in religion at **www.hers.com/water**.

[78]Graciela Pujol, "Miracles from Shared Gardens," trans. Sally Hanlon, *WATERwheel* 11 (Winter, 1998-99): 6.

[79]In addition to the thinkers discussed above, several other Catholics who have contributed substantially to ethics are also represented in the anthology, *Feminist Ethics and the Catholic Moral Tradition*, including Sidney Callahan, Toinette Eugene, Christine Firer Hinze, Susan A. Ross, and Maura A. Ryan.

[80]The Minnesota author, Carol Bly, has shown leadership here by publishing *Changing the Bully Who Rules the World: Reading and Thinking About Ethics* (Minneapolis: Milkweed Editions, 1996).

[81]Hans Küng and Karl-Josef Kuschel, eds., *A Global Ethic: The Declaration of the Parliament of the World's Religions* (New York: Continuum, 1993), 24-26.

[82]Ibid., 36.

Ethics/Civil Law in the New Millennium

M. Cathleen Kaveny

I. INTRODUCTION

How should we understand the relationship of law and morality? As a preliminary matter, let me emphasize that no one denies either that there is some relationship between the two realms, on the one hand, or that they do not entirely overlap, on the other. For example, no one doubts the immorality of many criminal activities, such as robbery, rape, and murder. Moreover, the very reasons that we consider them immoral, which generally have to do with the grave and unjust harm they do to other people, are the reasons that the full weight of the law is brought to bear against them.

However, not every activity that is immoral can or should be made illegal; conversely, not every act that is morally required can be legally mandated. Noncontroversial examples of arguably immoral activities that are beyond the scope of the law to remedy include wishing others ill, even hating them, breaking promises, and betraying or lying to friends and family. It is uncontroversial that the power of the civil and criminal law should not be used to prevent most garden variety manifestations of the seven deadly sins that appear in the lives of those we know and in our own lives. Many moral duties also lie beyond the province of law, such as the personal obligation to provide aid to the poor, to comfort the sick, and to perform the other corporal and spiritual acts of mercy. However, despite the significant agreement about most cases, there are examples of arguably immoral activity whose legal status has generated a great deal of controversy.

One cluster of these cases revolves around the role that consent should play in eliminating activity from eligibility for legal prohibition. For example, some people doubt whether the law should prohibit any consensual sexual activities, including prostitution. Doubts also exist about criminalizing harmful activities in cases where the person being harmed has given her/his consent to the activity. In some cases, such as abusing drugs or refusing to wear a motorcycle helmet or a seatbelt, the agent harms (or risks harming) her/himself. In other activities, the agent harms (or risks harming) another party, who has also given her/his consent to the enterprise. Examples here can range from consensual duels to voluntary euthanasia.

A second cluster of cases revolves around the question of whether and how activities must be harmful before they are eligible targets for legal prohibitions. A key question is what counts as "harmful" behavior. Is the loss of a community's traditional way of life harmful? Is the fact that other people are privately and consensually engaging in immoral acts (e.g., incest, watching pornography) harmful to those who know or suspect it is occurring? Is it necessarily harmful to a person to corrupt her/his moral character?

A. Practical Limits

How, then, do we decide which part of morality should be backed by the sanctions of law? Everyone agrees that certain *practical considerations* must be considered in making the decision. These include:

1. *The Logistics of Enforcement*

Legal precepts are not self executing. Once promulgated, they must be enforced. Violations must be detected before they can be punished. One reason that it is imprudent to enact laws prohibiting a significant range of immoral activity is that it would be virtually impossible to detect its occurrence. What tools, for example, will allow law enforcement officers to detect the countless times that one individual formulates an uncharitable or unjust attitude toward another individual, provided that those attitudes do not manifest themselves in concrete actions? Moreover, it is practically impossible for law enforcement to detect most instances where unjust or unkind intentions do result in immoral actions. Do we really expect the State to send a representative into every house to monitor the cruel words, thoughtless behavior, and day-to-day injustices that family members inflict upon one another?

2. *The Expense of Enforcement*

It costs money to detect crime, deter crime, prosecute accused criminals, and imprison convicted ones. Money is a finite resource; if it is spent on these activities, it cannot be dedicated to advancing other aspects of the common good (e.g., food, housing, education, the arts). Before deciding to criminalize a given activity, wise lawmakers must consider whether it is appropriate to spend money on deterring, detecting, and prosecuting instances of it. In the case of some actions, such as murder, rape, and robbery, the threat to the integrity of the person and property of the victims is so great that no State could credibly claim to be fulfilling its basic responsibilities to its citizens without attempting to prevent and punish these actions by means of the criminal law. But, the requirements of the common good are not so clear with respect to so called "victimless" crimes, such as prostitution or even drug use. Moreover, the imperative to deploy societal resources wisely can arise in the context of activity that triggers the machinery of the civil, as opposed to the criminal, law. To establish new private causes of action means that public resources will be devoted to adjudicating claims arising under them and that private resources will be dedicated to bringing and defending those claims.[1]

3. *Threat to Other Values*

The very act of investigating alleged violations of the law has other costs that cannot be measured in money. Sometimes, the very means required to enforce certain laws will destroy other values we want to protect. For example, in *Griswold* v. *Connecticut*, the Supreme Court of the United States considered the constitutionality of a state law that prohibited the use of contraceptives by married couples. Writing for the Court, Justice William O. Douglas held that the statute was unconstitutional, because it violated the right to privacy. In so holding, he focused on the fact that the very act of investigating alleged instances of this crime would require the police to invade the marital bedroom.[2]

B. Moral Limits

In addition to the practical limits outlined above, are there also *moral limits* to the manner in which law should endeavor to enforce morality? To put the question another way, is it *morally wrong* for the law to enforce certain moral prohibitions or requirements? If so, which ones? What aspect of morality can the law morally enforce? In the remainder of this essay, I will look at two fundamentally different answers to this question that legal theorists have given over the centuries, which are captured in two different metaphors about the nature of law: law as police officer and law as teacher.

"Law as police officer" is the metaphor that evokes the basic approach of much contemporary liberal legal theory. In essence, this approach to the relationship of law and morality says that the role of the law as an enforcer of morality is extremely limited, and essentially negative, in function. Properly understood, law should function like a police officer guarding the boundaries of a piece of property. Its purpose is to keep people from acting in ways that wrongfully harm others, not to inculcate a vision of the way they should live and flourish together. Moreover, in this view, not only is the inculcation of such a vision beyond the scope of law's purpose, but it is actually inconsistent with it. According to liberal legal theorists, it would be no more appropriate for the positive law to tell its members which view of human flourishing to adopt than it is for the security guard protecting the boundaries of your neighbor's property to tell you what type of grass to grow on your lawn.

A contrasting metaphor for the nature and purpose of law is "law as teacher" and, more specifically, law as teacher of virtue. This metaphor encapsulates the basic jurisprudential approach found in the work of Saint Thomas Aquinas. At its core, this approach to law is essentially positive. It understands the general purpose of law as furthering the common good which, in turn, furthers the good of the particular individuals who live within the community.

More specifically, in the "law as teacher" model, law is a crude, but nonetheless effective, way of teaching persons some of the habits of behavior that are required for living within the community. Certainly, negative prohibitions, such as "do not murder," "do not rape," and "do not rob," are central features of the law, particularly the criminal law. But, they are situated within, and point toward, the more positive goals of insuring that all people possess the basic character traits that will allow them to participate in, and flourish within, the society and that the society itself is the sort of place in which it is worthwhile to live.

In the remainder of this essay, I will explore these two fundamentally different metaphors for law in more detail. First, I will suggest that the "law as police officer" model is seriously inadequate in several respects. Second, I will argue that the major challenge posed to American jurisprudence in the new millennium is to recover an understanding of law as a teacher of virtue that is flexible and sophisticated enough to work in our diverse and pluralistic society. Third, taking the Americans with Disabilities Act as a case study, I will suggest that the model of law as a teacher of virtue already accounts for existing strands in American law better than does the "law as police officer" model, strands which need to be strengthened as we move into the twenty-first century.

II. LAW AS POLICE OFFICER

The model of "law as police officer" is embodied in most liberal legal theory, particularly its application of what has come to be known as the "harm principle." By "liberal legal theory" I mean that strand of legal thought that owes its basic insight to John Stuart Mill's *On Liberty*. Its most eloquent and effective contemporary advocate is the late philosopher, Joel Feinberg.[3] Rather than adding to the countless generalities that have been made about "liberalism" and "liberal theory" in the past decade or so, I will develop my points with reference to Feinberg's work.

A. The Harm Principle

As the name suggests, liberal legal theorists, including Feinberg, place great moral value on the liberty of each individual to live life in the manner that she/he sees fit. Threats to individual liberty can stem from many sources, including peer pressure to conform to the prevailing standards of thought and behavior. Nonetheless, the most serious threat to liberty comes from those who control the government, for they can deploy the coercive measures of law (particularly the criminal law) to limit the liberty of others. It is one thing to resist informal peer pressure to live life according to one's own lights; it is an entirely different matter to risk capture, trial, and even imprisonment to do so.

Consequently, liberal legal theorists maintain that the circumstances in which the State may legitimately interfere with individual liberty must be stringently limited and clearly defined. The most important such limit on State authority (or more accurately, set of limits) is frequently called the "harm principle." At its core, the harm principle holds that the sanctions of the criminal law should be used only to prevent people from wrongfully causing harm to others. What precisely does this mean, at least according to Joel Feinberg?

First, it is important to note that, in his articulation of the harm principle, Feinberg defines the "harm" that is the appropriate target of the criminal law in a highly specific way. The term encompasses only *setbacks to a person's interests* that are at the same time a *violation of that person's rights.*[4]

Feinberg's account of human interests is, in the end, individualistic and subjective. More specifically, he maintains that our ulterior interests are valuable because we want them, not because they are good in and of themselves. Generally speaking, however, it is beyond the power of law to promote the ulterior interests that each of us has developed. Instead, the law focuses its energy on protecting our *welfare* interests which include a predictable span of life, health, absence of pain and disfigurement, financial security, and a certain amount of freedom.[5] Welfare interests are necessary instruments to the achievement of a wide variety of ulterior interests; consequently, in protecting them, the law indirectly promotes our ulterior interests.

But, according to Feinberg, an act has to do more than set back someone's interests in order to qualify as a harm. It also has to be a wrongful act. On one level, this requirement clearly makes sense. For example, it obviously hurts a professional athlete's interests to lose rather than to win; but, unless some wrongful act was performed, the better player does her/his opponent no harm in beating her/him in the competition. It obviously harms both a thief's immediate and long term interests for me to resist her/his attempts to "liberate" my money for her/his own use. My resistance, however, does not qualify as wrongful.

What can the law do, then, if it is primarily charged with preventing and punishing wrongful setbacks to the interests of individuals? On Feinberg's interpretation of the harm principle, the State has abundant moral authority to function as a police officer, which centrally includes preventing physical harms to people and property. The State can criminally prohibit and punish such tangible harms to persons as murder, rape, kidnapping, and assault. It can also prohibit theft of both tangible and intangible property, because such theft involves a setback to a person's interest that at the same time violates her/his rights.

Feinberg's definition of "harm," however, does eliminate a great number of morally questionable activities from the pool of morally appropriate targets of the criminal law. For example, the first component of that definition, which requires a harm to be a setback to an individual's "interests" as Feinberg defines them, rules out the possibility of criminalizing activity that corrupts the morals of another. On the basis of his subjectivist understanding of "interests," Feinberg maintains that to corrupt someone else's character is not properly speaking to harm her/him. He maintains that being morally upright is in the ulterior interest only of those who have an antecedent desire to have a sterling character; it is not in the ulterior interest of those who do not have such a desire.[6]

The second prong of Feinberg's definition of harm, which requires setbacks of interests to be "wrongful," also rules out the criminalization of a significant range of morally suspect activities. For example, the maxim from Roman law, "*volenti non fit injuria*" ("to the one who has consented no wrong is done"), concisely expresses the view that the law should not provide a remedy for "victims" who consent to participate in the activities that cause them harm. On the basis of the *volenti* maxim, one could challenge the laws that give the losers of foolish bets recourse against those who took their money from them.[7] One might also challenge laws that punish the victors in fisticuffs or consensual duels.[8]

For Feinberg, the harm principle, together with the offense principle (which allows the criminal law to prevent behavior that is seriously and wrongly offensive to others), exhaustively describes the type of activity that the State may rightly prohibit and punish using the machinery of the legal system. He rejects proposals to make illegal "free-floating moral evils," a category which he proposes to include moral evils that do not constitute a "personal harm, offense or exploitative injustice." They include violation of societal and religious taboos, discrete and harmless immoralities (e.g., extramarital and homosexual sex), moral corruption, evil and impure thoughts, the wanton squishing of bugs or other small wriggling creatures in the wild, and the extinction of a species.[9]

Feinberg also contends that free floating evils connected with social change do not warrant legal prohibition. These include the extinction of a national or cultural group, drastic changes in the moral and aesthetic climate, or general environmental ugliness or drabness. Although he is willing to stipulate that such phenomena are evils, he does not believe that, in and of themselves, they constitute harms to any identifiable persons. Obviously, some of these changes can be accomplished through means that wrongfully violate the rights of others; the Nazi effort to extinguish the Jews and gypsies is a clear example. But, if social change takes place in a more evolutionary fashion, so that each step is gradual and voluntary, there is no wrongful harm to be remedied by the criminal law.[10]

B. Problems with the Harm Principle

For Feinberg, law functions more or less like a police officer, indeed, like a police officer patrolling a city beat. Its primary goal is to protect individual citizens from discrete and identifiable wrongful setbacks to their interests. Feinberg's understanding of the

meaning and application of the harm principle is elaborate and sophisticated; he anticipates and attempts to respond to many of the
criticisms mounted against liberal legal theory. Nonetheless, I
think that his understanding of the moral limits of the criminal
law, which is designed to protect individual liberty, fails to do justice either to the essentially social nature of human beings or to
the demands of the common good. Furthermore, his theory is inadequate to account for the deference he gives to the common
good in the one example where he does attempt to justify legal
prohibitions with reference to the social obligations of human
beings — good samaritan statutes.[11]

1. *A Subjectivist Account of Interest*

A key prong of Feinberg's framework is his subjectivist account
of individual interests. Ultimately, according to Feinberg, an individual's desires determine what is in her/his interests; a goal or an
aim is in my interest because I want to achieve it, not because it is
in some sense good for me to do so. But, it is not clear that this
account of human interests is persuasive. Instead, it seems that our
interests are not good because they are desired, but they are desired
because we perceive them to be (in some sense) good, as Joseph
Raz has persuasively argued.[12]

2. *An Individualistic Account of Interest*

A distinct, although related, problem with Feinberg's account of
interest is its atomistic individualism. By "individualism" I mean
that the interests Feinberg believes eligible to trigger the pro-
tections of the criminal law are those of discrete individuals. By
"atomistic" I mean that very little in Feinberg's account accommo-
dates the fact that an individual is not born with a full blown set of
interests that are distinctly her/his own. Instead, each of us acquires
the vast majority of our interests through the process of socialization into a particular familial network and surrounding culture.
Interests are made far more than they are inborn.

Feinberg's atomistic account of individual interests fails to account for the fact that one of the basic decisions a society must
make is which interests and options to foster and which ones to
discourage. He sidesteps this problem, mainly by insisting that his
focus is merely the moral limits of the criminal law, not the moral
limits of law in general. More specifically, he allows that it is appropriate for a liberal society to foster the choice of good options
through the mechanisms of the civil law, but not through the use
of penal sanctions.

But, it is not clear that such a sharp distinction between the civil and the criminal law can be justified on Feinberg's own terms. First, it is important to remember that the primary goal of the criminal law is not to impose sanctions on individuals after and because they performed the prohibited acts, but to deter them from performing such acts in the first place. The criminal law succeeds if it dissuades the vast majority of people from pursuing their interests by engaging in the acts that it prohibits. The threat of punishment, in other words, deters persons from pursuing their interests in particular ways.

Consequently, from a perspective that places paramount value on autonomy, a societal choice not to provide the social context that supports a particular ultimate interest does not differ greatly from a choice to block fulfillment of that ultimate interest by prohibiting an action integrally connected with the fulfillment of that interest. In either case, an individual's ability to pursue the ultimate interest in question is thwarted. In fact, that ability may be thwarted to a greater degree by the lack of appropriate institutional context and support than it is by the existence of a (mere) criminal prohibition.

3. *Harms to the Common Good*

A third and related failure of Feinberg's view of law as police officer is that it is unable to account for acts whose aggregate effect harms the common good in a consistent manner. For example, Feinberg believes it is permissible for the criminal law to target such activities as tax evasion. But, he has not developed a way of justifying such laws that does not seem arbitrary. Why is one person's failure to pay her/his taxes any more harmful than the so called "harmless immoralities" that he believes cannot be rightly criminalized? Why is failing to contribute $10,000 to a multibillion dollar national budget more harmful than is torturing bugs or small wriggling creatures, or destroying a species, or engaging in consensual sexual relations?

More specifically, Feinberg attempts to defend the legitimacy of criminalizing tax evasion based on: 1) the extent of the actual or threatened impairment to the institution in question and that institution's function; and 2) the strength or importance of each individual's interest in the institution.[13] But, this framework does not accomplish the work he needs it to do. One might argue, for example, that the relaxing of the prohibition against extramarital sex and contraception greatly threatened the stability of the institution of marriage, in which a great many people in this society have some sort of stake (as parents, spouses, and children).

Nonetheless, consensual extramarital sex continues to be his paradigmatic example of a harmless immorality. Why the inconsistency? A second difficulty is that Feinberg is inadequately able to protect goods that a society holds in common, because he is not willing to recognize that they are not in principle reducible to goods that can be divided and ascribed to the interests of individuals.[14] Feinberg attempts to rebut the claim that his thought is unable to take into account the importance of community. He writes that

> there is nothing in the liberal's ideology that need blind him to the social nature of human beings and the importance to all of us of community relationships. . . . [H]e can, indeed he must, concede what is plain fact, that most of what we fulfill when we fulfill ourselves are dispositions implanted by our communities, and most of what we exercise when we exercise our autonomy is what our communities created in us in the first place.[15]

But, in the end, Feinberg's approach allows virtually no community centered concerns to trump the application of the harm principle. While at some points in his argument he pays lip service to the importance of culture and communal context, at other points he is shockingly blind to their claims on us. For example, he writes that "even if the family as we know it should in time become extinct, however, and even if that would be an evil, it doesn't follow that any given individual would be wrongfully harmed in the transition."[16]

In the end, Feinberg acknowledges his respect for community values and moral traditions in the abstract, but takes every step necessary to insure that they do not compromise his version of autonomy.

C. Blinding Effects of Law as Police Officer

To view law exclusively as a police officer, through the lens provided by the harm principle, blinds us to very important aspects of human existence. First, by forcing us to look at each action and its effects atomistically, the harm principle blinds us to the cumulative effects of our actions upon our character, which, in turn, shapes the way we go on to perform other actions. Feinberg claims, for example, that the "wanton and capricious" destruction of a beetle or a small wriggling thing in the wild counts as a "harmless immorality" which is in principle beyond the scope of the criminal law. It may, of course, be true that, all things being equal, the criminal law should not devote its energies to stopping such activities. In fact, the example is deceptive, because it is hard to imagine any legal theory, liberal or not, that would argue that squishing bugs should be criminalized. What about persons who wantonly and capriciously destroy wild cats and dogs? Such animals do not have "interests," according to Feinberg's theory, so destroying them does no more "harm" (in Feinberg's sense) than does destroying small, wriggling bugs. But, thinking about the question in terms of animals that could be pets forces us to focus on the interconnection of acts, character, and future acts. What happens to the character of those who torture animals for fun? What sort of persons do they become.

Second, thinking about law exclusively as a police officer blinds us to the fact that human beings are essentially social and that our actions affect the well being of others in intricate ways. How do the changes in our character affect the way we interact with others, including what sort of influence we have on their own character development? For example, one result of the sort of brutalization that occurs when one makes a habit of torturing animals may be an increase in uncivil and uncooperative behavior that cannot be criminally prohibited, for all the practical reasons noted above.

Many of our actions have a broad impact on others, for good or ill. Some actions may have symbolic functions that extend far beyond their ramifications. For example, consider the copycat crimes that are frequently triggered by highly publicized evil doing. Conversely, acts of heroism also have a power that extends far beyond their physical effects, as the witness of the leaders of the Civil Rights Movement testifies. The living of any individual human life is in many senses a social enterprise. The knowledge that other people are making certain choices or engaging in certain activities shapes our imagination and alters our sense of the possibilities that are open to us.

For example, consider the way those wishing to participate in the institution of marriage are affected by contemporary American culture, where the divorce rate hovers near fifty percent. Even for the most committed couples, it is extremely difficult to enter into marriage with the intent of its being an indissoluble relationship; the possibility of divorce always hovers at the back of one's mind.

Third, the view of law as police officer fails to account for the fact that, because individuals are essentially social, they find the point of their autonomy, the point of their freedom, by living in community. Feinberg's approach stresses negative freedom — the freedom from restraint so that one can do what one wants to do. But, that is not enough. As the legal philosopher Joseph Raz points out, the ultimate rationale of negative freedom is positive freedom: the freedom to construct an identity and to live a life that authentically represents that identity.[18] No one, with the possible exception of a few hermits, can do that alone. The identity that one constructs depends on the forms of life available in the community and culture. For example, one cannot aspire to be a warrior in an Amish community. The identity of a warrior is a social identity; it has no place in a society committed to pacifism. Moreover, one cannot even aspire to an autonomous life in Raz's sense, e.g., in the sense in which one is part author of one's own life, unless one is part of a culture that values autonomy in general and for the subgroup to which one belongs. How could I, for example, be an autonomous woman trying to become a better scholar in a social context that had few, if any, opportunities for women to be educated?

Relatedly, once one recognizes that the point of freedom is not just negative freedom from constraint, but freedom to shape a cultural environment that reflects one's commitments, then Feinberg's understanding of the relative weight of community and individual choice appears inadequate. People exercise their autonomy in part by founding institutions, creating communities, and implementing their vision of the good life together. Consequently, these collective artifacts cannot be construed solely as a threat to autonomy; they also constitute its fruits. To refuse to give them any weight adopts a purely prospective vision of autonomy. It concerns itself with securing the conditions for the next choice to be made, rather than protecting the results of the last one. This is not, of course, to say that institutions and practices cannot become reified in a way that unreasonably strangles choices about the future. But, it is important to note that autonomy cannot be construed only in a way that places it in opposition to tradition, community, and culture.

D. A Case Study: Cloning and the Harm Principle

1. *NBAC Report*

In June, 1997, the National Bioethics Advisory Commission issued a Report, entitled *Cloning Human Beings: Report and Recommendations of the National Bioethics Advisory Commission.*[19] The *Report* was a response to the public furor precipitated by the announcement of the existence of Dolly, the world's first mammalian clone. Among other things, the *Report* recommends a federal legal ban (with a three-to-five-year sunset clause) of "attempts to create a child through somatic cell nuclear transfer," which is a primary technique involved in cloning.

2. *The Report and the Harm Principle*

For our purposes, what is crucial is the basis of the *Report's* recommendation: the harm principle. The Commission argues that a ban on cloning was justified because the untested procedure could result in harm to the cloned baby or its gestational mother. The Commission's definition of harm is extremely narrow: it includes only *physical harm*, not psychological harm. It also fails to include any consideration of the more diffuse social harms that might result from the practice of human cloning. In short, the Commission employed a definition of harm that is consonant with that developed by Joel Feinberg in his *Moral Limits of the Criminal Law*.

But, to deal with the prospect of human cloning in a jurisprudentially responsible way, we need to consider far more than the prospect of physical harm to the cloned child or the woman who carries it to term. More specifically, a jurisprudence that values human liberty in all its complexity will carefully scrutinize the way the origins of a cloned child are likely to affect her/his capacity for freedom.[20]

The legal philosopher, Joseph Raz, suggests that the human capacity for autonomy encompasses three components. First, in order to be autonomous, we need the raw mental capacity to consider, make, and carry out our choices. Consequently, we require a basic amount of intelligence and psychological stability. Second, we need independence, understood as the absence of manipulation as well as of coercion. Third, we need a range of morally worthwhile choices from which to choose.[21] Before our society decides to permit human cloning, we should ask how the process is likely to affect the cloned child's threefold capacity for autonomy. Unfortunately, it is a question that the harm principle, at least as it is narrowly construed by the *Report* (and by Feinberg), is unlikely to permit.

First, how will the knowledge of the circumstances of her/his generation affect the cloned child's conception of her/his own dignity and uniqueness? Will the fact that she/he was brought into being modeled on a template chosen by her/his parents contribute to the sense that she/he is a "product," not a person"?

Second, consider the circumstances under which parents are likely to clone a child. Possible scenarios have ranged from parents' cloning an admired figure from politics, the arts, or sports, to cloning themselves, to cloning an older child (perhaps one who is terminally ill). Under any of these circumstances, will there not be a great temptation for parents to exert pressure on the child to turn out as they expected?

Third, will not some such parents seek to clone a child in order to limit the uncertainty associated with parenthood? Will not a natural consequence of this motive be to limit the options available to the child in order to achieve one's purposes? For example, a couple would probably clone Mozart to get a child who is a musician, not a math genius. Given the effects of environment on personality, it is entirely conceivable that a clone of Mozart might choose to develop a set of interests and talents different from those of his famous template. But, would it not be at least tempting for the clone's parents to believe they know the child's talents better than he himself/she herself does and, on that basis, make a restricted set of options available to him/her?

A related set of questions that the harm principle is inadequate to raise, let alone address, involves the way the emergence of human cloning will affect the general meaning of parenthood in our society. While cloning is not likely to be widely practiced in the foreseeable future, the fact that it is known to be done at all will exert its grasp on the minds and hearts of far more people than those who are directly involved in the procedure. If it proceeds without opposition, the practice of human cloning might alter our understanding of the nature and purpose of the parent-child relationship. By allowing some parents to choose to produce a child who meets their specifications, whose biological and temperamental makeup is in some sense test driven or prelived, the law will erode social support for the delicate goal of encouraging parents, not only to pass on their values to their children, but also to provide them with the intellectual tools, the range of options, and the freedom from manipulation that will allow them to make their values truly their own. In particular, a law permitting cloning could suggest to *all* parents that they need not resist their understandable temptations to conform their children to their own expectations. In my view, the serious flaws in the law as police officer model, and in the harm principle that is its centerpiece, are revealed by their inability to deal with the real problems posed by the prospect of human cloning.

III. LAW AS A TEACHER OF VIRTUE

The practical questions that arise when we attempt to discern the appropriate stance for the law to take toward human cloning reveal that the law does far more than set up fences protecting citizens from one another. The law teaches; it says something to each of us about the way we should live and not live our lives. In fact, most people think that the law and morality are rather tightly knit together. If it is legal, they reason, how can it be (too) immoral?

I believe that the jurisprudential challenge at the turn of the millennium is to take responsibility for the law's pedagogical function. Law teaches. What should be its lessons? Only if we recognize the gravitational thrust of the law — its effect on those individuals who do not fall directly under its prohibitions — will we be able to begin addressing problems that arise in connection with such novel technologies as cloning.

What, then, do we need to do to correct the deficiencies of a liberal account of jurisprudence? In my view, we need to accomplish two tasks. First, we need to consider in more detail what it means to see law as a teacher of virtue, specifically the virtue of justice. The very fact of seeing law as a teacher of virtue will force us to consider the social implications of law in a way that the view of law as police officer does not. Second, we need to consider the way to modify the liberal understanding of justice, so that we move away from individualism toward solidarity.

A. Meaning of Seeing Law as a Teacher of Virtue

In his *Summa Theologica*, Saint Thomas Aquinas writes: "It is evident that the proper effect of law is to lead its subjects to their proper virtue; and since virtue is that which makes its subject good, it follows that the proper effect of law is to make those to whom it is given, good, either simply or in some particular respect."[22] Thomas goes on to say that the purpose of the divine law is to make men and women good in and of themselves; but, the purpose of the human law is to make them good with respect to their lives in a particular government, a particular community.

Note two fundamental differences between seeing law as a teacher of virtue and seeing law as a police officer. First, seeing law as teacher of virtue is inherently positive, not negative; its regulating vision is ultimately the wholeness of each person within the context of the whole community.

Second, seeing law as a teacher of virtue is inherently more respectful of the dignity of those to whom it applies. More specifically, on the law as police officer model, it is irrelevant *why* an individual refrains from committing acts that harm others; its only concern is that she/he *does refrain* from doing so. In contrast, the model of law as a teacher of virtue is bound to care about the "why."

Being a virtuous person means that it is not enough that one does the right thing or avoids doing the wrong thing, when viewed from an external perspective; it is also important that one's externally correct activity spring from the right intention. A virtuous person refrains from killing and maiming other persons because such actions are inconsistent with respect for their dignity, not because she/he is afraid of going to jail. In other words, a virtuous person internalizes the purpose of the law; she/he intentionally adheres to the goods internal to legal practices and institutions.[23] In order to develop the right intentions, however, those asked to participate in the practices must first be given an explanation of their point. In other words, lawmakers must explain the nature and purpose of legislation to the citizenry before it is enacted and while it is in effect. They cannot merely exact blind obedience from citizens and expect them to develop virtue.

B. Three Caveats

Even as we begin understanding law as a teacher of virtue, it is also important to recognize that it is not the only such teacher. In fact, its lessons are primarily for the least advanced students. Becoming virtuous is a long process; it takes training by, and inter-action with, those further along in that process. For most persons, paternal and maternal training suffices to deter them from fatal mistakes and to point them in the right direction on the long path to virtue. Others, however, need more help. According to Aquinas, a primary purpose of the criminal law is to provide those who are too obstinate to be trained by friends and family with a forceful introduction to the rudiments of virtue (which largely consists in refraining from the major vices).[24]

Second, it is important to remember that law is also subject to very significant practical limitations in its quest to inculcate virtue. Aquinas quotes Isidore of Seville about the practical constraints that good law always takes into account: "Law shall be virtuous, just, possible to nature, according to the custom of the country, suitable to place and time, necessary, useful, clearly expressed, lest by its obscurity it lead to misunderstanding; framed for no private benefit, but for the common good."[25]

In light of the practical limitations on law, how do we formulate the moral limits of the criminal law? What guide to these limits do we use to replace the liberal harm principle? I believe that we should recognize that the moral limits of the criminal law in any particular culture are the limits of ordinary virtue in that culture. The practice of virtue is like the practice of any good habit; it needs to be built up gradually. An analogy to exercise is helpful here. If our goal were to raise the average fitness level among American adults, a significant number of whom are sedentary and overweight, it would be a bad idea to make all of them comply with the exercise régime used by Jane Fonda herself. It would be much better to get them to purchase and use the exercise videos she designed for beginners.

The same is true with virtue. St. Thomas says:

> The purpose of human law is to lead men to virtue, not suddenly but gradually. Wherefore it does not lay upon the multitude of im-perfect men the burdens of those who are already virtuous, viz., that

they should abstain from all evil. Otherwise these imperfect ones, being unable to bear such precepts, would break out into yet greater evils. The precepts are despised, and those men, from contempt, break out into evils worse still.[26] Thus, the limits of legal sanctions are the limits of ordinary virtue.

C. Which Virtues?

If law is to function as a teacher of virtues, which ones should be considered within the scope of its pedagogy? According to Aquinas, the purpose of law is to promote the common good. The primary virtue concerned with promoting the common good is called "general" justice, also called "legal justice," because it is the paramount concern of the law.[27]

Unlike the virtues of fortitude and temperance, which focus their efforts internally on regulating the passions of the individual who possesses them, the virtue of general justice as such focuses primarily on the *external* features of human actions in particular, our relationship with other people. Aquinas describes justice as the virtue that is primarily concerned with "operations," the way the effects of our actions affect the just claims of others. He writes: "Accordingly, the directing of operations insofar as they tend toward external things, belongs to justice, but in so far as they arise from the passions, it belongs to the other moral virtues which are about the passions."[28] The object of general justice is *jus*, the right, which is best understood, not in contemporary terms as a single individual's moral property, but as a *situation* of right relations among two or more people, described from an external point of view.[29]

What, then, is the relationship between general or legal justice and the other virtues? Does Thomas mean to imply that law should be concerned only with promoting the virtue of justice and not at all focused on inculcating the other virtues, particularly those that fall under the cardinal virtues of fortitude and temperance? The answer to this question is no.

According to Thomas, legal justice is a general virtue, not because it constitutes part of each virtue by definition, but because it directs the acts of all the virtues toward the common good.[30] To begin to see the way this is the case, one will find it easier to start with vice rather than with virtue. The virtue of general justice looks at acts as they affect the common good, whereas the other virtues look at them as they affect the person who commits the act. To put it another way, the virtue of justice and the other virtues frequently judge and find the same actions wanting, but from different per-

spectives. Aquinas gives the example of the relationship of liberality and justice: "Hence justice hinders theft of another's property,
in so far as stealing is contrary to the equality that should be maintained in external things, while liberality hinders it as resulting
from an immoderate desire for wealth."[31] Justice is concerned with
the outbreak into the external world of disordered passions.
Aquinas writes that "external operations [with which justice is con-
cerned] are as it were between external things, which are their
matter, and internal passions, which are their origin."[32] At some
point, virtues and vices lead us to take actions that affect the
broader community. At this point, the law steps in. To quote
Thomas again, "There is no virtue whose act cannot be prescribed
by the law. Nevertheless human law does not prescribe concerning
all the acts of every virtue: but only in regard to those that are or-
dainable to the common good..."[33]

So, the law targets its attention on acts of virtues or vices as they
intersect with general justice, the virtue of acting rightly with
respect to the common good. Another question now becomes
pressing: Assume that the law's primary target is those actions
falling in the intersecting purview of legal justice and some other
virtue. Is the law's concern in targeting these actions limited to the
respect in which they violate justice, or can it also attempt to reinforce the other virtues at the same time? This question is
important, because it directly involves the degree to which the law
can take into account motive in fixing punishment. Is the degree
to which a prohibited act violates another virtue relevant to its
seriousness, or is the gravity of every prohibited act determined
from the perspective of its relationship to justice?

I believe that careful consideration of Thomas's understanding
of law as teacher demonstrates that, while the law might generally
target only those acts inconsistent with the other virtues that also
violate justice, it exerts its pedagogical force on behalf of all the
virtues. Thomas writes:

> An act is said to be an act of virtue in two ways. First, from the fact
> that a man does something virtuous; thus an act of justice is to do
> what is right [from an external perspective]; and an act of fortitude
> is to do brave things; and in this way law prescribes certain acts of
> virtue. Secondly an act of virtue is when a man does a virtuous thing
> in a way in which a virtuous man does it. Such an act always proceeds
> from virtue; and it does not come under a precept of law, but is the
> end at which every lawgiver aims.[34]

Thus, the law legitimately attempts to encourage its subjects to
adopt an internal perspective toward the goods of all the virtues,
not just justice. This view is consistent with Aquinas's understanding of the connection among the virtues. Aquinas states explicitly

that, at the highest level, the virtues are unified. If we are unable to control our passions in accordance with the demands of reason, we are likely to take actions that are hurtful to others, as well as to ourselves. In order to act consistently in a just manner, we need to cultivate the other virtues. While the vices against temperance and fortitude spring from disordered passions internal to the person (e.g., an individual is moved in an inordinate way by desire or fear), those disordered passions frequently give rise to actions that violate justice. A person who cannot control lust might be tempted to commit adultery, which undermines the virtue of justice. A person who cannot control the vice of daring might be tempted to take excessive risks, thereby recklessly endangering the lives of others. On this view, the law has very good instrumental reasons for encouraging the virtues and discouraging the vices opposed to them.

Finally, however, there is a noninstrumental reason for the law to be concerned with the development of all the virtues in individual citizens. This reason has to do with the relationship between the individual and the community, which Thomas frequently describes in terms of the relationship between a whole and its parts. Fundamentally, the common good encompasses and supports the good of each individual within the community; it does not limit its *concern* to the external effects that are the fruits of a good or bad character. Accordingly, while the law customarily focuses on external acts, the internal acts that prompt them are not entirely beyond its authority. At the very least, they are appropriately considered in the context of determining the aggravating and mitigating factors of a criminalized action.

In his development of the relationship of justice, the other virtues, and the law, Aquinas recognizes the essentially social nature of human beings in a way that Feinberg's thought never adequately takes into account. Development of the virtues is necessary, not only for us to be well ordered with respect to the order in our own souls, but to be well ordered with respect to the community in which we live. The law can concern itself with virtues other than justice, primarily because the external acts we perform at the prompting of our passions frequently affect other people. But, because each person is indeed a "member" of the community, the fact that she/he develops in virtue in and for herself/himself is also of concern to lawmakers.

In addition, according to Aquinas, legal justice has a holistic, integrative function; it orders the virtues possessed by individuals toward the common good. When Feinberg describes acts that are potentially subject to legal strictures, he presents them as if they have no context in the life of the individual who performs them or in the life of the broader community. But, the virtue of legal justice, precisely because it is concerned with the well being of the entire community, invites us to see the way all of our actions and character traits impinge upon the community as a whole. This, in turn, encourages us to look at our legal structures holistically, not solely in terms of isolated prohibitions and requirements. In fact, a holistic approach to describing the nature and purpose of law may have far greater explanatory and predictive power in the contemporary era. Many major pieces of legislation enacted in the last half of this century (e.g., the Civil Rights Acts) are not merely concerned with requiring and prohibiting a set of discrete, unconnected actions, but with fundamentally transforming the way we view our relationships with one another.

D. Using Solidarity to Specify Justice

Another challenge facing us in the new millennium is the way we are to understand the virtue of justice. As recent discussions in political theory have made increasingly clear, no understanding of justice exists in the abstract; it is interlocked with a corresponding political anthropology and conception of practical rationality.[36] I believe that the conception of justice that is most urgently needed at this point in time is one that supports an anthropology forcefully advocated by recent Catholic social teaching. All human beings are essentially embodied as well as essentially social. Dualist anthropologies, along with those that support an atomistic individualism, are seriously inadequate. Each human being is endowed with an innate dignity and called to a unique vocation by our Creator, to echo the words of the Declaration of Independence.

What would it look like to understand justice through the prism of solidarity (and its corresponding anthropology)? First, it would call us to be attentive to three aspects of human existence in designing our social structures, including our legal systems. First, solidarity would require us to make sure that each person's basic needs as *an embodied individual* are met, i.e., that everyone has access to food, clothing, shelter, and basic medical care.

Second, solidarity would require us to honor each person's *social nature* by insuring that no one is isolated from the community. In particular, this would mandate providing persons with physical, mental, and social disabilities with the assistance they need to insure their integration into the social world that surrounds them.

Third, and finally, solidarity would require our best efforts to enable each person to contribute to the community. Confident in the recognition that each of us is called to a particular vocation, to give something back to the community in which we live out our lives, each must realize that it is imperative to facilitate meaningful opportunities for work for every adult member of society. The Pastoral Letter on the Economy of the Bishops of the United States makes these points eloquently.[37]

IV. EXAMPLES FROM AMERICAN LAW

A. Generalizations

Finally, I would like to suggest that the view of law and justice I have developed can find several points of contact in existing American law, points which need to be fostered and expanded. To summarize, that view comprises three key planks. First, law should be understood, not as a police officer, but as a teacher of virtue, pointing toward the flourishing of both individuals and the community. Second, since the purpose of law is to further the common good, the primary virtue with which law will be concerned is justice. The founding and maintenance of a just society, however, depend upon inculcating other virtues, falling under the cardinal virtues of prudence, fortitude, and temperance. Finally, the concept of justice needs to be specified in accordance with an anthropology that recognizes that individuals are essentially social. At the end of the second millennium, the most appropriate specification of justice was solidarity.

I believe that this conception of law already animates some of the most significant legislation passed during the second half of the twentieth century, including the Civil Rights Act,[38] the Family and Medical Leave Act,[39] and the Americans with Disabilities Act.[40] In my view, these important pieces of legislation share three important characteristics.

First, they are holistic in approach. They point toward a vision of the way our lives should be lived in common. They do not simply target a disjointed set of actions that are recognized to cause harm to others, in the manner contemplated by law as police officer. Moreover, they do not support a jurisprudence that would sharply separate the strictures of the criminal and civil law. In the case of the Civil Rights Act, the criminal and civil penalties work together in tandem to implement its vision of a society free from invidious discrimination. (Needless to say, the criminal penalties are reserved for the more egregious violations.)

Second, the guiding virtue of all three pieces of legislation is justice, understood as solidarity. Each strives to insure that some members of society, formerly excluded from full participation in (and contribution to) the economic life of the community, are enabled to take some steps toward unity and are encouraged to overcome their marginalization.

Third, these pieces of legislation do not attempt to penalize the subjects of the law for failing to exhibit the full range of relevant virtues. As Aquinas recommends, they generally limit their requirements and proscriptions to specified external actions; they do not try to reach the full range of purely internal acts and dispositions that we would like to encourage and discourage among the members of the community. Also in accordance with Thomistic jurisprudence, they limit their requirements and prohibitions to what can be expected of persons or institutions of ordinary virtue, not of extraordinary or heroic virtue. For example, the Family and Medical Leave Act requires only that workers be given unpaid leaves to respond to family emergencies, despite the fact that a virtuous company would provide paid leaves in such circumstances (provided, of course, that doing so was financially feasible).

On the other hand, the three pieces of legislation signal the hope that the subjects of the law will move beyond mere compliance with the external requirements of the law to an appreciation of the broader vision of community that it seeks to begin establishing. More specifically, individuals and communities may initially obey the law to avoid the penalties attached to violations. To use Alasdair MacIntyre's terminology, they would be motivated by the goods external to the practices required by the law.[41] In time, however, some individuals or corporations might come to appreciate the goods internal to the practices which, in the case of all three laws, is broader participation of marginalized groups in the life of the community. Coming to appreciate these internal goods, they might find themselves obeying the "spirit," rather than just the "letter," of the law.

B. The Americans with Disabilities Act

In order to illustrate the general points made in the foregoing paragraphs, I would like to take a closer look at the Americans with Disabilities Act, which was passed in 1990. The purpose of the ADA is encapsulated in its title; rather than calling the law the "Disabled Americans Act," its sponsors chose the title the "Americans with Disabilities Act." They thereby emphasized the paramount goal of activists in this area: encouraging all Americans to see the whole person before they see the disability.

1. *Findings and Purposes*

The first section of the statute articulates the reasons that the lawmakers believe this law to be necessary. The "findings and purposes" section begins by reflecting upon the status of persons with disabilities in contemporary America. It states that "some 43,000,0000 Americans have one or more physical or mental disabilities, and this number is increasing as the population as a whole is growing older."[42] It also proclaims that

> individuals with disabilities are a discrete and insular minority who have been faced with restrictions and limitations, subjected to a history of purposeful unequal treatment, and relegated to a position of political powerlessness in our society, based on characteristics that are beyond the control of such individuals and resulting from stereotypic assumptions not truly indicative of the individual ability of such individuals to participate in, and contribute to, society.[43]

Next, the section articulates the purpose of the law: "The Nation's proper goals regarding individuals with disabilities are to assure equality of opportunity, full participation, independent living, and economic self-sufficiency for such individuals."[44] This purpose is fully moral in nature and fully consonant with the requirements of justice, understood as solidarity.

Why, some might ask, is it necessary to enact legislation to implement this moral vision? Why not simply encourage individuals and businesses to fulfill their moral obligations to those people with disabilities? In part, because law always teaches, for good or for ill. The lessons that the law has taught about our obligations in this regard have not always been morally sound. They need to be unlearned before a better approach can take root and grow. For example, it was not until 1973 that the City of Chicago repealed its ordinance prohibiting persons who were "deformed" and "unsightly" from exposing themselves to public view on the streets.[45] The law is an extremely powerful teacher; sometimes the only way to counteract the mistaken pedagogy of past legislatures is to enact new law that forcefully proclaims a different moral vision.[46]

2. Mandates

The mandates of the ADA must be understood in light of its general purposes. They are not isolated prohibitions or requirements, but fundamental planks in a program that implements a vision of the common good in a way that aims to overcome the marginalization of persons with disabilities.[47] The ADA covers two basic aspects of social existence: employment and accommodation in facilities accessible to the public.

In the employment context, the general rule provides that no employer shall discriminate against a qualified individual with a disability. This requirement, however, is not merely a negative prohibition against discrimination, but also encompasses a positive

requirement that the employer make "reasonable accommodations to the known physical or mental limitations of an otherwise
qualified individual with a disability who is an applicant or employee."[48] The law recognizes an exception in cases where an
employer can "demonstrate that the accommodation would impose
an undue hardship on the operation of the business of such
covered entity."[49] Restrictions on the use of preemployment medical
tests help enforce this requirement.

It is necessary, but not sufficient, to enable persons with disabilities to take their place in the work world. It is also essential to
allow them to participate more generally in the public sphere, to
become active and visible parts of the common life of Americans.
The second and third prongs of the ADA attempt to facilitate just
this sort of participation.

In Subchapter II, which deals with public services, the ADA not
only prohibits discrimination against persons with disabilities, but
it also requires those who operate public transportation to adopt
plans to insure they have equal access.[50] In Subchapter III, the ADA
imposes significant obligations on private entities who operate
public accommodations and services.[51] By "public accommodation," the Act means to include all the business establishments we
patronize as part of our day-to-day lives: hotels, restaurants, movie
theaters, laundromats, hairdressers, museums, parks, offices of
doctors, and other professionals.[52] The ADA prohibits public
accommodations from discriminating against persons with disabilities, which includes providing them with less than equal services
and separating them from nondisabled persons.[53] It also requires
them to remove barriers to access and to install assistance devices,
unless doing so would fundamentally alter the nature of their
establishments, result in an undue burden upon the business, or is
for some reason not readily achievable.[54]

3. Enforcement Mechanisms

How does the ADA propose to enforce its requirements? The
enforcement provisions are modeled on some of those included in
the Civil Rights Act. Available remedies include equitable relief,
including injunctive relief to force entities to modify their policies
or their facilities, as well as monetary damages.[55]

4. Limits of the Law

The ADA does not attempt to instantiate a perfect world from
the perspective of persons with disabilities. It does not, for example, require any type of affirmative action on behalf of those with
disabilities: "Employers are still able to hire any employee without

a disability who can do the essential functions of a job marginally better than a person with a disability can, as long as that person has received reasonable accommodations."[56] Moreover, the ADA does not change the fact that employment services for adults with disabilities frequently focus on those who suffer from the least severe problems and who are thereby likely to be counted as "success" stories without much effort on the part of the agency.[57]

It does, however, produce a context where employers can begin to recognize the point of the law, to begin to appreciate the goods internal to the practice of solidarity. Taken together, the three prongs of the ADA attempt to bring into existence a culture where all of us are more accustomed to seeing persons with disabilities in public places and overcome our sense of uncomfortableness about them. That may encourage us to begin looking beyond their disabilities to see the gifts and talents that they offer to our community. Once we reach this stage, those who are bound by the ADA's strictures (and those who are not) might find themselves willing to go beyond the law's requirements in order to implement its ultimate goals. In other words, the ADA points us toward, and attempts to teach us to believe in, an expansive vision of economic and social participation of persons with disabilities, a vision that the law itself only partially instantiates.

V. CONCLUSION

I believe that the jurisprudential challenge facing the United States in the third millennium is to move beyond the constraints of law as police officer toward the more expansive vision available to us if we appropriate Aquinas's view of law as a teacher of virtue.

The attitude toward the purpose of human law offered by this view accounts much better for some of the more significant pieces of legislation that have been passed in the latter half of the twentieth century, including the ADA, the Civil Rights Act, and the Family and Medical Leave Act. The law as police officer approach, with its subjectivist and individualistic anthropology, cannot account for the manner in which these laws attempt to transform the cultural context for certain marginalized groups, not merely to prohibit isolated "harmful" acts.

More importantly, if we see law as a teacher of virtue, it will encourage us to take responsibility for the virtues — or the vices — that our laws are actually teaching. One can imagine a liberal legal theorist, such as Feinberg, reacting to a Thomistic view of law with a great deal of worry: Who, he might ask, is to decide what the law teaches? What is to prevent the majority from unjustifiably imposing its morality upon minorities?

In my view, this is the fundamental question about the legitimacy of law. One can attempt to answer this question in two ways.
Feinberg's approach is to limit the scope of the criminal law, to
attempt to justify the provisions he supports in ways that do not
make normative judgments about varying visions of the good life,
but depend ultimately upon each individual's conceptions of
her/his own interests. A major difficulty with this approach, as I argued extensively in the foregoing pages, is that he is unable to
achieve those goals.

The overarching virtue law should teach is justice, as identified
by Thomas Aquinas. But, justice needs to be understood, not in
the isolated, atomistic way of the liberal tradition, but in the community enhancing way of Catholic Social Thought. Justice, in other
words, needs to be understood as solidarity.

NOTES

[1]The criminal law embodies the obligations that private people owe to
the community as a whole. In contrast, the civil law embodies the obligations that people owe to each other as private individuals (or
corporations).

[2]*Griswold* v. *Connecticut*, 381 U.S. 479 (1965).

[3]Joel Feinberg, *The Moral Limits of the Criminal Law* (New York: Oxford
University Press): *Harm to Others* (vol. 1, 1984), *Offense to Others* (vol. 2,
1985), *Harm to Self* (vol. 3, 1986), and *Harmless Wrongdoing* (vol. 4, 1988).

[4]Joel Feinberg, *Harmless Wrongdoing*, xxvii-xxix.

[5]Feinberg, *Harm to Others*, 37.

[6]Ibid., 65-70.

[7]Ibid., 115-18.

[8]Feinberg would support outlawing duels to the death, in part because
he believes that the choice to engage in them is not voluntary and in part
because he recognizes that the practice of dueling left dependent spouses
and children without support (*Harm to Others*, 221). I do not believe his
position is consistent with the antipaternalistic thrust he adopts in the rest
of his work.

[9]Feinberg, *Harmless Wrongdoing*, 20-25.

[10]Ibid., chap. 29.

[11]Unlike most liberal legal theorists, Feinberg would allow the criminal
law to be used against "bad samaritans" who fail to come to the rescue of
others when they can do so with virtually no risk to themselves. See
Feinberg, *Harm to Others*, 126-30.

[12]Joseph Raz, *The Morality of Freedom* (Oxford: Oxford University Press,
1986), chap. 6.

[13]Feinberg, *Harm to Others*, 63.

[14]Feinberg, *Harmless Wrongdoing*, 89.

[15]Ibid.

[16]Ibid., 73.

[17]Ibid., 21.

[18]Raz, 410.

[19]National Bioethics Advisory Commission, *Cloning Human Beings: Report & Recommendations* (June, 1997).

[20]I have made this point more extensively in my "Cloning and Positive Liberty," *Notre Dame Journal of Law, Ethics, & Public Policy* 13:1 (1999): 15-35.

[21]Raz, chap. 14.

[22]Thomas Aquinas, *Summa Theologica*, I-II, q. 92.

[23]Alasdair MacIntyre makes this point in *After Virtue: A Study in Moral Theory* (Notre Dame, IN: University of Notre Dame Press, 1984), chapter 14.

[24]Thomas Aquinas, *Summa Theologica*, I-II, q. 95, art. 1.

[25]Ibid., art. 3.

[26]Ibid., I-II, q. 96, art. 2, rep. ob. 2.

[27]Ibid., II-II, q. 58, art. 5.

[28]Ibid., art. 9, rep. ob. 2.

[29]Ibid., q. 57, art. 1.

[30]Ibid., q. 58, art. 6.

[31]Ibid., art. 9.

[32]Ibid.

[33]Ibid., I-II, q. 96, art. 3.

[34]Ibid., rep. ob. 2.

[35]Ibid., II-II, q. 58, art. 5.

[36]See, e.g., MacIntyre, *Whose Justice? Which Rationality?* (Notre Dame, IN: University of Notre Dame Press, 1988).

[37]"All work has a threefold moral significance. First, it is a principal way that people exercise the distinctive human capacity for self-expression and self-realization. Second, it is the ordinary way for human beings to fulfill their material needs. Finally, work enables people to contribute to the well-being of the larger community. Work is not only for one's self. It is for one's family, for the nation, and indeed for the benefit of the entire human family" (National Conference of Catholic Bishops, *Economic Justice for All: Pastoral Letter on Catholic Social Teaching and the U.S. Economy* (Washington, D.C.: U.S. Catholic Conference, Inc., 1986), ¶ 97).

[38]Civil Rights Act of 1964, Pub.L.No. 88-352, 78 Stat. 241 (codified as amended in scattered sections of volumes 28 and 42 of the United States Code) and Civil Rights Act of 1968, Pub.L. No. 90-284, 82 Stat. 73 (codified at 25 U.S.C. SS 1301-1341 (1994) and in scattered sections of volumes 18, 28, and 42 U.S.C.).

[39]Family and Medical Leave Act of 1993, Pub.L.No. 103-3, 107 Stat. 6 (codified as amended at 2 U.S.C. §§ 6om-on; 3 U.S.C. §§ 2601, 2631, 2651 (1994)).

[40]Americans with Disabilities Act (ADA), Pub.L.No. 101-336, 104 Stat. 328 (1990) (as amended in scattered sections of 42, 47, and 29 U.S.C.).

[41]MacIntyre, *After Virtue*, 175-76.

[42]ADA, § 12101(1).

[43]Ibid., (7).

[44]Ibid., (8).

[45]Mark C. Weber, "Beyond the Americans with Disabilities Act: A National Employment Policy for People with Disabilities," *Buffalo Law Review* 46 (1998): 123-74, at 132.

[46]Of course, the most compelling example of the need to enact new law to eradicate the moral evils embedded in society by old law is the Civil Rights legislation, which has proved an essential, if not all powerful, tool to overcome the effects of centuries of racism endorsed and *taught* by the legal system. On the legal pedagogy of racism, see John T. Noonan, Jr., *Persons and Masks of the Law: Cardozo, Holmes, Jefferson, and Wythe as Makers of Masks* (New York: Farrar, Straus, and Giroux, 1976), and his *The Antelope: The Ordeal of the Recaptured Africans in the Administration of James Monroe and John Quincy Adams* (Berkeley: University of California Press, 1977).

[47]I do not mean to suggest that the ADA cannot be criticized for being an ineffective or inefficient means of achieving this end. For example, some people have criticized the ADA for defining "disability" so broadly that it does not effectively target the population it aims to help.

[48]ADA, § 12112 (5) (A).

[49]Ibid.

[50]Ibid., § § 12131-12165.

[51]Ibid., § §12181-12189.

[52]Ibid., § 12181 (7).

[53]Ibid., § 12182 (b) ((1) (A) (i)-(iii)).

[54]Ibid., ((2) (A)).

[55]Ibid., § 12188.

[56]Mark C. Weber, at 137-38.

[57]Ibid., at 141.

Index of Persons